QUEST FOR DEVELOPMENT IN MANIPUR

Books published for Centre for Alternative Discourse, Manipur

- Look East Policy: India's North East Polemics and Perspectives edited by Thingnam Kishan Singh
- Location Space and Development edited by Konthoujam Indrakumar & Homen Thangjam

---

About the Editors

Homen Thangjam teaches Political Science at the Department of Political Science, the Maharaja Bodhchandra College, Imphal. He received his doctoral degree from the School of International Studies, Jawaharlal Nehru University, New Delhi. He has co-edited, *Location, Space and Development: Development Trajectories in India's North-East,* New Delhi: Concept Publishing Company Pvt. Ltd., New Delhi, 2010.

Hanjabam Isworchandra is ICSSR doctoral fellow. He is working on Agrarian Economy and Rural Non-farm Employment of Manipur for his Ph.D. programme at the Department of Economics, Manipur University, Canchipur.

Quest for Development in Manipur

Continuity, Constraints and Contradictions

Edited by

Homen Thangjam

and

Hanjabam Isworchandra Sharma

Published for

CENTRE FOR ALTERNATIVE DISCOURSE, MANIPUR

by

CONCEPT PUBLISHING COMPANY PVT. LTD., NEW DELHI-110059

ISBN-13: 978-81-8069-908-5

First Published 2013

Published and Printed by

Concept
Since 1974

Concept Publishing Company Pvt. Ltd.
A/15-16, Commercial Block, Mohan Garden
New Delhi-110059 (India)
T: 25351460, 25351794, *F*: 091-11-25357109
E: publishing@conceptpub.com, W: www.conceptpub.com
Editorial Office: H-13, Bali Nagar, New Delhi-110 015, India.

Cataloging in Publication Data--Courtesy: D.K. Agencies (P) Ltd. <docinfo@dkagencies.com>

Quest for development in Manipur : continuity, constraints and contradictions / edited by Homen Thangjam and Hanjabam Isworchandra Sharma.
p. cm.
Contributed articles.
Includes bibliographical references and index.
ISBN 9788180699085

1. Manipur (India)—Economic conditions. 2. Economic development—India Manipur. 3. Manipur (India)—Economic policy. I. Thangjam, Homen. II. Sharma, Hanjabam Isworchandra. III. Centre for Alternative Discourse, Manipur.

DDC 330.95417 23

Preface

The present edited volume is a compilation of select-updated articles published thematically in the Volume III (No. 2) of the *Alternative Perspectives*, a quarterly journal published by the Centre for Alternative Discourse, Manipur (CADM). The issues, as a whole, attempted to critically intervene into the debates surrounding the development trajectory of Manipur from the pre-colonial days to present (since Manipur became a part of the Indian Union). Principal reasons cited for underdevelopment of the State in many of the development discourses are that it is land locked, geographically occupying a formidable mountainous terrain. Apart from the geographical factors, which recent policy initiatives for trade had debunked, for example, the Look East policy, the situation of "law and order" (in official vocabulary) or insurgency that thrive upon "extortion" and "looting" (in the official vocabulary, again) has been cited as the root cause of underdevelopment in the State. Being so, development efforts are arduous and nearly impossible. Apart from initiating a sustained academic engagement on the said issues, as a challenge, insights have been provided by the authors on why development remains elusive in the State, inspite of existing potentials. Thus, the present edition aims at providing critical and constructive evaluation of the existing conditions and policies that are detrimental to development of Manipur.

As an academic journal, *Perspectives* aims to provide critical and constructive evaluation of the existing conditions and circumstances surrounding the North-East. It also offers informed debates on issues crucial to the material realities in the region.

The *journal* represents the recognition of the historical necessity of accepting the twin challenges of to critique and to explore various alternatives for ushering in a new order. The journal is published by the CADM, which is run by Research Foundation Charitable Trust, a registered body, constituted under the Indian Trust Act, 1882, and registered under Registration of Societies Act 1908. CADM is an outcome of year-long discussion and consultation initiated by the academicians, intellectuals, scholars, thinkers and social activists of the State with the objective to promote a sensible, systematic and informed study on various issues confronting the North East Region through the publication of an academic journal. The very inception of the idea of establishing the centre came from the recognition of a need to critique the realities surrounding our social existence. The establishment of the Centre for Alternative Discourse, Manipur in September 2005 represents our understanding that we belong to a critical historical epoch. An acutely felt need to engage the emerging as well as persisting realities is crucial behind the genesis of the centre.

The present book is the third in a series of publications by CADM. Taking due cognizance of the widespread appreciation and acknowledgement that we received from the academic community across the country for our humble initiatives, we at the CADM, deeply felt the need to produce the third volume of the published works in book form. The present publication has also been necessitated by the reality of underdevelopment in the region, which is mainly due to misplaced difficulties given to the geographical space and misdirected policies ensuing from such a fallacy by policy formulators in New Delhi as well as in various capitals of the States in the region. The result of such policies on the region needs to be properly scrutinized *vis-à-vis* the growing aspirations of the indigenous people.

We look forward to positive criticism and suggestions from readers for further improvement of the present volume.

Homen Thangjam
Hanjabam Isworchandra Sharma

Acknowledgements

The Centre for Alternative Discourse Manipur (CADM) acknowledges the help and assistance extended by members in finalising this volume in the shape of a book. Foremost, we thank our esteemed readers, for their constant support and criticisms, which has helped us in improving ourselves. We thank *Oja* Monoranjan (Associate Professor, The Maharaja Bodhchandra College, Imphal) for his critical insights and comments. We also thank Moirangthem Prakash, (Asst. Professor, IRMA, Gujarat), Laishram Nadalal (Sub-Editor, *The Pioneer,* New Delhi), Hidam (O) R.K. Smejita (Asst. Professor, Gargi College, New Delhi) for going through the manuscripts and critical comments.

Finally, we would like to thank Mr. Ashok Kumar Mittal of Concept Publishing Company Pvt. Ltd., New Delhi for his friendship and publishing the book.

Homen Thangjam
Hanjabam Isworchandra Sharma

Contents

Contributors

E. Nixon Singh is Associate Professor in the Department of Management, Mizoram University. He had worked on aspects of entrepreneurship for his doctoral research.

Hanjabam Isworchandra is ICSSR doctoral fellow. He is working on Agrarian Economy and Rural Non-Farm Employment of Manipur for his Ph.D. programme at the Department of Economics, Manipur University, Canchipur.

Hidam Premananda is a doctoral scholar working on governmentality for his Ph.D. programme at the Centre of Comparative Political Theory, School of International Studies, Jawaharlal Nehru University, New Delhi.

Homen Thangjam teaches Political Science at the Department of Political Science, the Maharaja Bodhchandra College, Imphal. He received his doctoral degree from the School of International Studies, Jawaharlal Nehru University, New Delhi. He has co-edited, *Location, Space and Development: Development Trajectories in India's North-East,* New Delhi: Concept Publishing Company Pvt. Ltd., 2010.

Kangujam Sanatomba has submitted his thesis on comparative insurgencies for the award of doctoral degree at the Department of Political Science, Manipur University, Canchipur.

Laishram Churchill, an environmentalist, is Sr. Sub-Editor, *The Sangai Express,* a leading English daily based in Imphal.

Lourembam Sanatomba Meetei teaches Economics at DM College of Commerce, Imphal. He had worked on "Impacts of Industrial Policies on Industrialization in Manipur" for his doctoral thesis.

N. Manichandra Singh teaches Economics at Ram Lal Anand (E) College, University of Delhi. He is Consulting Editor, *Eastern Quarterly*.

Oinam Ranjit Singh is Guest Faculty, Department of History, Manipur University, Canchipur. He had worked on ancient Manipuri history for his doctoral research.

Potsangbam Kumar Singh, a renowned ethnobotanist in India, is Associate Professor at Department of Life Science, Manipur University, Canchipur. He has published a wide range of articles on medicinal plants of Manipur in national and international journals.

Soibam Haripriya is working on cultural memories for her doctoral thesis in the Department of Sociology, Delhi School of Economics, Delhi University, Delhi. She has worked as a health activist with a Delhi based NGO for more than five years.

Th. Joychandra Singh teaches Economics at Imphal College, Imphal.

List of Tables

List of Figures

Introduction

Homen Thangjam and Hanjabam Isworchandra Sharma

Economic development has continued to form the backbone for social change and as a process, policy intervention has been embraced in the historical process of nation building all over the world. But the world has witnessed non-uniformity in the historical process of economic development. For example, majority of the western countries have experienced rapid development whereas the third world countries have lagged behind. The aftermath of the industrial revolution witnessed heightened process of economic development in the newly industrialised or western countries driven by market oriented capitalism. The so-called process of development in the developed countries began to affect the global economy through its colonial expansion. Economies of the third world were largely exploited or made redundant by the expansionary and exploitative process of the developed countries. Third world countries could not evolve its own economic development process and policy, and were largely dictated by the economy of the developed countries. The hunger for ever increasing surpluses of capital in newly industrialised countries opened the floodgate for proliferation of colonies. Advanced industrial countries embodied in a dominant colonial power and using its superior military power colonised most of the underdeveloped region of the globe. Economies of the newly colonised country were reduced to captive markets for the manufactured exports of its metropolitan capitals. Subjugation and exploitation of the third world economy increased manifold. And third world economy were not only reduced to captive economy but also their natural resources were exploited to feed the manufacturing and consumption needs of the metropolitan capital. Economy of the colonies were transformed into a passive state and transformed into a peripheral economy for the metropolitan capital. A process of underdevelopment and immiserization of the people of the colonies were taking shape and were integrated to global capitalism with a weak internal economy. Colonization phase witnessed the emergence of a bipolar economic world in terms of development operating in a zero sum framework—development of the colonizer at the expense of underdevelopment of the colonies (third world countries).

Even after the decolonization phase, though the third world countries gained political freedom, their economic relationship with the metropolitan capital remains unchanged. The Western capitalist still have hegemony over the economy of the third world. Even the processes of economic development were adopted from the policy prescription of the developed countries. Supranational institutes like IMF, World Bank, MNC controlled by erstwhile colonial powers straggled third world economy through capital investment, loans, aid, etc. Not only the *status quo* relationship between former colonies and Western capitalist, the incidence of economic domination by metropolitan capital over the third worlds had been the inheritance of colonial/capitalist type within the colonies. India's development experienced from the British colonialism may serve as a case in point. In the colonial period, an embryo of indigenous capitalist class was nurtured to smoothen colonial rule. This class served as intermediaries or middleman for metropolitan capital. Colonial rulers had also created indigenous elites, viz. government officials, professionals associated with trade; they were the emerging ruling class of the newly independent India. Post-independent India followed a state backed capitalist development aiming at establishment and strengthening of indigenous metropolitan, and at the same time, neglecting peripheral area. Emerging scenario witnessed a colonial anatomy within the country — a metropolitan and periphery. Regions like north-east proliferated to the status of peripheral economy.

Manipur's economy from its association with British colonialism has been a long journey of peripheral economy and its economic destiny being dictated by exogenous factor failed to evolve its own. Manipur during the pre-colonial period had a rich history of self-sufficient, self-regulating, self-sustaining and stable economy leaving aside few critical phase of hostility with neighbouring countries especially Burma. Its economy during the pre-colonial period was characterized by peasant economy; household manufacturing and trade, both internal and external, formed the other important aspects of the economic life of the people. Strength of the economy was on its productive base and supplemented by exchange. The core of the peasant economy, crop husbandry reached its zenith way back in the early pre-colonial period with the people mastering the art of irrigation for paddy cultivation. Rice economy formed not only the backbone of the agrarian economy but for the economy as a whole. Export of livestocks and forest products formed the other important source of income. Though the use of currency was evident in the pre-colonial period, the economy was not monetized thoroughly as a result there was no commoditization and commercialization. Mode of production which existed in the pre-colonial period was non-exploitative and progressive in nature and existing institutional set-up of that time complemented the smooth and efficient working of the economy. Notwithstanding its smallness, the economy had the potency for transforming into a structurally well balanced economy in the long run. Economy was self-regulating and external element determining the working of the economy was negligible.

Advent of British colonial rule after the Anglo-Manipur War of 1891 brought about major structural changes in the economy subservient to their interest. The thrust of British colonial rule was to penetrate the pre-capitalist formation to organize the condition of surplus extraction and accumulation. This was possible through introduction of private ownership in land, monetization of economy through commercialization of agriculture and taxation. British colonial rule managed to extract huge surplus from rice export and taxation and the revenue generated were utilized for colonial administration rather than for the welfare of the native people. Monetization of the economy had serious implication breaking the cycle of reproduction existed before colonial economic system. Class distinction emerged with the introduction of outside trading class for smoothening rice export and influx of consumer goods from the British India and Europe. With the breakdown of the internal strength of economy after British rule, its economy was slowly but surely transformed into a dependent economy followed by external forces and agents consolidating its base. Institutions in the pre-colonial period that served as an engine of reproduction cycle were dismantled rather than modernized. British colonial rule reduced Manipur into peripheral economy for the metropolitan capital of British India.

Manipur experienced a short stint of independent nation from 1947-49. During this period the agrarian economy of erstwhile pre-colonial period was reviving from the ravage of Second World War. British colonial rule had left an economy that was structurally distorted but possessed a strong agricultural base from where a development path could have evolved. Merger with Indian Union only worsed the already fragile economy with Indian State continuing the trend of colonial legacy. The newly independent India which claimed to be a modern-nation state in the making, had not shed away the colonial policy followed with regard to Manipur but rather appropriated and internalized the colonial policy. Merger with India had implication of a small economy integrating with a big economy. Notwithstanding its smallness, Manipur's economy had a rich history of self-sufficient economy. But merger with India completely undermined its importance not only in the national arena but also for the local populace. Manipur's economy was completely reduced to a peripheral status through the complete monopoly of its development destiny in the mercy of the Centre as the State was union territory. Manipur's economy was completely reduced to a peripheral economy and served as captive market for the newly emerging metropolitan capital of India. More precisely, merger with India was an economic tragedy. Centralized planning of the immediate post-merger was a continuation of British legacy which was evident from the sheer neglect of productive base of the economy. Policy followed after merger only derided the aspiration of the people and helped in consolidating external agents and few section of local elites. Free flow of fund in the region in the post-statehood phase with the inception of NEC and DONER helps only the vested interest group and neglect of productive base continues.

Emerging contours of Manipur's economy depicts a disturbing picture. Worth mentioning are, firstly, the economy is sustaining on inordinate growth in the tertiary sector propelled by central fund, the contribution of agriculture and industry is diminishing.

This trend of central fund backed tertiary growth can collapse anytime. Evolving trend is an outcome of long-term neglect of productive base of the economy. Secondly, economic planning regarded as the ultimate tool for economic development has been reduced to end itself not means. Five Year Plan in the State are not meticulously framed and is devoid of physical and clear-cut targets and lack direction. Economic planning has been merely reduced to economic rituals and it has not contributed significantly to economic health of the region. Regional planning under the aegis of NEC has also not contributed to the growth especially the productive base of the economy. Funds are largely invested in infrastructural and administration for appeasing the ruling elites. Thirdly, there is not a concrete policy for strengthening the productive base of the economy, viz. agriculture and industry. The State has not a draft agricultural policy which will have a long run impact in pursuing for a self-reliant economy. Development policies for agriculture and industry of the State are *ad hoc,* piecemeal and ceremonial in nature which impacts are not filled. Strengthening of these two sectors will create a long chain of linkages both backward and forward helping in generating gainful employment and income. The focus has been on infrastructure and government services that too without a long-term vision. Infrastructure cannot be neglected but disproportionate attention reflects the interest of commission mongering vested interest ruling elites. And finally, development process of the region is shaping in a top down developmentalism of the Indian State. Its destiny and mapping of the course of economic development is being framed by intellectual hegemony of the mainland India devoid of people aspiration. The economy of the region has never been made to stand on its own and its potential is being externalized and underutilized.

The persistence of underdevelopment of the region in general and Manipur in particular cannot be meaningfully explained in a very narrow economistic approach but rather through a historically oriented political economy. The historical roots of the economy must be traced with care; social set-up should be kept in mind; development within sectors and organic linkages among these sectors must be analyzed; the emergence of new class and shifting class relation and the role of the State must be incorporated. The present volume is a humble effort in that direction.

The present volume titled *Quest for Development in Manipur: Continuity, Constraints and Contradictions* is divided into three sections. The first section titled "Evolution and Transformation" has four essays. The first essay by Oinam Ranjit Singh and Elangbam Nixon Singh "Economic Profile of Manipur (33 AD–1652 AD)" provides a glimpse of Manipur's economy as it grows and develops from the early times to the seventeenth century. Tracing the historical development through the help of various sources including *Cheitharol Kumbaba* or the Royal Chronicles, edicts, texts both literary and non-literary, Oinam and Elangbam surveys the economic system in Manipur as it has evolved over the centuries. Pointing out the fact that the land and its people lived in a self-sufficient and self-reliant economy in the period under survey, the essay scrutinizes the different components of the economy. Agriculture and allied activities in the primary sector exhibited remarkable progress during the period. Productivity was substantial in the sense that it could support both consumption demands and commercial demands for export. Other sectors of production like pottery, carpentry and metallurgy also find mention in this essay. Scientific and technological advancements witnessed during the period had profound impact on the economy of Manipur, as significant move towards industry was evident. The essay substantiates the self-sustaining capacity of Manipur's economy during the period surveyed.

The second essay in the collection by Laishram Churchill titled "Trajectory and Transformation of Economy: Before and During the British Period" argues that prior to the British occupation, Manipur was self-sufficient in all its basic requirements. With subsequent structural changes brought about by the British such as abolition of Lallup system and monetisation of the economy, Manipur started losing its self-sufficient status. As manufactured goods imported from outside made inroads into the country, its agricultural products were also exported in large quantities resulting in a quantum rise in the volume of cross-border trade. As elsewhere in the colonial world during nineteenth and twentieth centuries, the increased State revenue was never used for the welfare of the native country but went to the coffers of the British Empire. Despite the positive Balance of Payment enjoyed by Manipur throughout the British period, people became more miserable economically, politically and socially. Taxes imposed by the British Government were comparatively exorbitant. Even though the country as a whole had considerable quantity of surplus food, no village or household had surplus food in stock except those belonging to State officials and royal families. Earlier before the British occupation, each and every village had surplus food stock for at least two years. With the people compelled to produce marketable products that could earn hard money, people neither had time to work for other products of daily requirements nor their products could compete with the imported goods. As such, Manipur became more and more dependent on imported goods. In fact even the self-sufficiency in food, despite producing surplus, was threatened after the entire rice export trade was monopolised by Marwaris and Bengalis. Manipur is still unable to recover from the adverse economic changes brought about by British rulers which were perpetuated by New Delhi after the country's merger with the Indian Union.

The Third essay by Oinam Ranjit Singh titled "Pre-Colonial and Colonial Source of Revenue" argues that for a stable and prosperous state or country, healthy finances are absolutely indispensable. This importance was well understood by the rulers of Manipur. Manipur had a stable source of revenue from different sources. Of the various sources of income, revenue from land, mines, forest, herds, fishery and tributes were paid in kind. But in British Manipur, revenue from land and fishery were paid in cash. The tributes from the vanquished were also abolished during the British rule. Manipur also had ample revenue from duties on trade and commerce, foreigners' tax and fines from convicts, etc.

The last essay of the first section by Hanjabam Isworchandra Sharma titled "Post Statehood Economy: A Critical Analysis" looks into the persistent underdevelopment of the State even after the attainment of statehood and establishment of central agencies like NEC and DONER. Economy of the State which was shattered by centralized planning during the pre-statehood and was expected to be on the right track after the attainment of statehood as economic planning and preparation of budget became the prerogative of the State government. Not only this, parallel to the attainment of statehood, the NEC regarded as a catalyst of development for the North East region was also established. But the emerging scene does not reflect the desired result. Important sectors of the economy, viz. agriculture and industry did not kick off but rather remained stagnant throughout the period. Both the sectors never received adequate attention in the State's Five Year Plans. Hanjabam further argues that foodgrain production, especially rice in the post-green revolution, increased significantly with the intensive use of HYV and fertilizers, however, the State is far from self-sufficient in foodgrain production. Lack of proper irrigation system, demographic pressure, and prevailing land right system in the hill areas are some of the important problems facing the development of agriculture. Industrialization process was initiated immediately after the attainment of statehood but did not last long as it was engulfed both by endogenous and exogenous factors. He further argues that the maximum thrust of the Five Year Plans has been on the development of infrastructure but the State is far from maintaining a quality infrastructure for all-round development. The onset of NEC did not bring about any remarkable change as it also neglected the productive base and rather focussed more on the infrastructural development. The trend continues even after the inception of DONER, clearly indicating the Central Government's intention for nurturing the region as dependent economy.

The second section subtitled as "Problems and Prioritizations" has five essays. The first essay titled, "Foodgrain Economy and Food Security" by N. Manichandra Singh was written behind the reality of foodgrain crisis faced by the global community. He provides an incisive analysis on the role of primary sector in the economy of Manipur. Drawing on the emerging scenario of an inflated government services sector which accounts for the quantum of the total service sector, the essay records the grim realities of a declining agricultural sector and far-reaching consequences and ramifications. Pointing out several factors including demand and supply forces and consumption patterns, Manichandra strongly contends that the issue of food security can be overcome through reduction or minimising deficit in foodgrain production. He elaborately suggests several means of addressing foodgrain productivity in terms of increasing output ranging from expansion of net sown area, intensive land usage and technological improvements. The essay reiterates the urgent need of the Government to formulate a policy for agriculture to pull the State's economy out of the current impasse. Asserting the conspicuous role of such a policy to minimise food deficit through enhanced production as the only way to propel the economy towards self-reliance, the essay tangentially raises the issue of making the cultivated areas in the hills of Manipur agriculturally productive.

The second titled "Industrialization in Manipur: Retrospect and Prospects", essay by Lourembam Sanatomba Meetei foregrounds the importance of industrialization for the development of Manipur. He traces the history of industrialization in Manipur when in 1074 AD a particular division of labour system was introduced in the kingdom by assigning different names in respect of the particular mode of occupation of the people. He is of the opinion that even after 55 years of economic planning and after having put into practice various development programmes and implementations, Manipur still remains industrially backward. She is one of the least industrially advanced States of India. All the nine districts of the State have been categorised as 'No Industries Districts' by the all India standard. Manufacturing sector contributes hardly nine per cent of the State domestic product and a mere 10 per cent of the total working population are found to engage in this sector. There is no large and medium industry in the State. The only industries existing in the State are in the form of small and village industries of which handlooms and handicrafts are worth mentioning. He identifies the prospective sectors where investment can be made. Given the market and abundance of raw materials, industrialisation of Manipur need not be an unrealizable dream, the author argues.

The third essay "Educated Youths and Issues of Unemployment" by Th. Joychandra Singh examines the increasing number of unemployed educated youths in Manipur. As per the 2001 Census, Manipur has a higher rate of literacy than all India average. However, the qualitative uplifting factor needs to be translated in terms of giving an opportunity to earn a livelihood whereby the contributory role (empowerment) becomes more meaningful. In the face of rising educated people in India as well Manipur, an appalling situation is the corollary rise in the number of unemployed educated persons. The accommodative power of the job market remains low. In such a situation, educated persons remain an unproductive human capital.

The fourth essay by Soibam Haripriya, "Invisible Workforce: Role of Women in Economy", makes an assessment of women's contribution to the growth and development of Manipur's economy in different sectors. She provides the historicity under which women started to enter the public space and argues that taking up such roles was necessitated as a way of positioning against colonial policies. She critiques the dominant narratives responsible for silencing gender issues in the economic arena. Debunking popular romanticized images of Manipuri women, Soibam asserts women's role in the evolution of its economy by citing instances of resistance to colonial exploitation which underscores economic currents vital to the welfare of the people. She gives a detailed treatment of women's contribution in the domestic sphere which ironically has not been properly augmented in clear cut economic terms and women's participation in both organised and unorganised sector. Highlighting several issues like underpayment, adverse working environment and conditions, Soibam's essay captures the nuances of economic production *vis-à-vis* women's active engagement in different economic activities. Traditional practices and institutions exclusively handled by women speak volumes for the serious need to generate a debate on the area of women's role in financial and capital generation and management.

The last essay titled, "Medicinal Plants of Manipur: A Potential Sector of Economy" by P.K. Singh explores the rich biodiversity of Manipur and highlights the various medicinal plants in the State. The author argues that Manipur having hundreds of valuable medicinal plants is sitting on a gold mine if properly exploited with due consideration for their preservation can enrich the State's economy. The article mentions the name of valuable medicinal plants found in the State which were used by inhabitants for curing several diseases and ailments since time immemorial. He argues that despite having many medicinal plants in the State, lack of proper government policy and guidelines, has pushed these plants to the brink of extinction. Hence, a policy guideline for the promotion, protection and preservation as well as a marketing support system for commercial exploitation is the need of the hour.

The last section of the book titled as "Developing the 'Development' in Manipur: Towards a Counter Mapping" has four essays. The first essay in the section by Hanjabam Isworchandra titled 'Deconstructing Development Politics' provides different trajectories of development politics. The author brings out how actual development has been missing in the post-independent India. The article brings out some inherent contradictions in India's planning when it comes to the North East India. For example, land lockedness was identified as the main cause of underdevelopment of the region. But in the wake of India's infatuation with Look East Policy, the author argues, geographical location of Manipur has been cited as an opportunity. The author also brings into light how the hegemony of the domestic capitalist class over the economy of the region was established, not by the interplay of market forces, but by coercion and the introduction of non-market factors. The article critiques the ongoing 'militarization of employment' in the form of extensive recruitment of security personnel in the State of Manipur. As an alternative to the existing development paradigm, the article explores the post-development perspective in order to emphasize 'local' empowerment.

The second essay 'Democratic Decentralization of Economic Development' by Homen Thangjam thoroughly investigates into why there is a need for having reciprocity between 'intention' of development and local needs. It is the contention of the author that there is a deeper disillusionment with the notion and practice of development hitherto experienced at the theoretical as well as policy realm and at the pragmatic level in Manipur. While questioning neo-liberal agenda of economic development, Thangjam uses primary data to build upon his arguments. The article advocates for a meaningful utilization of arable land and immediate stoppage to further shrinking of the same. He emphasises that land is the most important asset/capital and its meaningful utilization is important if Manipur aspires for self-sufficiency and comes out of dependency. As a basis to durable economic development, the article advocates for strengthening 'local' manufacturing units. He discusses important sites of alternative economic development in the State of Manipur. The author goes on to suggest for a better site of setting up of a manufacturing units in Jiribam with substantial database. Thangjam's article is suggestive as it points out the lack of political will on the part of the political leadership which according to the author is source of contemporary discontentment.

The third essay by Sanatomba Kangujam's titled 'Contesting Statist Version of Underdevelopment: Development and Conflict' expounds the correlation between the existing conflict, officially described as insurgency, and development in the State. The author provides a counter narrative to what he calls the statist version of underdevelopment, which attributes underdevelopment to the existing conflict. Kangujam raises some of the intriguing questions such as: Does insurgency really hinder economic development or does it serve as a mere pretext for prolonging underdevelopment? Is development not possible in the presence of conflict? Would there be rapid economic development in Manipur had there been no insurgency? Countering the rationale behind the establishment's allegation of underdevelopment in Manipur as a result of insurgency or law and order problem, the author asks why development failed to take root during the period prior to the emergence of armed opposition groups in the State of Assam and Manipur.

Finally, Hidam Premananda's article titled 'Resistance and Development: Shaping of Counter-Discourse' is an exposition on the relation between development discourse and resistance. Hidam's article endeavours to show the ways in which development discourse becomes an interplay between promotion and resistance. Citing the importance of power and politics, the author defines development as a politically constituted discourse. As the author argues development is a language and constitutive of the social reality within which experiences of difference, dissent and aspiration come to play as a force to become what can be considered broadly as the reality of politics. The article further argues that unproblematic nature of development need to be dismantled because development is a complex form of knowledge that produces domination and hegemony with the help of various welfare projects. The author critically assesses the role of resistance to the notion of development which brought a serious rupture within the establishment of development thinking. Resistance as a form of critique contributes to an understanding of how to make crucial transformation by referring it to the terms of debate of development discourses. In the concluding part the author emphasizes the importance of bringing to the fore an understanding of the politics of resistance in order to see that development can be a negotiated discourse, to see that development is not the product of grand narratives but of diverse struggles that nonetheless become organized into coherent patterns of domination, representation, repression and liberation.

SECTION-I

Evolution and Transformation

1

Economic Profile of Manipur (33 AD–1652 AD)

Oinam Ranjit Singh and Elangbam Nixon Singh

Introduction

The economy of Manipur in the early period of its development has been an area of concern for many scholars involved in studying the history of this ancient Asiatic kingdom. It is an interesting area, which still remains to be explored critically. It deserves the attention of the scholars for a systematic study. In this chapter an attempt has been made to present a picture of the economic profile of Manipur in the period preceding contact with the British especially from the reign of Pakhangba to Khagemba (33 A.D. to 1652 AD).

Known through various names in the region between South Asia and South-East Asia, history records its existence as a sovereign Asiatic kingdom since ancient times. Known as Kathe to the Burmese, Meklee to the Ahoms, Mooglie to the Cacharies, Cassey to the Shans, the people of this land have undergone several ordeals in the course of its long drawn civilizational history. It is generally accepted that the history of Manipur begins from 33 AD. *Cheitharol Kumbaba* records the ascension of Nongda Lairen Pakhangba to the throne at Kangla, the ancient seat of power in Manipur in 33 AD (Singh, 1986, 4). Historically evolved practices over the centuries exhibit unique civilizational trends in its socio-economic and cultural milieu. Confluence and convergence of various cultural crosscurrents *vis-à-vis* the interactions with neighbouring civilizations produced an economic system, which included trade and commerce with neighbouring kingdoms or countries. Its geographical location provided the basis of a functional standpoint in terms of the historic Silk Route traversing China, Myanmar and present Bangladesh. Economically, Manipur was self-sufficient and self-reliant in the long span of time from Pakhangba's reign to Khagemba's.

Agriculture

Agriculture was the primary occupation and mainstay of the people of Manipur. In the early period of its civilization, the mode of cultivation was primitive and production was for local consumption. Traditions and myths recorded in a number of literary texts indicate that the ancient Manipuris practiced shifting cultivation. According to the ancient text, *Naothingkhong Phambal Kaba*, the Shelloi Langmai tribe of Nongmaiching Hill was shifting cultivators. *Loyumba Shilyen*, the edicts of King Loyumba (1074–1122 AD), mentions the adoption of wet rice cultivation by the Meiteis during his reign. Another ancient text, *Panthoibi Khongul*, refers to the plantation and cultivation of varieties of crops and paddy by Nongpokningthou and Panthoibi. Chronicles such as *Panthoibi Khongul* refers to several irrigation works by dredging the rivers and making drainages to drain out the water from low-lying marshy areas. King Taothingmang was well-known for his work of draining the marshes of valley and dredging its rivers and stream (Singh and N. Khelchandra Singh, 1967, 2). Located in the tropical region, endemic to heavy rainfall, rains would cause flood as the marshes could not be drained away by the narrow rivers and streams, thus affecting agricultural production (Kabui, 1991, 97).

Prior to the coming of Muslims in Manipur in the medieval period, knowledge and practice of transplantation (*Lingthokpa*) method of cultivation was limited in Manipur. Only two traditional methods, viz. *Punghul* and *Pamphel* were widely practiced in the valley of Manipur (Ali, 1988, 66–7). *Punghul* method was generally applied in dry land. Under this method the land was to be tilled first and the seeds were strewn over it, and finally the seeds were covered with soil through tilling. *Punghul* was done in the month of May and June every year (Ali, 1988, 66–7).

Pamphel was adopted in wetland. In this method, land was first tilled to make it muddy and the field was to be properly levelled. Seeds were soaked with water and packed into an air-tight bag till the seeds germinated. After the seeds germinated, they were sown properly. Generally, June and July are the suitable months for the practice of *Pamphel*.

Another method known as *Lingthokpa* (transplantation) was introduced during the reign of Khagemba (1597–1652 AD). Agricultural technology improved with the introduction of transplanting system of paddy cultivation, introduced in a large scale by the Muslim immigrants from Bengal. Under transplantation method, the farmer at first had to grow the paddy in a nursery and then transplanted them to the fields (Ali, 1988, 66–7).

While the above-mentioned methods were practiced in the valley areas of Manipur, in the case of the hill areas, *Pamlou Uba* (shifting cultivation) was the common agricultural practice. Also known as slash and burn cultivation or *jhum* cultivation, under this method, trees, bamboos, shrubs, etc. grown in the prospective cultivation area were cut down. When they were totally dry it was burnt down and reduced to ashes. In tilling the area neither plough nor cattle could be employed. They scratched up the surface with little hoes and mixed the soil with the ashes (Brown, 1975, 17–8). Another method of farming followed by the hill people was terraced cultivation. Under this method, strips of levelled plots were arranged, which were embanked with mud and trunks in parallel lines (Ali, 1988, 69). This was a less popular method of farming.

Varieties of rice were grown in Manipur, which included early (*Anganphou*) and late crops. *Sajikhong*, *Tumai*, *Kabaw Phou* and *Phourel Anganba* were varieties of early crops. Late crops included *Phourel*, *Luining* and *Yenthik* (Sharma, 2002, 86). A new variety of paddy known as *Taothabi* was introduced by King Khagemba, and planted in the swamps in 1634 AD (Kabui, 1991, 219).

Since very early times, the people of Manipur seemed to have been cultivating varieties of crops. In addition to the cultivation of rice, the people of Manipur also indulged in cultivation of other crops. Traditionally, food crops such as chilli, pumpkin, ginger, millet, sweet potato, cucumber, onion, cabbage, cauliflower, beans, pulses, peas, etc. were cultivated for domestic consumption. But later on, these crops were grown on a large scale for commercial and export purposes (Jhalajit, 1965, 245). Traditional commercial crops cultivated by the Manipuris were mainly confined to cotton, tea, sugarcane, tobacco, etc. There are no available sources indicating the import of these items during the early phase of Manipur's history.

Silk weaving was an ancient agro-related art and its manufacturing was a continuation of the popular tradition in Manipur. Silk was considered an important item for export. Remarking the significance of the silk industry Brown observed:

> About 300 persons are employed in the silk culture, and they pay for the privilege some rupees 300 annually; they are for this payment excused from the operation of *lallup*, or forced labour. The raw silk is disposed of by ... a weaver class called 'Kubbo' – they having originally, it is said, emigrated from the Kubbo Valley in Upper Burma ... the Burmese traders who frequent Munnipore, buy up greedily all the raw silk they can get; this speaks well for the quality of silk, as the silkworm is plentiful in and near the Kubbo Valley (Brown, 1975, 25ff).

Cotton, another important crop for manufacture, was also grown in Manipur. The excellence of Manipuri art and manufacture has been given testimony by several observers. In the treaty concluded in 1762 with Governor Verelst, mention is made of the products of the country: silk, iron, kupass, dammer, black thread, wood oil, wax, elephants' teeth, agar, sandal wood, camphor, red ditto, blue ditto, white ditto, black coss, Meklee cloths, Meklee gold rupees (Pemberton, 2005, 42).

Indigo, bixa and alba, etc. were also cultivated in the villages and homesteads (Brown, 1975, 1). The Manipuris grew a rich variety of garden crops such as tobacco, opium, and different types of plantain, vegetable and a few varieties of spices. Mangoes, pineapples, apples, peaches, jackfruits, etc. were cultivated. Mention also must be made that the agrarian landscape of Manipur was enriched with the coming of the migrant Muslims popularly known as Pangals or Meitei Pangals. Acknowledging their expertise in gardening skills, the then king of Manipur inducted them into the larger Manipuri population by bestowing

Manipuri *Sagei* (surname) names such as Hawai-Ingkhol-Mayum. The Pangals introduced varieties of fruit seeds. They opened a garden called Ningthem Inkhol at Khumidok Heinou Khongnembi by the order of King for cultivation of fruits and vegetables (Singh, and M.A. Janab Khan, 1973, 52–3).

Granary

Several granaries were established by King Mungyamba (1562–1697 AD) to store foodgrains at different places of Manipur. The state godown or granary was known as *Kei*. The objective of the establishment of the *kei*s was to distribute the foodgrains to the needy people during famines or lean seasons (Kabui, 1991, 208). King Khagemba also established state godown at various places to store foodgrains to meet the requirements of the people during famine, drought or other calamities. The places where King Khagemba established granaries were Kakyao, Langpok Leihao, Tingri, Koireng Kei, Mongsang Kei, Kiyam Kei, Wangoo and Yihari Kei (Kabui, 1991, 9). The chief of the village was appointed as *Keirakpa* (keeper of granary).

Handloom

From the earliest times down to the 17th century, there was a slow but steady development of technology in Manipur, which is testified by archaeological findings and historical evidences. The art of spinning, weaving and dyeing had already been developed. *Panthoibi Khongul* speaks about spinning and weaving of varieties of clothes. King Naothingkhong (663–765 AD) innovated coronation costumes such as *Leiruthak* (a head dress), *Chareiningkham* (a triangular piece of cloth with a brocade hanging on the back from the waist), *Phirel Phurit* (a long and loose shirt) for the King and *Leiren Leichao* (ornament of the hair), *Kumshang Phanek* (a sarong dark in colour) and *Kabrang Phanek* (a sarong made of silk) for the Queen (Singh, 1983, 42–3). Handicrafts witnessed immense development during the period of Loiyumba (1094–1122 AD). The task of weaving involving as many as 32 different designs of clothes was assigned to thirty families. The clothes were *Mung Phi, Chinphi, Lai Phi, Wana Kadeng Phi, Lai Phi Tangkap, Phirel, Langdom Phi, Yarongphi, Leirumphi, Dolaithanaphi,*

Purumphi, Taraophi, Pumthitphi, Phimmu, Phinin Lanphi, Leiyekphi, etc. (Kabui, 1982, 23).

Dyeing in eight different colours, based on colours of flowers was assigned to eight families. Historical records indicate silver crowns adopted during the reign of Mungyumba (1562–1697 A.D.) (Kabui, 1991, 207). A popular belief mentions that Queen Laisna, wife of Nongda Lairen Pakhangba had created several designs of clothes based on the pattern of python. Nongmainu Ahongbi, wife of Khuyoi Tompok discovered *Leimatil* (mulberry silk worm). The handloom industry was further developed with the introduction of shuttle locally known as *Pangandem.* Among the Muslim immigrants there were many skilled weavers who made great contributions to the development of handloom and handicraft in the kingdom. King Khagemba assigned *Phisabam Yumnak* (lineage or clan indicating the profession of weaving) to those Muslims who were skilful in the art of weaving.

Pottery

The people of Manipur knew the art of pottery since very early times. The immigrant Muslims introduced improved technology of pottery by using wheels in Manipur. They were given local *Yumnak* (surname) known as *Phusam* by the then King (Sanahal 1985, xv; Sharma and Badar-ud-Din, 1991, 27). T.C. Hodson observes:

> The household utensils consist of earthen pots manufactured for the most part by the *Lois* of Chairel and Shuganu, who also produce stone bowls . . . .which is blackened by lamp black and then wrought to a high polish. Brass, copper, and bell-metal cooking pots are in common use but are imported from Cachar. Plates, both of metal and cheap earthenware, are found in many houses (Hodson, 1989, 39).

Carpentry and Others

Carpentry works played an important role in the traditional economy of the land. Khuyoi Tompok introduced the drum, which was used during wartime, dance, music and other social and religious events (Singh and N. Khelchandra Singh, 1967, 1). Carpentry works including boat making, canoes, *kangpots*, beds, stools, spinning wheel, shuttle, *hookas*, other agricultural implements, making of bridges across the rivers and streams were done by the carpenters (Hodson, 1989, 33; Singh, 1976, 120). *Hijan Hirao* refers to boat making in Manipuri. The immigrant Muslims in Manipur also played a big role to the enhancement of carpentry work. They used *Phundrei* (lathe) for polishing of wood. According to their skill in the carpentry work, the then king of Manipur allotted their *Sagei* (clan or lineages) or *Yumnak* (surname) as *Phundreimayum* (Sharma and Badar-ud-Din, 1991, 28).

The art of making paper was brought by the Chinese to Manipur during the reign of King Khagemba (Sharma and Badar-ud-Din, 1991, 62). The Manipuris learnt the art of manufacturing gun powder from the Chinese merchants who visited Manipur in *circa* 1630 at the time of Khagemba (Hodson, 1989, 21). It is stated that Khagemba, in 1627 AD, "experimented to make big guns, and prepared one metal gun of big size" (Hodson, 1989, 21). The people of Manipur knew the technology of brick making since the time of King Khagemba. This art was learnt from the Chinese. The Chinese called brick as *chek*, which was included in the Meitei vocabulary (Kabui, 1991, 221). British records mention two brick-built walls called *hogaibi* constructed during the reign of King Khagemba. Bricks were used for building only royal houses and temples (Hodson, 1989, 26).

Mineral Ore and Salt

Mineral resources such as iron, copper, salt, lime, silver, gold, tin, etc., were found in Manipur. Many historical texts refer to these mineral resources. According to historians, the reign of Khuyoi Tompok appears to be an age of several technological developments. Technical innovation in metallurgy was also recorded in the chronicle that bronze was smelted and bell-metal was cast. There was a reference to a bridge (Kabui, 1991, 115) over the Naga River constructed with tin and copper. Iron, gold and silver were also used. *Senbung* or bell-metal gong was manufactured during his period (Kabui, 1991, 96–7). During his reign iron was discovered at Kakching, gold at Kongba and copper at Sibong (Sharma, 2002, 88). *Poireiton Khunthokpa* refers to the use of iron implements for the first time in the history of Manipur. British records mention that the Manipuris knew the art of metallurgy and produced metal works for domestic purposes (Dune, 1886, 7). Accounts of the coronation of Naothingkhong speak of iron weapons and metals like silver, gold, etc. The earlobes of Naothingkhong were bore by goldsmith and earrings of gold were put on. The introduction of bell metal currency (Kabui, 1991, 221) by Khagemba proved the development and prosperity of the kingdom.

Manipur produced salt to meet the demands of the people and the Meiteis made systematic arrangements to procure salt which was mainly obtained from the brine wells situated in the valley. Salt wells are situated at the villages of Ningen, Chandrakhong, Sikhong and Waikhong (Sharma, 2002, 91; Hodson, 1989, 33–6). Records indicate that nearly the whole of the salt consumed by the people of Manipur was obtained from salt wells situated in the valley (Brown, 1874, 22).

Fishing

Next to rice, fish constituted one of the most important food items of the people of Manipur. Fishery was an immensely important profession since the early times. The ancient text *Khongchomnupi Nongkarol* mentions six girls of the Luwang clan, who were intimate friends, going to Haoku Soy Lake to purchase fish. The same text also mentions of six youths known as Haoku Pakhang who used to catch fish in the lake and sell them to fishwives. Colonel McCulloch furnishes interesting particulars about the method of fishing employed by the fishermen at the Loktak Lake:

> The Loktak, the great resort of these aquatic birds, is covered with floating islands. Under these, amongst the roots of the vegetation of which they are formed, fish, in the cold weather, collect in great numbers, and are caught in the following manner: An island, having been cut into a manageable size, is pushed to a part of the lake where the water is not very deep, and where the bottom has been paved with stones. There it is fixed by means of long bamboo stakes; and when the fish have collected in sufficient quantity, a long strip sufficient to surround it is

> cut from some other of these floating masses of vegetation. With this the asylum of the fish is surrounded, and a row of stones being placed on the edge nearest the island, that edge sinks down to the prepared bottom, whilst the rest remains upright in the water and thus forms a wall all round. The fish are now driven out of their sanctuary; if small they are taken in nets, if large they are speared (McCulloch, 1980, 30–1).

T.C. Hodson also observes the significance of fish for the Manipuris. "As a large portion of the valley is still underwater, and as fish forms an article of food of the Meitei community, the gentle art gives employment to many people. At present, the State enjoys a large revenue from the fisheries" (Hodson, 1989, 44).

Systematised Economy

Operation of traditional economy existed in Manipur during the period between Pakhangba and Khagemba (33–1652 AD). The ancient text *Naothingkhong Phambal Kaba* mentions of better economic conditions during this period. Use of *Sangbai,* basket for measuring paddy, is also mentioned. It is stated that the King was strict about the paddy seedlings. A slave was killed by tying him to a pole under water for spoiling paddy seedlings kept at the crown land which was tilled by the slaves. People husked the paddy by use of mortar and stick. The women did weaving with spinning of cotton yarn and silk. Animal husbandry was also developed with substantial poultry maintained in almost every household both in the hill and valley (Kabui, 1991, 114). Rearing of cattle like cows and buffaloes was widespread. During the period of King Loiyumba (1094–1122 AD), handicrafts made rapid strides. Agriculture made substantial improvements during Khagemba's reign. A number of technological changes took place during his reign.

The ancient text, *Nongsamei Puya,* refers to the contribution made by Muslim immigrants to a number of technological developments in different fields. For example, the Muslim immigrants during Khagemba's period introduced transplantation of paddy, plough drawn by the bullock and buffalo, etc. King Khagemba took interest in providing irrigation facilities to the farmers and cultivators. Rivers and streams were dredged, canals were dug and bunds were constructed to control flood. Marketing centres were established at different places which facilitated the selling and buying of commodities. The emergence and establishment of markets in Manipur testified existence of surplus produce. There are references to the existence of many artisans of different occupations in the period under survey.

Land Tenure System

In the pre-colonial period all the land in the State belonged to the king. Lands in the valley were classified into two categories, i.e. *ingkhol* (homestead land) and *Lou* (cultivable/agricultural land). These *ingkhols* were distributed in a number of villages. The cultivable lands were classified as (i) *Taonalou,* (ii) *Ningthoulou* or *Sarkari,* (iii) *Phumlo* (*Ihamlou*), (iv) Sepoys (*Siphailou*), (v) *Manaro* (*Manalou*), (vi) Brahmins (*Lugun-lou*), (vii) Royal family, and (viii) Maharani and Temple (*Lairou*), etc. (Howell, 1891, 9) R. Brown states as follows:

> The whole land system of the valley starts with the assumption that all the land belongs to the Raja. Under the Raja is an official named the Phoonan Saloomba, whose duty is to look after all matters connected with land cultivation; he looks after the measurement, receives the rent in kind, and transacts all business matters connected with the land on behalf of the Raja. The land is sub-divided into villages and their surroundings; the head man of each division or village looks after the cultivation, and is responsible for the realization of the tax payable by each cultivator; he holds no interest in the land, and is merely an agent of the Raja (Brown, 1874, 11–3).

It is said that a member of one community was not allowed to cultivate any part of the land owned by another community (Hodson, 1982, 105). *Tounalou* may be regarded as land brought under fresh cultivation. People were allowed to bring land under cultivation with the permission of the king. *Tounalou* holding was generally divided into two: (i) holding through purchase and (ii) holding through clearing of jungles or forests with permission.

The person who possessed *Tounalou* through the latter mode was exempted from payment of tax for one year (Sharma, 2002, 78–9). Under normal circumstances the king could not evict the land-holders without paying proper compensation.

Sarkari-lou was government land. The lands were cultivated by the slaves or free man. If a landholder failed to pay the land tax, he could be deprived of the same (Ali, 1988, 62). *Phamlou* was the service land. It was granted to the state officials. Those people who got land by virtue of their service could get rent for the land given to them. *Siphailou* was the land of the sepoys. Sepoys who were in the service of state were not paid in cash and in lieu were given lands. Size of land holdings varied according to their rank (Sharma, 2002, 79).

The king used to grant land to those who rendered valuable service to the state. This type of land grant was known as *Manalou* and was granted for a period covering only the lifetime of the recipient. It is stated that Brahmins on taking the sacred thread (*Lugun*) were entitled to get one *pari* of land from the king. The land received under this system could not be disposed of or sold out to any other person (Sharma, 2002, 80). This type of land was known as *Logun-lou.*

In addition to the above categories of land, there is another one, which can be broadly defined as land for the royal family. This type of land consisted the landed property granted by the king to his relatives such as sisters, brothers, children and others. They owned such land, more or less, permanently.

Another land tenure system in Manipur was assignment of lands to the temples and Sylvan deities. Govindaji, an important deity of the royal family was assigned one hundred *pari* of land. These lands were cultivated by the slaves of the temple who dwelt in the village of Charangpat, Thinunggei, and Uyan (Howell, 1891, 9). The king also gave lands to those who rendered distinguished service in war. These land grants were called *Pangallou,* i.e. land acquired through merit and strength.

Tounalou, the Raja's own *Lou* and *Phamlou* were taxed. Each household cultivator had to pay tax in kind to the Raja from 2 to 13 baskets of paddy for each *pari.* According to British records, two baskets of paddy was the normal tax to be collected. Only from his favourites and from others, it was set down at twelve baskets annually; this was seldom exceeded, except in rare emergencies such as war. In cases where lands are held by officials, etc., as middlemen, the burdens are more severe, running as high as 24 baskets per *pari* (Brown, 1975, 11–3).

> No one is prohibited from cultivating, but rather the contrary, for every male who comes on duty is entitled to cultivate one *pari* of land, paying a rent for the same. The state rent is nominally 2 baskets of rice in the husks, the basketful weighing 50 or 60 pounds; but usually 12 or 13 baskets are taken. Considering, however, that the worst *pari* of land yields 100 baskets and the best from 160 to 200, the 13 baskets is not a high rent; but so long as the rent taken by the state is given out as two, every basket over this is an exaction, and may be made a matter of grievance, as it is now. But this grievance can only be one as long as the *pari* of the cultivator is of the standard measure, which is very seldom the case indeed, it has sometimes been found nearer two, and until a survey has been made, neither the Raja nor the people can be satisfied (Brown, 1975, 11–3).

The rate of rent of *Sarkari-lou* was very high as compared with other tenures. The cultivators had to pay sixty baskets of paddy as rent. The rent of Pham Lou per *pari* was 24 baskets of paddy as the officers in turn gave revenue of 2 baskets to the state (Howell, 1891, 9).

The systematization of *Lallup* system by King Loiyumba (1074–1122 AD) had drawn the kingdom towards a more stable and organized polity. *Lallup* (*Lal* = war, *Lup* = organization) means war organization. This system emerged during the reign of Taothingmang (264-364 AD), while he engaged labour service of his subject in dredging the Imphal River. *Lallup* covered all the work relating to the state, i.e. both military and civil.

Conclusion

Naothingkhong Phambal Kaba furnishes a good account of Manipur's economy in ancient times. In retrospect, we find several technological developments which appeared during the reign of King Khuyoi Tompok (154-264 AD). Invention of silk rearing, boat making with the help of Luwang chief and exploration of minerals were also ascribed to his reign (Singh, 1967, 196–201). The Ningthouja kings took up major irrigation works in the kingdom. King Taothingmang was well-known for his work of draining the swamplands of the valley of Manipur and dredging its rivers and streams (Singh, 1967, 4–6 and 17–21). Cheitharol Kumbaba refers to the dredging of the Imphal and the Iril rivers by Taothingmang and his brother. *Ningthourol Lambuba* refers to the abundant harvest of paddy. During the reign of King Loiyumba (1094–1122 AD) handicrafts had greatly prospered. The period of Khagemba (1597–1652 AD) was a landmark in the history of Manipur for a number of technological transformations. Growth and development in various economic fields could be witnessed in Manipur from 33 to 1652 AD. In other words, agricultural and industrial life witnessed remarkable development with the rise of diverse arts, crafts and improved technologies.

CITED WORKS

Ali, Ashraf. 1988. *Economic History of Manipur*. Ph.D. Thesis, Manipur University, Canchipur.

Brown, R. 1975. First published in 1873. *Statistical Account of Manipur.* New Delhi: Mittal Publications.

Dune, E.W. 1981. First published in 1886. *Gazetteer of Manipur,* Delhi: Vivek Publishing Company.

Hodson, T.C. 1989. First published in 1911. *The Naga Tribes of Manipur.* Delhi: D.K. Publishers.

Hodson, T.C. 1989. First published in 1908. *The Meitheis.* Delhi: B.R. Publishing Corporation.

Howell, A.A. 1891. *Short Account of Land Revenue in Manipur*. Unpublished archival record.

Kabui, Gangmumei. 1982. *Loiyamba Shilyen: A Royal Decree on the Social Distribution of Economic Occupation*. Proceeding of third session of the North East India History Association.

Kabui, Gangmumei. 1991. *History of Manipur,* Vol. 1. Delhi: National Publishing House.

Khongchomnupi Nongkarol. Unpublished manuscript.

Loyumba Shilyen. Unpublished manuscript.

McCulloh, M. 1980. 1st published in 1959. *The Valley of Manipur.* New Delhi: Gian Publishing House.

Naothingkhong Phambal Kaba. Unpublished manuscript.

Nongsamei. Unpublished manuscript.
Panthoibi Khongul. Unpublished manuscript.
Pemberton, R.B. 2005. First published in 1835. *Report of the Eastern Frontier of British India*. New Delhi: Mittal Publications.
Poireiton Khunthokpa. Unpublished manuscript.
Sanahal, R.K, (ed.) 1985. *Pangal Thorakpa*. Imphal: R.K. Book House.
Sharma, B. Kullachandra and Badar-ud-Din. 1991. *Meitei Pangal Haorakpam*. Imphal: R.K. Book House.
Sharma, K. Ruhinikumar. 2002. *Social and Polity Formation in Pre-Colonial Manipur in the Eighteenth and Nineteenth Century*. Ph.D. Thesis, Manipur University, Canchipur.
Singh, Ch. Manihar, (ed.) 1983. *Naothingkhong Phambal Kaba*. Imphal: Manipur Commercial Co.
Singh, L. Ibungohal and N. Khelchandra Singh, (ed.) 1967. *Chaitharol Kumbaba*. Imphal: Manipur Sahitya Parishad.
Singh, N. Ibobi, 2003. First published in 1976. *The Manipur Administration: 1709–1907*. Imphal: Friends & Co.
Singh, O. Bhogeshor and M.A. Janab Khan, (ed.) 1973. *Nongshamei*. Imphal: XYZ.
Singh, O. Bhogeswar. 1967. *Ningthourol Sheireng*. Imphal: Manipur Commercial Co.
Singh, O. 1966. *Ningthourol Lambuba*. Imphal: Manipur Commercial Co.
Singh, R.K. Jhalajit. 1965. *A Short History of Manipur*. Imphal: R.K. Jhalajit Singh.
Singh, W.I. 1986. *The History of Manipur*. Imphal: Manipur Commercial Co.

2

Trajectory and Transformation of Economy: Before and During the British Period

Laishram Churchill

Manipur as it stands today is virtually dependent on the Government of India for its survival both politically and economically. Though it was once a sovereign kingdom having indigenous economic institutions, at present it subsists itself on centrally allocated funds. One reason is, with the introduction of central planning after it became a part of India, the State's indigenous economic institutions were either marginalised or incapacitated. This emanated primarily from the inability on the part of the planners in New Delhi to comprehend the priorities and fundamentals vital for the growth of indigenous economy while undertaking economic planning. Over and above, the subsequent assimilation and merger of the State's economy with the larger economy of the Indian Union ruined almost all the indigenous economic institutions. Since then, Manipur has become a sort of captive market for the industrial and agricultural goods produced in the more affluent regions of India. Finally, the closure of ancient trade routes between Manipur and the East Asia by India on account of its deep rooted suspicion of the racially different eastern neighbours further muffled the economy of Manipur.

Of recent, there has been initiative from India to open up the eastern corridor to East and South East Asia for trade and commerce. Interestingly, it comes at a time when the indigenous economy of Manipur has been incapacitated and any sound infrastructure and manufacturing units are preesent in the State. Moreover, so far the Government of India has not come out with a suitable or workable economic policy in this regard. In such a scenario, it remains highly doubtful if the much publicised Look East Policy can breathe in any fresh air into the ailing economy of Manipur.

Leaving aside concurrent and contemporary economic issues, the essay will focus on the economic condition of Manipur during the British period with reference to the immediate period before their advent. The essay is an attempt to trace the trajectory of Manipur's economy from being a self-reliant economy, albeit small in capacity, to the present status of dependency. To understand the contemporary dynamics of the economy of Manipur, it is crucial to grasp the economic picture of Manipur during the British period and prior to it.

Manipur's Economy before the British Conquest

Economic status of Manipur in the pre-British period can be broadly described as a self-sufficient local economy. Although lives of the people can never be termed as rich, they were fairly self-sufficient as far as their basic needs were concerned. While many erstwhile kingdoms of India endured famine on numerous occasions during and before the British rule, Manipur experienced no such misfortune. There is no historical evidence of any major famine in the long history of Manipur even as there were records of crop failure.

Though self-sufficient in terms of the basic requirements, Manipur as might be expected from its small geographical size and population and frequent wars with neighbouring countries particularly Burma (now Myanmar), the State revenue's was not large. That the monetary revenue of the State including the compensation of Rs. 6,370 per annum paid by the British Government for the surrender of the Kabow Valley to Burma is estimated to be between Rs. 25,000 to Rs. 30,000 annually from all sources (Brown, 1873, 88). Taxes and duties levied on import-export trade with neighbouring countries constituted a major share of the kingdom's revenue. Annually, Manipur could earn close to Rs. 1,975 as revenue in the form of taxes levied upon goods imported from Cachar. Another Rs. 3,533 came from export duties on goods exported from Manipur. This was in addition to the annual revenue of Rs. 100 earned as duties for export of silk from Manipur to Burma.

Manipur had its own currency system before British occupation. For trade within Manipur and beyond, the kingdom used a currency system with *Sel* being its common unit. Each *Sel* coin weighed about 16 grams. It was made of bell metal and was small in size. Each coin was inscribed with the word *'Sri'*. The market value of *Sel* varied when rupees were plenty, the *Sel* is cheap, whence scarce, it got dearer. During the reign of Chourajit Singh at about 1815 silver coins of square shape were minted in Manipur. It was of the same size and weight as the British rupee. The British and Burmese rupees, both representing the same value were also freely circulated in Manipur as well as smaller silver coins, such as four anna and two anna pieces (Brown, 1873, 89). Manipur enjoyed a favourable position in its cross-border trade with neighbouring countries. In 1868–69, a surplus of Rs. 1,657 accrued to Manipur excluding the compensation for Kabow Valley.

Table 2.1: Balance of Payment, Manipur 1868–69

Export	Rs. 3,632
Import	Rs. 1,975
Balance	Rs. 1,657

Source: R. Brown, 1873. *Statistical Account of Manipur.*

During that period, the export items of Manipur included ivory, wax (bees), silk, dyed thread, mosquito curtains, silk clothes, cotton fabrics (*lashing phi*), thread carpet (*lairoom*), jute fabric (*thowri phi*), chaddar, fabrics from Moirang (*moirang phi*), bed sheets, buffaloes and pony, etc. The import basket consisted of betel nuts, American clothes, long clothes, satin clothes, steel, iron, brass, copper, paper, soap, iron pan, iron nails, Swiss chaddar, velvet, salt (rock), woollen chaddar, umbrella, etc.

Introduction of Tax System

A landmark change brought about by the British after the occupation of Manipur following Manipur's defeat in the Anglo-

Manipur War of 1891 was the abolition of the institution of *Lallup* (British authors roughly defined it as a system of forced labour). In 1892, *Lallup* system was replaced by tax system, which heralded monetization of the entire economy. With the introduction of tax system, there was marked shift in the economic life of the people and revenue collection pattern of the country. For the first time, people felt the necessity to earn money-income for which production of marketable surplus was vital.

A promising beginning could be seen in the composition of exports from Manipur prior to 1949. Industrial products such as cloth, yarn and silk accounted for 20.15 per cent of the overall economy while primary products constituted 79.85 per cent. The Imperial Gazetteer of Manipur (1909) recorded that Manipur was China's contemporary in the production of silk (Mohendro, 2005, 2). However, silk, which was an important item of export, and cotton, which Manipur had the potential for large scale production, given that handloom was an important economic activity of the country, suffered setback on account of misplaced policy orientation and implementation. Moreover, finished goods from these two raw materials could not survive competition from outside imports, and consequently Manipur became a captive market. Moreover, if the King had not imposed restriction against cultivation of silk by the common people other than *Lois*, the Manipuri silk industry would have advanced and could have become the mainstay of the economy of Manipur. Of the silk manufactured, R. Brown commented:

> The cultivation of silk which if properly developed, would form a most important article of export is unfortunately much restricted. The silk culture is entirely in the hands of the *Loi* section of the population. The fact of the *Loi* being the cultivator of silk is fatal to its extension, as by the custom of the country, which so much associates position or caste with the nature of the various employments pursued, anyone wishing to engage in silk culture must lose his position and become a *Loi* (Brown, 1873).

Hodson further adds, 'The Manipuri silk was of fine quality and this was evident from Burmese traders' great demand for raw silk. They would greedily buy all the raw silk they could get' (Hodson, 1908, 31).

Although cotton was not an export item for Manipur, it was grown in the country to meet domestic demands. Weaving being the most important occupation of Manipuri women and every household owning a loom, the quantity of cotton produced in the country was quite considerable. Cultivation of cotton was very popular among the Kuki tribes of Manipur in the South West hills of the country from early period (Hodson, 1908, 45). In 1915, with a view to introduce new varieties of crops in Manipur, the British opened an experimental farm in the northern part of the Manipur valley at Kanglatongbi and cotton was selected to be one of the most important commercial crops to be grown there. Also, it was pointed out that new varieties of cotton could be introduced successfully on the soil of Manipur (Annual Administrative Report, Manipur, 1915, 16). But later on, it was found that the local varieties were more suited to the climate and soil of the country than the foreign varieties and the yield of the new variety of cotton was not satisfactory on account of unfavourable rainfall (Annual Administrative Report, Manipur, 1915–16, 17).

However, with the beginning of import of cotton yarn from outside after the British occupation, the demand for raw cotton dwindled. This subsequently led to a sharp decline in cotton price. Thus, cultivation of cotton which once constituted a crucial factor in the economy of Manipur became no longer profitable. If cotton cultivation should be revived and made profitable once again, it was rightly felt that large quantities should be cultivated and produced in the hills and some in the valley on the higher lands (Letter from the Vice President, Manipur State Durbar to the Political Agent Manipur, No. 881, dated 18-3-1919). In 1942, the Government of India virtually instructed provincial authorities to replace at least half of the existing area under cotton crop by food crops in view of the declining cotton price. This measure led to total disappearance of cotton plants from Manipur where the area under cotton cultivation was already reduced to a great extent. Shortly after, Manipur became wholly dependent on imported raw cotton for its handloom industry. The situation only got aggravated after the lapse of British paramountcy and with the subsequent merger of Manipur to India. The country only changed its position from being a captive market of the cotton mills of Manchester to those of cotton mills located in Bombay and Calcutta.

Trade

Trade, in terms of internal and cross-border, flourished prior to the advent of the British as well as during their rule. On the one hand, internal trade was characterised by exchange of goods between the hill and valley. For example, cotton grown in the hills of Manipur, which were considered of excellent quality, found its way to the bazaar of the valley. In addition to cotton, oilseeds, pepper, vegetables, potatoes, ginger, Indian corn, tobacco, pan leaves, etc. were also sold to the valley. On the other hand, Manipur, on account of its strategic location served as a centre of trade activity for countries such as China, Burma, Cachar, Trepperia and others. For the purpose of trade exchange, as mentioned above, *Sel* was the currency of the country. However, British Rupee and Burmese Kyat, both representing the same value were circulated. Smaller silver coins of four-anna and two-anna were also used. Besides, bartering of articles in the bazaar was also common (Brown, 1873, 90).

A distinguishing feature of the internal trade was that women did all the marketing. Typically, women gathered in open areas to sell goods. Collections of women were to be found throughout Imphal, but the most prominent one was on a vacant plot of ground to one side of the brick bridge over the Nambul River. In the morning, women congregated with their wares for sale. In the afternoon, this market place became deserted after the women moved to the side of the road leading to the Raja's enclosure. All the daily requirements and the produces of the country were sold or bartered at these places.

Manipur's constant war with Burma, especially the seize by Burma, known as Seven Years' Devastation, had crippled her economy. Resurgent recovery of the economy was witnessed during the reign of Gambhir Singh starting from 1826. This period of relative peace and stability were the years of reconstruction of Manipur's economy. Many of those who fled the country in the wake of Burmese invasion returned back. Construction activities were undertaken on a wide scale as devastated villages were rebuilt. And a new capital was built at Langthabal, about 8 km. from Imphal. At the same time, increasing areas of land were reclaimed for cultivation. Along with reopening of old markets, new markets were created and damaged roads were mended. The signs of growth were manifested in the growth of population, increased degree of specialization and diversification of productive activities, raising of new crops, increasing volume of monetization in transactions, commercialization of agricultural products, increasing volume of internal and external trade (Hodson, 2005, 3).

The volume of trade between Cachar and Manipur and also with Burma saw a substantial increase. Once again, goods from the hills including cash crops such as ginger, cotton and pepper, etc. found their way to the markets in the valley or in Cachar. Brisk trade picked up with the Burmese inhabitants of the frontier through the Kabow Valley. Chinese merchants from Yunan occasionally visited Manipur bringing with them the same description of articles they took to Ava and carrying away, in return, ivory, wax, cloth, cotton and ponies of the country.

With the exception of woollen clothing, Manipur produced every article essential for the comfort and prosperity of its inhabitants.

Pemberton wrote:

> Had the same facilities of communication existed between Manipur and the British territories which are found on the opposite or eastern quarter, it would now in all probability have been a densely populated and fertile country; but this unfortunately was not the case, and it was doomed, like every other minor contiguous state, to the devastating visitations of Burmese armies, which have nine or ten times swept the country from one extremity to the other, with the apparent determination of extirpating a race whom they found impossible permanently to subdue (Pemberton, 1835, 35).

Pemberton's observation is misplaced on two accounts. First, after Manipur and Burma became parts of British India and hostility between the two countries ceased, however, Manipur did not witness any remarkable economic growth. Second, even after the lapse of British paramountcy and merger of Manipur into the Indian Union, the connectivity of the State with other Indian States and neighbouring countries continued to be poor. This is in spite of the fact that Manipur occupies a strategic position for commercial purposes, which was well noted by the British even before they occupied the country.

Manipur did not contribute much to the merchandise sought by the Burmese and people of Bengal. This was primarily due to its natural poverty, reduced number of population resulting from frequent wars with neighbouring countries, and finally on account of its political chaos. With regard to trade with Burma, the level of commercial intercourse was highest among inhabitants residing on the banks of the Ningthee River and in the doab of the latter and Irrawady River. However, as in the case of Bengal, it was marked by restrictions. Before 1833, a Manipuri leaving the country had to deposit Rs. 80 as security of his return and had to pay a fine of Rs. 5 for each day of delay. Every Indian trader coming to Manipur had to pay one anna and another 12 annas before leaving the country. Over and above, Manipur's access to the west at that time was restricted to those proceeding on pilgrimages to western India and Nadia.

Situated in the very heart of the great chain of mountains which separate the British (India) and Burmese territories, the valley of Manipur presents a most convenient point of assemblage for the traders on either side. Pemberton opined, 'The centrical situation of Manipur, its peculiarly fine climate, fertile field and its intimate connection with the British Government then, marked it as a spot peculiarly fitted to become the centre of trade between Burma and Bengal (Pemberton, 1835, 168).

Transformations during British Period

After the British occupation of Manipur since 1891, western institutions and colonial structures necessary for the universal colonial goal of economic exploitation and surplus extraction were promptly established. Not long after establishment of their rule in Manipur, the British administrators affected profound changes not only in the political system but also in economic and social sectors. Foremost among them were the introduction of new land and administrative system and setting up of new revenue and commercial structures. Along with the monetization of the indigenous economy, modern infrastructure for trade and commerce were initiated. The relatively closed and agrarian economy was opened up. Such changes were necessary for a conducive transformation towards a market-based economy, which would give a favourable return to the colonial rulers. Along with the monetization and opening up of the economy, the British rulers and their agents (Marwari and Bengali traders) had monopoly over export-import trade.

Raiyatwari systems of land tenure were introduced in the Manipur valley. Under the *Raiyatwari* system, no intermediary proprietors were recognised and settlement was undertaken with the *raiyats* on an individual or collective basis for temporary periods. The *raiyats* were vested with inheritable and transferable rights of property and made individually or collectively responsible for revenue payments (Joshi, 1987, 4). The new land system, with taxation in money, heralded the process of monetization and marketization of economy and commercialization of agriculture. The revenue assessment for one *pari* of land (2.5 acres) was Rs. 5 and Rs. 2 for each homestead. There was a rush for *pattas* (legal ownership documents) and agricultural land which was only 26,500 *paris* in 1881 rose to 75,370 *paris* by 1941. The population of the valley rose from 1,35,782 in 1891 to 3,43,694 in 1941. Thus, the man-land ratio increased from 0.195 to 0.219. In other words, one *pari* of land supported 5.12 persons in 1891, which was reduced to only 4.56 persons by the end of the British rule (Chongtham, 2005, 48).

Table 2.2 gives a concise picture of the quantitative dimensions of changes in the agrarian sector during the British period.

From Table 2.2 it can be inferred that during the period from 1891 to 1941, Manipur had exportable surplus of rice close to 34 per cent of the total produced in each year. The Administrative Report of 1894–95, states that every village in the Manipur valley had surplus food stock for two years.

Table 2.3 shows the export of rice and *chira* from Manipur in the corresponding years. Rather than encouraging the native traders, the British rulers handed over the entire export business to Marwaris and Bengalis, particularly the former. Thus, the lion's share of the rice export business went to the Indian business men. In short, the native cultivators were exploited only to benefit the colonial rulers and their agents. The profitability of the trade in Manipuri rice was evident from the large number of Kabuli traders who visited the country and by the fact that they made heavy remittances to the Imperial Government (Administrative Report of Manipur Political Agency, 1892–93).

The most important road before the British occupation of

Table 2.2: Area, Production and Rice Surplus in Manipur Valley (1891–1941)

Year	Valley population	Area (ha)	Demand (MT)	Production (MT)	Surplus (MT)	Surplus demand (%)
1891	1,35,782	26,500	28,107	38,160	10,053	26
1901	1,91,207	42,283	39,580	60,887	21,307	35
1931	2,86,843	71,316	59,376	1,02,695	43,319	42
1941	3,43,694	75,370	71,145	1,08,533	37,388	34

Source: Administrative Reports for Population and Area under Paddy.

Manipur was the one leading from Manipur to the British province of Cachar. This road was constructed by the British Government shortly after the Burmese War and was maintained by it until 1865 after which the maintenance was done by the Manipuri kings (Brown, 1873, 97). However, after 1891, the cart road from Imphal to Dimapur gained more prominence with the extension of Assam-Bengal Railway till Dimapur. Apart from these two routes, a third road leaves the valley to the South, passing through Tumu and reaches the valley of Chindwin in upper Burma. Of the three roads connecting Imphal with Tumu, Kohima and Silchar, the first-two were maintained by Manipur Government and the last by the Assam Government (B.C. Allen *et al.*, 1979, 622). By the second decade of British Rule the vital road links to Cachar, Dimapur and Tumu had become fully operational. Coupled with the extension of the Assam-Bengal Railway till Dimapur, there was a sharp increase in the import volume along Imphal-Dimapur road through Mao. Consequently, there was decline in the import along Imphal-Silchar road through Jirighat. Nonetheless, the Imphal-Silchar route remained the most important export route from Manipur.

As reflected in Table 2.4, Manipur saw a quantum increase in its cross-border trade by the second decade of British Rule. The

Table 2.3: Rice and *Chira* Export from Manipur during 1901–1940

Year	1900–01	1911–12	1924–25	1932–33	1934–35	1938–39
Rice (MT)	2655	4107	7589	10542	9334	14143
Chira (MT)	–	–	–	–	5331	7551
Total	2665	4107	7589	10542	14645	21694

Note: *Chira* (pound rice) data recorded 1933–34 onwards only.
Source: Administrative Reports of relevant years.

increase in import was well corresponded by the rise in export volume and as such, Manipur enjoyed positive trade balance in most of the financial years except for some in between. The enhanced cross-border trade may be accounted by increased productivity and better connectivity established after the British conquest of Manipur. The increased productivity was largely a result of complete monetization of Manipur's economy, which impelled farmers to pay taxes in cash as against the earlier practice of paying taxes in kinds or agricultural produces. The British legislation compelled people to produce marketable surplus products.

However, despite producing more, the people did not see any improvement in their economic life rather they became more miserable due to two reasons: first, imposition of high taxes by the British rulers and second, complete monopolization of cross-border trade by Marwaris and Bengalis. The miseries and economic insecurity of the Manipuri people were testified by the two open revolts by women, popularly known as the Women's Wars, the first against forced labour and the latter against man-made foodgrain scarcity.

Conclusion

Prior to the British occupation, although the economy of Manipur was not prosperous, it was self-sufficient in all its basic requirements. *Lallup* system had a direct bearing on the economy of the kingdom and compensated paucity of State revenue for undertaking public works. Moreover, the *Lallup* system made every male population of the Manipuri society militarily fit. Most often they (men serving under the system) formed a basic component of the Manipuri army and at times, they constituted a formidable reserve army against the ever-lurking threat of Burmese aggression.

With the abolition of *Lallup* system and monetization of the economy, Manipur started losing its self-sufficient status. As manufactured goods imported from outside made inroads into the country, its agricultural products were also exported in large quantities resulting in a quantum rise in the volume of cross-border trade. As elsewhere in the colonial world during nineteenth and twentieth centuries, the increased state revenue was never used

Table 2.4: Import-Export through Jirighat and Mao, Trade Balance of Manipur 1901–07

(in Rupees)

Year	*Jirighat*	*Mao*	*Total*	*Jirighat*	*Mao*	*Total*	*Balance*
1901–02	1,21,608	68,988	1,90,596	1,21,985	1,20,822	2,42,807	(+) 52,211
1902–03	89,825	1,22,185	212,010	112,228	78,257	1,90,485	(–) 21,525
1903–04	1,00,271	2,46,064	3,46,335	2,58,730	1,36,817	3,95,547	(+) 49,212
1904–05	1,28,416	1,21,064	2,49,480	95,154	95,183	1,90,337	(–) 59,143
1905–06	93,998	1,16,029	2,10,027	1,64,422	1,38,637	3,03,059	(+) 93,032
1906–07	87,535	2,57,405	3,44,940	5,41,891	2,64,422	7,06,333	(+) 3,61,393

Source: Administrative Reports of relevant years.

for the welfare of the native country but went to the coffers of the British Empire. Despite the positive balance of payment enjoyed by Manipur throughout the British period, people became more miserable economically, politically and socially. Taxes imposed by the British Government were comparatively exorbitant. Even though the country as a whole had considerable quantity of surplus food, no village or household had surplus food in stock except those belonging to the state officials and royal families. Prior to the British occupation, each and every village had surplus food stock for at least two years. With the people compelled to produce marketable products that could earn hard money, people either had no time to work for other products of daily requirements or their products could not compete with the imported goods. As such, Manipur became more and more dependent on imported goods. In fact even the self-sufficiency in food, despite producing surplus, was threatened after the entire rice export trade was monopolised by the Marwari and Bengali traders. Manipur is still unable to recover from the adverse economic changes brought about by the colonial British, which was perpetuated by New Delhi after the country's merger with the Indian Union.

CITED WORKS

Allen, B.C., E.A. Gait, H.F. Howard and C.G. Allen. 1979. *Gazetteer of Bengal and North East India*. New Delhi: Mittal Publications.

Brown, R. 1873. *Statistical Account of Manipur*. New Delhi: Mittal Publications.

Chongtham, Priyoranjan. 2005. *Agrarian Structure and Production Relations in Manipur*. Ph.D. Thesis, Manipur University.

Hodson, T.C. 1908. *The Meitheis*. Delhi: Low Price Publications.

Joshi, P.C. 1987. *Institutional Aspects of Agricultural Development*: New Delhi: Allied Publishers.

Manipur State Administrative Report 1873–74.

Manipur State Administrative Report 1915–16.

Manipur State Administrative Report 1916–17.

Manipur State Office File; 'Letter from the Vice President', Manipur State Durbar to the Political Agent Manipur No. 881 dated 18-3-1919.

Meitei, Oinam Somorendro. 2005. Economic History of Manipur (1826–1891)'. www.manipuronline.com

Mohendro, N. 2005. Development experience in Manipur (1891–1969)', www.manipuronline.com

Mohendro, N. 2005. The Lost Article of Self-Reliance. www.manipuronline.com

Pemberton, R.B. 1835. *The Eastern Frontier of India*. New Delhi: Mittal Publications.

3

Pre-Colonial and Colonial Sources of Revenue

Oinam Ranjit Singh

Introduction

For a stable and prosperous state, healthy finances are indispensable. The importance of this proposition was well realised by ancient political thinkers. Kautilya's *Arthasastra* remains an important source for revenue administration of ancient India. It states, "The treasury should be able to stand the strain of expenditure during times of adversity. Without treasury it is not possible to maintain the army and to keep it loyal" (Shamasastry 1929, 1). Many writers, too, accept the significance of revenue. G.P. Singh states, "It was one of the six virtues as well as the primary duty of the king to replenish the treasury, amass the wealth by all pure means and to increase the resources for not only consolidating his own financial position, but also to promote the growth of the state and welfare of his subjects" (Singh, 1993, 103). So, an efficient administration is closely related with a sound system of revenue. Ungaonkar adds that treasury is the breath of the king's existence, and not the air he breathes (Ungaonkar, 1986, 171). Even in the theories of state formation, it is accepted that the institution of the state had emerged only when a community produced more commodities or surplus which could be given as revenues by the people.

The present essay examines the sources of revenue of the Manipur state before and during British colonial rule. Ample historical evidences for the reconstruction of the history of revenue system in ancient Manipur is scarce. For the purpose of the study and as far as revenue system during ancient Manipur is concerned, four major works are consulted. First is the royal edict of King Loiyamba popularly known as "Loiyamba Shinyen". And the other ancient texts are "Mashin" and "Loina Shinlon" and "Loiyumba Sinyen". After Manipur lost her sovereignty in 1891 to the British, notable changes were introduced not only in the structure of the economy but also in the realm of revenue system. For example, traditional form of revenue system which was based on payment in kinds was replaced by payment in cash. Moreover, tributes from the vanquished were also abolished during British rule in Manipur.

Overview of the Sources of Revenue of Manipur

The Manipur state grew up gradually to become a consolidated and well ordered feudal state in the fifteenth century. Under feudal rule, the basic assumption is that all the land belongs to the Raja, and in the case of Manipur too, the king can "give away or retain (*sic.* land) as he pleases" (Brown, 1874, 11–3). A well organised system of taxation emerged during this period in Manipur. In the discussion of the principles of taxation in Maipur, N. Ibobi Singh says that king had the right to impose and accumulate taxes from the people as a price for the services rendered to them (Ibobi, 2003,148). In the case of India, Hindu political thinkers are of the opinion that, the king had the right to collect one-sixth of the total produce from the cultivator in exchange for his services of protection. The Raja was, however, expected not to be greedy and thereby, not to become an engine of oppression. He should pluck the ripe fruits from his kingdom just as one gathered them from a garden, but should not take unripe fruits which caused provocation, lest this should bring about his own ruin (Ghosal, 1929, 17). It is pointed out that taxation must not be vexations. If the cow is milked too much the calf would not nourish. The milkman should also behold that the udders of the cow is not hurt. The king should act like a gardener and like the maker of charcoal. So taxes should be imposed at the time and place most suited for the subjects. Usually, taxation should not be levied on the capital. Kings in Manipur were informed by similar sense of justice while imposing taxes upon the subjects.

The main sources of income of the Manipur is pre-colonial and colonial periods may be classified as: tax on land, tax on forest, tax on mine, tax on fisheries, tax on herds, duties from trade and commerce, foreigner's tax, fines, tributes from the vanquished and revenue in the form of services.

Tax on Land

In a primitive economy, land is the most important asset of the people. When people practiced shifting cultivation and were living under subsistence economy, no tax was imposed on lands. But when settled agriculture was practiced, the state imposed taxes in the forms of certain quantum of paddy as tax. In the case of Manipur, too, revenue from land was the major source of income. Next to the *Lallup* duty, land revenue was the most important source of revenue of the state of Manipur (Ali, 1988, 194). The main occupation of the people was agriculture. And agriculture played a big role in the development of the economy. In the beginning of the eighteenth century nearly one half of the valley was fit for raising crops of various kinds and about half was under cultivation. Every individual who was subjected to the operation of *Lallup* was entitled for his support one *pari* of land equivalent to about three English acres, subject to the payment of the regular tax in kind (Hodson, 1989, 85–6).

Chronicles such as "Cheitharal Kumbaba", "Loiyamba Shillon", and "Poireiton Khunthokpa" throw some light on the socio-economic and political life of the people of Manipur, and also provides an account of the introduction of agriculture and use of land in ancient times (Singh, 1963, 11). These sources indicate that since the time of Pakhaba, the first king of Manipur, there existed a systemic pattern of land use system and the valley of Manipur was divided into four *Pannas* for the purpose of administration. Agricultural lands were divided as: *Ningthu Lou, Lugun Lou, Siphai Lou, Mana Lou, Pangal Lou, Lai Lou, Pham Lou, Touna Lou, Sarkari Lou* (Howel, 1891, 9).

In the above categories, there were lands for which the owners did not have to pay any tax. These included *Ningthou Lou, Lugun Lou, Siphai Lou, Mana Lou, Lai Lou* and *Pangal Lou*. Following Table 3.1 shows the categories of tax-free land along with estimated area as found in 1891:

Table 3.1: Categories of Tax-free Land

Type of land	*Estimated area (in Bigha*)*
Ningthou Lou	12,000
Lugun Lou	18,750
Siphai Lou	67,500
Mana Lou	22,500
Lai Lou	3,750
Total	**1,24,500**

* 1 *Bigha* = 0.33 Acre = 0.13 *Pari*.

Source: Singh, N. Khelchandra, 1979. Lam in Sahitya. *Manipur Sahitya Parishad Quarterly* 10–11, 40–41, May to August.

The lands from which taxes were levied included *Pham Lou, Touna Lou* and *Sarkari Lou*. As is found in 1891, the respective areas covered by *Pham Lou, Touna Lou* and *Sarkari Lou* were 9,000 Bighas, 37,500 Bighas and 27,750 Bighas, respectively. So the total areas covered by these categories of lands were 74,250 *Bighas*.

Lands owned by civilians were subject to payment of revenue of "one Chengkok (about 20 seers) of rice to the Raja every year" (Singh, 1963, 96). The tax in kind realised from each cultivator is liable to many modifications, however, in theory, the tax was a fixed one. Generally, 12 baskets (each basket containing about 30 seers) of paddy was collected from each *pari* of land as tax (Allen, 1905, 114). "The tax, as given by McCulloch varied from two baskets to 13 from each *pari*". Hodson notes that the two baskets which nominally should be only taken from every one alike, is realised from favourites, and that the average from others may be set down at 12 baskets yearly; this is seldom exceeded, except in rare emergencies, as war. He further stated that this again was applicable only to land cultivated for the Raja or held by those subject to *Lallup*. In cases where lands were held by officials, such as middlemen, the burdens were more severe, running as high as 24 baskets per *pari* which was the outside limit (Hodson, 1989, 86).

The average yield per *pari* was about 150 baskets annually: each basket contains about 60 pounds. Colonel McCulloch wrote in his report to Government, dated February 28, 1867:

> The state rent is nominally 2 baskets of rice in the husks,

> the basketful weight 50 or 60 pounds; but the worst *pari* of land yields 100 baskets and the best from 160 to 200, the 13 baskets is not a high rent, but so long as the rent taken by the state is given out as two, every basket over this is an exaction, and may be made a matter of grievance, as it is now (quoted in Hodson, 1989, 86).

This pattern of collection of land revenue existed till 1891 (Singh, 2003, 151). The estimated land revenue in that year was 85,000 maunds of paddy (Shakespeare, 1907, 1). The King appointed a sub-collector with some subordinate staff such as Phourungba, Pana Sanglen Lakpa, Leiyat Lakpa, Khullakpa, Lambus and Lamchaba for the purpose of revenue collection (Devi, 2002, 148). Revenue collection was carried out throughout the year. But the peak season was *Poinu* or month of harvesting, which was extended up to the two succeeding months without fine or reduction of Uchikhang (damage by mice) (Singh and Singh, 1967, 96 and 101). Fine was imposed in proportion to the amount of grains damaged by mice but relaxation might be made on the mercy of the King (Devi, 2002, 148).

Land owners paid taxes in the form of paddy starting from the reign of Khagemba (1597–1652 AD), during whose reign the revenue system was systematised. The suppliers of foodgrains were exempted from military service and the *Lallup* system (Gangmumei, 1991, 218–19). The administration of revenue circles were undertaken by the *Panas*. The department of revenue was kept under the "Lourungpurel Achouba" who supervised the work of "Pana Puren" and "Lourungba Macha" (Kabui, 1991, 220). The villagers had to supply certain quota of paddy to the state after keeping their requirements, and the rent of the land was 12 pots of paddy per hectare. The Lourungshang Office undertook land measurement and census of the individual holding lands, land record keeping of settlement and agricultural areas, custodian of land records, to allot land to applicants, etc. (Chandrasekhar, 1975, 7; Devi, 2002, 149).

Beginning from the year 1892, land revenue was purposed to be amassed partially in kind and partially in cash. But payment in kind was dropped and land revenue was paid in cash at the rate of rupees five per *pari* since the year 1892. It is estimated that the total receipt from land revenue was Rs. 1,24,382 in 1892 and it increased to Rs. 2,81,291 in 1906. The cost of collection raised from 3 per cent of the gross receipt in 1899 to 9.57 per cent in 1906–07 (Singh, 2003, 152). The percentage of land revenue collection was increased from 72.32 per cent in 1894–95 to 96.08 per cent in 1898–99 (Administration Report, 1898–99, 5) and to 98.24 per cent in 1907.

Revenue from Forest

Out of the total area of Manipur, about 90 per cent is in the hills, which is covered by forest. Forests have provided sustenance for the people for ages. It is believed that principality which had control over forest in the hills built-up strong government. Pemberton writes:

> I know no spot in India in which the products of the forests are so varied and magnificent but their utility is entirely local, as the nature of the country precludes the possibility of transporting to foreign markets... Every village is surrounded by a grove of forest trees (Pemberton, 1835, 11–20).

E.W. Dune also opines:

> The climate at once rainy and temperate cover the hills in the western portion with thick forests and induces the inhabitants to grow rice, causes numerous rivers, streams and marshes and encourage aquatic and water loving plants. Forest in the east is not thick as in the west. Oak replaces bamboo, firs for Nageshwar, a drier climate produced a lighter and different kind of Jungle (Dune, 1981, 6).

Forest products like honey, wax, wood oil, ivory, timber, silk, etc. were good source of income of Manipur. Since 1892, there had been a regular income from forests. In 1892–93 an income of Rs. 4,037 came from the forests. In the year 1904–05 forests fetched an income of Rs. 39,529.

Tax on Mines

Another important source of income of the state was the mines of salt, lime, iron and gold. Salt being a scarce commodity, the state made systematic arrangements to procure the precious item. Principal salt wells were located at the villages of Nigel, Chandrakhong, Sikhong, Waikhong, Chalou, Torbung and Chibu. 30 per cent of the quantity of salt manufactured went to the king; the remaining 70 per cent was distributed among the workmen (Hodson, 1989, 35). The salt wells belonged to the king and tax was imposed on those people who produced salt from these wells (Ali, 1988, 195). In 1867–68, the monthly yield was 150 maunds of which more them half was furnished by Ningel (Hodson, 1989, 35). The wholesale price of salt before January, 1869 was about Rs. 6 and 4 annas per maund (Hodson, 1989, 36). The workers employed in salt production were from the *Loi* community and their *Lallup* duty was for six months in a year. But longer period of engagement in *Lallup* was remunerated by the state.

Limestone deposits were found in Khangoi and Nungshangkhong in the country. It is said that lime pits were also available at Tangjeng, Toupokpi, Khubungkhunou and Kangbung near Shugunu, Aimol Khunyai, Nungjaopokpi and Soubam near Kakching (Government of India, 1964, 10). In the pre-colonial period, these areas supplied the state with lime. Since the year 1891, no substantial income came to the state (Singh, 2003, 155). Hodson says that the comparative abundance of limestone outcrops in the valley, occurring at places many miles apart, is significant of the presence of this valuable mineral beneath the alluvial deposits of the valley and some of the limestone deposits were worked one hundred and fifty years ago (Hodson, 1989, 32).

Historical references to iron are found in literatures such as "Poireiton Khunthokpa" and "Naothingkhong". During the period of Khuyoi Tompok (154–264 AD) iron was found at Kakching, gold at Kongba Meirembi and copper at Sibong. The accounts of Poireiton refer to the use of iron implements for the first time in the history of Manipur. Use of iron implements in agriculture, weaponry like swords, spears, *dao* and other tools testified the availability of iron and the development of blacksmithy in the kingdom. Accounts of the coronation of Naothingkhong mentioned about weapons made from iron and other metals. So iron was found in the valley of Manipur and Kakching was the main iron ore producing centre (Singh 2003, 155).

Pemberton remarked:

> Iron, the only metal yet ascertained to exist in Manipur, is found in the form of titaniferous oxydulated ore, and is obtained principally from the beds of small stream south of Thoubal and the hills near Langathel. The principal articles manufactured are such as would be thought of in the earliest stages of civilization–axes, hoes, and ploughshares for felling timber and preparing the ground for agricultural purpose, spear and arrow heads for self-defence and blades which fixed in a wooden or metal handle under the name of *dao* forms the inseparable companion of the Manipuris, Burmese, Shan and Singpho (Pemberton, 1966, 27).

Accounts of the earliest use and availability of gold is mentioned during the reign of Naothingkhong (663–763 AD). The King wore earrings made up of gold. Gold was also used as decorative pieces of households. For example, King Khagemba feasted off gold vessels (Hodson, 1986, 30). Five hundred Manipuri gold pieces were valued at Rs. 12 each in the treaty alliance of Raja Jaee Singh with East India Company (Pemberton, 1966, 42–3). Gold was produced at Shokpao and is found in almost all the rivers of Manipur (Chowdhuri, 1959, 370).

Revenue from Fishery and Herds

Fish and herds formed important sources of revenue for the state before 1891. Fish is one of the most important food items of Manipur. The fishermen had to supply fish to the royal kitchen and also to the nobles and the sepoys.

Ngarungba, the fishery officer was responsible for looking after the lakes from which fish tax was regularly collected (Singh, 2003, 186). About eighty-seven fisheries were under surveillance, which were given to favourites and nobles of the King. These fisheries were regularly auctioned by the British after their rule commenced over Manipur. The Waithou Shorien and the Waithou Phoomnow were two lakes which in 1903–04 fetched an income of Rs. 6,450 and Rs. 1,475, respectively. The Ekop Lake in the same year fetched Rs. 3,170 and the Kajipat Lake Rs. 1,410 and the Pumlen Lake Rs. 1,000

(Allen, 1905, 121). The income from fishery in the year 1892-93 was Rs. 14,522 and it was Rs. 35,283 in 1906–07 (Singh, 2003, 166).

In case of the rivers, a cess was occasionally levied on each net employed. Hodson says, "The policy of letting the fisheries by public auction is attractive to the sections of the community who have means, but it has on occasions given rise to a conflict of the interests of the fishery lessees and of the villages, many of which enjoy rights over weirs and streams" (Hodson, 1989, 46). Herds played an important role in the economy of the state. The King had different sheds for bulls and cows, buffaloes, horses and elephants. In 1870 income from sale of elephants was Rs. 7,000 (Singh, 1965, 244).

Duties from Trade and Commerce

There were trade and commerce among the native people and also with people outside the state before the coming of the British in Manipur. But trade and commerce could not be carried out in a large scale due to poor road condition and transportation system. Moreover, trade was confined to specific articles such as salt, clothes, agricultural produces, cattle and so on. British Rule in Manipur brought about changes in the traditional system of trade and commerce.

Duties from trade and commerce constituted an important item of income of the state. These were imposed on different goods exported from and imported to the state. In the year 1868-69, the state collected as duty a sum of around Rs. 1,975 from imported articles and Rs. 3,633 from exported articles. The amount received on account of licenses for cutting wood in the Jiri forest was estimated at Rs. 7,406 (Singh, 2003, 157). The tax on pony was increased to Rs. 23.40 to Rs. 23.80 but it was reduced to Rs. 20.00 again.

During the reign of King Gambhir Singh unauthorised tolls at Chandrapur were imposed on the Kacharis who were accustomed to proceed up to the Barak River for cutting grass, timber and bamboos. "The king forced the Kala Nagas to dispose of their cotton, ginger and pepper at an arbitrary valuation fixed by himself or by his agents" (Barpujari, 1963, 76).

Manipur produced a good quantity of silk. A village called Leimaram was specialised in production of high quality silk. Brown said:

> The cultivation of silk which if properly developed, would form a most important article for export. The silk culture is entirely in the hands of the *Loee* .... About 300 persons were employed in the silk culture and they paid for privilege some rupees 300 annually. Only a small quantity of silk cloths finds their way into Cachar. The Burmese traders purchased greedily all the raw silk they could get (Brown, 1973, 25).

Pemberton also notes:

> The principal article of manufacture in Manipur consisted of coarse Khess cloths, perfectly white; a very soft and light description of muslin worn by women as scrafs; a coarser description for turbans and jackets and their silk manufactures which were remarkable for their strength, and brilliancy of their colours, were made up principally into petticoats, jackets and large scarfs, the last of which were only worn by the higher orders of the male sex; some of these scarfs were very richly embroidered, and though the work was coarse, they were highly prized in Ava (Pemberton, 1966, 33).

Foreigner's Tax

Foreigner's tax was another important item of revenue of the state. A sum of Rs. 5.00 was imposed on all adult foreigners living in the state who were neither in government service nor in the employment of the Manipur state. During the year 1900–01 an amount of Rs. 4,429 was collected under the head. In the year 1907–08 the amount was increased to Rs. 9, 256 due to immigration of a number of outsiders (Administrative Report 1900–01, 7). In addition to the personal tax on foreigners, grazing fees were also levied in 1894–95 from foreigners who kept cattle for trading purposes at a rate of 4 annas per year per head of cattle.

Fines

In early days, forced labour was the most widely practiced form of punishment. Flogging for men and *Khungoinaba* for women (in which a half-naked woman was exposed in different markets) were more customary modes of punishments too. When British rule was established in Manipur, imposition of fines became more important than forced manual work. Besides, ostracism, and exile and beating, fines were collected from wrong doers. The only penalty Panchayat courts could inflict was fine and that must not exceed Rs. 50 in rural areas. The town Panchayat at Imphal could impose fines up to Rs. 100 and decide civil and criminal cases (Shakespeare, 1907, 2). The Cherap Court could order as many as 500 lashes to a person for not obeying the Manipuri custom (Administration Report, 1895–96, 14) and award two years' imprisonment, a fine of Rs. 500 or flogging. Receipt from "Law and Justice" varied from Rs. 893 in 1892–93 to Rs. 14,705 in 1906–07.

Tributes

Tribute was a very important source of revenue of the state. The conquered communities were compelled to pay tribute in the form of clothes, cattle, baskets, forest products, herbs, agriculture products and so on. "Loiyamba Shinyen" fixes the quantum of tributes to be paid to the state by different communities. Revenues were collected, generally during the time of harvest. All the clans of Manipur except the Ningthouja clan paid tribute to the king of Manipur. The Moirang paid "Leishang" creeper as tribute to Ningthoukhomba (1432–67 AD). It is mentioned that the tribute of Moirang contained *Mushumphi* (a cloth), *Shareng* (Wallago attua big and fairly good eating fish) and fifteen pitchers of *Hentak* (a preserved edible food prepared from small fish). When a child was born to the King, headmen of villages of Moirang supplied or offered bowls, dishes and clothes to the queen (Singh, 2003, 170). In the fifteenth century Moirang King was given a status of tributary chief (Kabui, 1991, 188). The people of Kakching gave swords, iron ores, bowls and dishes as tribute. The village of Sugunu paid pines in tribute. The pottery-making villages like Chairel, Thoubandong, etc. provided earthen pots annually. Wine manufacturing villages like Sekmai supplied pots of paddy and pitchers of wine especially for the Kuki soldiers of the King (Singh, 2003, 170).

Besides tribute from different clans in the valley of Manipur, the King of Manipur received tributes from tribes of Manipur. In case, if any tribe refused to pay tribute to the King, they were subjugated or punished. For example, tribal villages of Haoku disagreed to pay tribute to King Loiyumba (1094–1122 AD). So the King deputed his half brother Khamlang Pansaba to conquer the tribal villages of Haoku and the chief of Haoku was defeated (Kabui, 1991, 124) King Kyamba (1467–1508 AD) raided the village of Chingsong which was earlier a tributary to the Meitei King. They used to supply timber for making boat to the King (Kabui, 1991, 126).

The Nagas paid tributes on two occasions: during Mera Houjongba and at the time of coronation of the King. The former was the annual tribute whereas the latter was a token of recognition of the suzerainty of the King.

There was a third kind of tribute (rather offer), that was paid in kind, at the time of birth of a son or daughter to the King (Singh, 2003, 170). It is also mentioned that a big Tangkhul village would provide one pot of cotton, ginger and pulses and also offered clothes at the coronation of the King. The Marrings supplied one *pon* (a big basket) of *Kumna* (a useful herb used for binding articles), two pieces of iron ores, one *pon* of chillies, one *Chi* (a known heap) of edible *arums*. They also offered clothes at the coronation of the King. The Anals offered annually one *Chi* of edible arums, one *Chang* of Sesamum, one husking pillar, one *pon* of tobacco and pines, and clothes at the time of the coronation of the King. The Kabuis also paid tribute which included one *Chi* of edible arums, one *pon* of cotton and sesamum, tobacco, chillies, *Heirabop* (a kind of edible fruit used in cooking curry and ginger) (Singh, 2003, 171). The tribute of Chothe included one *Chi* of edible arums, four *Kairen phis* (spotted clothes), one *Channg* of Sesamum, ten brooms, ten *Huitris* (a bow shaped implement meant for cleaning cotton) (Singh, 1979, 622), baskets and tongs. It also recorded that the "tribute varied from a little oilseed to a regular payment in money, which in the case of the Maram Nagas amounted to a sum of Rs. 100 per annum" (Administrative Report for the Year 1877–78, 4–5 and 12–6).

Revenue in the Form of Services

The early Manipur State did not realise or collect revenues as such from the subjects but services were rendered by the people to the state under *Lallup* system. *Lallup* was a feudal service rendered by the subjects to the King or the state. *Lallup* is the combination of two words, i.e. *Lal* = war, and *Lup* = organization. Literally *Lallup* means war organization. Originally it was a military service which was extended to other economic activities of the state (Kabui, 1991, 126). *Lallup* was a military organization, but in the times of peace it was made to play a part in the economic life of the country (Hodson, 1989, 59). *Lallup* system was introduced making it compulsory for every male members of the country between the age of 17 to 60 years to work for the state for 10 days out of every 40 days. The introduction of this system brought about considerable changes in the developmental activities of the state particularly in social and economic fields.

A new order of militia was introduced during the reign of King Loiyamba (1074–1112 AD). As the number of villages increased, King Loiyamba established a regular available force to render service to the state at any given time. The King and nobles decided to order every subject to spare a few days in a month, "each male belonging to age group between 16 or 17 years and 16 years of every household was supposed to render to the state 10 days labour out of every 40 days" (Allen, 1981, 115). "Cheitharol Kumbaba" also refers to *Lallup* system in Manipur (Singh and Singh, 1989, 8). T.C. Hodson recorded that "the person liable to duty under the *Lallup* system were the Meiteis, Brahaman and Pang-gans" (Hodson, 1989, 60). The native people had to sacrifice specified labours time for the state. Hence, the people who were on the *Lallup* duty were indispensable because they had to preserve and defend the sovereignty of the state. Moreover, they had to provide labour for developmental works of the state. Colonel McCulloch gives the description of the *Lallups* as follows:

> This population is composed of different classes. The principal is the Meiteis, next the Phoongnai, after whom the Teng-khul, the Ayokpa, the Kei, the Loee, and the Mussulman. The Meitei population is divided into four parts called, "Punnahs", which are designated in the order of their superiority, *Kaphum, Lai Phum, Ahulloop,* and *Niharoop*. The Punnahs perform *Lalloop* or service for ten days in rotation, thus bringing every male in the country above sixteen years of age on duty, ten days in forty. This

> service is due to the state; none are remunerated for it. The head of each family or tribe furnishes the proper persons for different services required of that tribe. The immediate family of the *Peepa*, or head of the tribe, is not called to perform any heavy duty. Its post is near the Raja, acting as *Ningthou Selba* or personal attendants. The family next in seniority has a heavy duty to perform in the *Laikai*. The third has the *Lalmee*, and the fourth the *Sungsa roi*. The *Lalloop* of the second and fourth families works generally in unison. Their chief duty is to make houses and bridges. The *Lalmee* was in former times the soldiers of Munnipore, but since the raising of the troops before mentioned in the time of the Raja Gumbeer Singh, the *Lalmees* duties have become civil. Of the families after the fourth the places are not fixed, some are "khoot naiba" or artificers, as goldsmiths, blacksmiths, carpenters, etc. who all have their *Lalloop* in which they perform any work in their respective lines they may be called upon to do ... The Brahmins even have the *Lalloop*, during which they cook for the Raja and their idol Govindjee ... Individuals belonging to any *Lalloop* who are anxious to remain at home, can do so by paying the chief officers. Sick people even have to pay if they miss their *Lalloop* (McCulloch, 1980, 11–3).

The *Lallup* duty was characterised by a form of direct tax levied in terms of service. Persons who were covered under the *Lallup* were to pay compulsorily that particular labour time to the state or for that matter to the King for which no special benefit could be determined in return. If anybody failed to perform *Lallup* duty, he was punished. Even a sick person was also liable to pay a fixed amount of money in case he was not able to discharge his *Lallup* duty (Ali, 1988, 192–93). However, those persons who engaged themselves as fishermen in the lake of Loktak were taken as exception as they were authorised to carry on their profession by paying some amount per month, fixed by the king from time to time, instead of rendering the duty of *Lallup* (McCulloh, 1980, 12 and 83; Brown 1975, 14).

R. Brown adds further:

> The general system of *Lallup* is based on the assumption

> that it is the duty of every male between the age group of 17 and 60 to place his services at the disposal of the state, without remuneration for a certain number of days in each year. The system of *Lallup* was first introduced, it is said, in the reign of Pakhangba, and it has undergone little change since. The number of days thus placed at the disposal of the state in 10 days in every forty.... There is no *Lallup* for woman (Brown, 1973, 83).

Each individual liable for *Lallup* for the state was entitled to cultivate for his support one pares of land subject to the payment of the regular tax in kind (Hodson 1989, 65).

N. Ibobi Singh mentions:

> All men attending *Lallup* were divided into sections, each of which was engaged in functions of the state. For instance, the Tokpam, the Ayum and the Akham (all were clans) were engaged in digging grave, burying and doing all customary duties connected with death of the Raja. The Tengkhul, the Phunganai and Ayokpa were engaged in gardening. Those who attended at the office of Humairoi were in charge of making fans. The institution of Shangsaroi was in charge of building huts .... Some villages like Undro, Sekmai and Chairel for one particular function or functions. All people of Chairel were engaged in making pottery. Sekmai was engaged in distilling wine Undro was engaged in making pottery and supplying the Raja with Charcoal (Singh, 2003, 163).

Thus, the *Lallup* duty was a form of direct tax levied in terms of service. It was not merely a warfare organization but also a public institution. There were no regular officers separately in the *Lallup* service in the ancient days. *Lallup* was feudal service to the state both for military and revenue purpose. Allen called it as corvee labour (Allen, 1981, 115).

In addition to the sources of income mentioned above, there were also other sources such as receipt from Kubo Valley compensation, revenue from tea, revenue from ferries, excise, stamps, jail, hill house tax, *Lallup* house tax, etc. Such income were similar to the revenues gathered by the *zamindars* in the British India.

Since the year 1892, a special house tax of Rs. 2 per house was imposed in the valley, without reference to its size or the number of inmates. An amount of Rs. 3 was levied as tax on each house among the hill tribes of Manipur since 1891. The income from *zamindaris* during the year 1891–92 was Rs. 5,891. The 1834 agreement declared that it was the intention of the Supreme Government to grant a monthly stipend of five hundred Sicca Rupees to the Raja of Manipur, to commence from the ninth day of January one thousand eight hundred and thirty four, the date at which the transfer of Kubo Valley took place (Aitchison, 1909, 197). From that time onwards Manipur received a monthly stipend of Rs. 500. But by 1893–94, the allowance was increased to Rs. 13,248 for the preceding two years (Singh, 2003, 168). In 1891, the income from ferries was Rs. 240 and the amount of revenue from excise was Rs. 950 in 1894–95. In 1893–94 stamps fetched an amount of Rs. 865 and so on.

Conclusion

It may be concluded that the State of Manipur derived its income from different sources. Of the various sources of income, revenue from land, mines, forest, herds, fishery and *Lallup* were paid in kind. This form of payment was prevalent until the beginning of British rule in Manipur. Thereafter, the primary mode of payment was transformed in monetary method. For example, revenue from land and fishery was paid in cash. Duties on trade and commerce, foreigners' tax and fines from convicts were also paid in cash throughout the period from 1709 to 1907. The *Lallup* and tributes from the vanquished were also abolished by the British.

CITED WORKS

Administrative Report of Manipur: 1877–78.

Administrative Report of Manipur: 1898–99.

Aitchison, C.U. 1909. *A Collection of Treaties, Engagements and Sanads: Relating to India and the States in Rajputana.* Calcutta: Superintendent Government Printing.

Ali, Ashraf, Md. 1988. *Economic History of Manipur: 1801–1951.* Ph.D. Thesis, Manipur University.

Allen, B.C. 1905. *Assam District Gazetteers, Vol. IX: Naga Hills and Manipur.* Calcutta: Mission Baptist Press.

Altekar, A.S. 1984. *State and Government in Ancient India.* Delhi: Motilal Banarsidass.

Barpujari, H.K. 1963. *Assam in the Days of the Company: 1826–58.* Gauhati: Lawyer's Book Stall.

Brown, R. 1973. *Statistical Account of Manipur.* New Delhi: Mittal Publications.

Choudhuri, P.C. 1966. First published in 1959. *The History of Civilization of the People of Assam to the Twelfth Century AD.* Gauhati: Department of Historical and Antiquarian Studies in Assam.

Devi, Sanoujam Somola. 2002. *Political Economy of Land Reforms in Manipur since Independence.* Ph.D. Thesis, Manipur University.

Dune, E.W. 1981. First published in 1886. *Gazetteer of Manipur,* Delhi: Vivek Publishing Company.

Ghosal, U.N. 1929, *Contributions to the History of the Hindu Revenue System.* Calcutta: University of Calcutta.

Government of India. 1964. *District Census Handbook.* Imphal: Directorate of Census and Population.

Hodson, T.C. 1989. First published in 1908. *The Meitheis.* Delhi: B.R. Publishing Corporation.

Howell, A.A. 1891. *Short Account of Land Revenue in Manipur.* Unpublished archival record.

Kabui, Gangmumei. 1991. *History of Manipur, Vol. 1.* Delhi: National Publishing House.

McCulloh, M. 1980. First published in 1959. *The Valley of Manipur.* New Delhi: Gian Publishing House.

Pemberton, Capt. R.B. 1966. First published in 1835. *Report of the Eastern Frontier of British India.* Gauhati: DHAS.

Poireiton Khunthokpa (Manipuri text).

Ruhinikumar Sharma, K, *Social and Political Formation in Pre-colonial Manipur in the Eighteenth and Nineteenth Century,* Ph.D. Thesis, Manipur University, 2002.

Shakespeare, J. 1907. *Manipur under British Management: 1891–1907.* Shillong: XYZ.

Shamasastry, R., ed. and trans. 1929. *Arthasastra of Kautilya.* Mysore: Weslayan Mission Press.

Sharma, R.S. 1968. *Political Ideas and Institutions in Ancient India.* Delhi: Motilal Banarsidas.

Singh, G.P. 1993. *Political Thought in Ancient India.* New Delhi: D.K. Printworld.

Singh, Kh. Chandrasekhar, ed. 1975. *Loiyumba Sinyen.* Imphal: Kh. Chandrasekhar Singh.

Singh, L., Ibungohal. 1963. *Introduction to Manipur.* Imphal: Sahitya Parishad.

Singh, L. Ibungohal and Singh, N. Khelchandra. 1967. *Cheitharol Kumbaba.* Imphal: N. Khelchandra.

Singh, N. Ibobi, 2003. First published in 1976. *The Manipur Administration: 1709–1907*. Imphal: N. Ibobi Singh.

Singh, N. Khelchandra. 1979. Lam in Sahitya. *Manipur Sahitya Parishad Quarterly* 10–11, 40–41, May to August.

Singh, O. Bhogeswor, ed. 1973. *Sanamahi Laikan.* Imphal: O. Bhogeswor Singh.

Singh, R.K. Jhalajit. 1965. *A Short History of Manipur.* Imphal: R.K. Jhalajit Singh.

Singh, Yumjao. 1950. *Manipur Itihas.* Imphal: Yumjao Singh.

Ungaonkar, P.B. 1986. *Political Institutions and Administration.* New Delhi: Motilal Banarsidass.

4

Post Statehood Economy : A Critical Analysis

Hanjabam Isworchandra

The essay seeks to explore possible reasons behind the persisting state of underdevelopment in Manipur even after attainment of statehood and establishment of the North Eastern Council (NEC). In the pre-statehood period, the power of state economic planning and preparation of budget were in the hands of the Central Government. However, during this period Manipur's economy *vis-à-vis* the country's dawdled behind in almost every aspect. Neither agriculture nor industry was in a laudable position for performance or as a launch pad for sound economic growth. Disproportionate emphasis on transport and communication and social sector reduced the economy to a state of dependency. Products ranging from agricultural to industrial had to be imported from mainland India. Negligence of sectors such as agriculture and industry seriously affected the livelihood of the local populace at large. Thus, one can say that centralised planning during the pre-statehood period was responsible for stagnation of Manipur's economy.

Changes in the economic climate were expected with the attainment of full-fledged statehood in 1972 as well as with the establishment of NEC. Concomitant with the attainment of statehood, NEC was conceived and established as a catalytic agent to bring integrated development in the region. Moreover, economic planning and preparation of budget, which were earlier in the hands of the Central Government, then became prerogative of the State Government. However, in spite of these institutional changes, the State continues to be caught in an inescapable condition of underdevelopment. One possible reason is that the State was faced with the Herculean task of restoring the economy, shattered by centralised planning and mismanagement, to keep pace with the rest of the country. An attempt is made to discern other factors responsible for the persisting state of underdevelopment in the State.

Towards the Path of Deterioration

Centralised planning during the pre-statehood period has left the economy of the State with a fragile productive base. There has been marginal endeavour from the State Government to fortify the productive base. In due course of time, economy could not withstand the forces of large influx of consumer goods. Therefore, intense tertiarization in the post-statehood period was inevitable. The evolving structure of the economy is not an autonomous development, but is explained mainly by inconsistency in planning and lack of policy coordination. For instance, up to the Tenth Plan only 6.6 per cent of the total outlay went to agriculture and 8.26 per cent to industry with the lion's share of 78 per cent to transport, water, power and the social sector. Rapid decline of agriculture in the contribution of Gross State Domestic Product (GSDP) and slow growth of secondary sector consequently leads to an inflated tertiary sector.

The usual trend of falling income share of primary sector especially agriculture to the total income as the economy progresses is witnessed in the context of Manipur (see Table 4.1). But the decline in the contribution of primary sector is very disturbing, since it has not been accompanied by a matching fall in the workforce dependent on agriculture (see Table 4.2). On the other hand, the secondary sector does not register any remarkable contribution to State Gross Domestic Product (GDP). Instead an inordinate growth of tertiary sector is encountered in the State.

As shown in Table 4.1, primary sector contributed the largest share (45.46%) with agriculture as its dominant component (41.98%) in the year 1980–81. Its contribution to GSDP/GDP declined uninterruptedly, i.e. from 30.23 per cent in 1990–91 to 29.18 in 1993–94 and to 22.76 per cent in 2001–02.

Table 4.1 : Percentage Share in GSDP/GDP by Industry of Origin at 1980–82 Prices

Sl. Industries	1980–81	1990–91	1993–94	2001–02
1. Agriculture	41.98	30.23	29.18	22.76
2. Forestry and logging	2.22	1.63	3.23	4.62
3. Fishing	1.26	3.31	3.08	2.18
4. Mining and quarrying	0.00	0.00	0.00	0.00
Primary	45.46	35.17	35.49	29.57
5. Manufacturing	4.76	6.09	0.57	0.1
5.1 Registered	0.29	0.18	0.28	0.05
5.2 Unregistered	4.46	5.91	7.91	8.35
6. Construction	6.31	7.66	6.68	10.72
7. Electricity, gas and water supply	0.84	0.04	4.49	3.98
Secondary	11.89	13.79	18.61	23.1
8. Transport, storage and communication	1.95	5.55	4.34	3.98
8.1 Railways	0.00	0.00	0.00	0.00
8.2 Transport by other means	1.72	5.3	3.7	3.23
8.3 Storage	0.01	0.01	0	0
8.4 Communication	0.23	0.24	0.64	0.58
9. Trade, hotels and restaurant	5.06	3.9	10.97	8.44
10. Banking and insurance	1.13	1.85	1.48	1.1
11. Real estate, ownership of dwellings and business Services	12.48	12.71	3.94	2.94
12. Public administration	10.26	12.68	13.94	15.05
13. Other services	11.75	14.36	11.23	16
Tertiary	42.65	51.04	45.9	47.33
14. Gross State Domestic	**100.00**	**100.00**	**100.00**	**100.00**

Source: Institute for Human Development. 2006. *Manipur State Development Report.* New Delhi: Planning Commission, p. 4.

Table 4.2 : Distribution of Workforce in Manipur by Occupational Sector Percentage

Census year	Primary sector	Secondary sector	Tertiary sector
1961	66.26	23.05	10.69
1971	71.27	14.53	14.2
1981	68.59	9.68	21.73
1991	69.97	9.69	20.34
2001	49.69	6.54	43.77

Source: Government of Manipur. Various issues. *Statistical Abstract of Manipur.* Imphal: Directorate of Statistics and Economics.

Secondary sector registered a slow growth from 11.89 per cent in 1980–81 to 13.79 per cent in 1990–91 and to 23.10 per cent in 2001–02. But the scene is not a praiseworthy one as construction amounts for the lion share, i.e. 6.31 per cent in 1980–81, 7.66 per cent in 1990–91 and 10.72 per cent in 2001–02. The second segment in the secondary sector to grow is unregistered manufacturing activity, i.e. 4.46 per cent in 1980–81 to 5.91 per cent in 1990–91 and to 8.35 per cent in 2001–02. Registered manufacturing failed to touch one per cent mark, i.e. 0.29 per cent in 1980, 0.18 in 1990–91 and 0.05 per cent in 2001–02 clearly indicating the regressive condition of medium and large scale manufacturing sector.

Agricultural Development

Topography has always been a major constraint in agricultural development of the State, with the valley occupying only 10 per cent of the total geographical area and rest being hills. In the valley permanent cultivation is practiced while in the hills it is terrace cultivation in few pockets and shifting cultivation or *Jhum*, which is not much productive. Agriculture, notwithstanding its high importance in the State's economy, did not receive much attention during the pre-statehood period. Efforts for agricultural development, to cite a few such as establishments of a number of farms and introduction of High Yielding Variety seeds (HYV seeds) in the Third Plan, were initiated (Singh, 1987). But it did not bring about any phenomenal change in agriculture, as the steps were marginal and limited.

Serious efforts for agriculture development were initiated immediately after attainment of statehood with thrust on irrigation—the most important infrastructure for agriculture. The first major irrigation project, the Loktak Lift Irrigation Project, was taken up in 1973–74. It was followed by medium river irrigation projects, viz. Imphal Barrage, Sekmai Barrage, Khoupum Dam, Singda Project and a number of minor irrigation projects. By the time Manipur attained statehood Green Revolution was already in place in other parts of the country. Post-statehood agricultural scenario witnessed intensified used of HYV seeds and chemical fertilizers. The result has been the State's modest participation in Green Revolution. Both production and productivity of the most important staple crop (rice) have increased substantially (see Table 4.3). However, self-sufficiency in foodgrains is still a distant dream, as production always falls short of the requirement (see Table 4.4).

Table 4.3 : Area, Production and Average Yield of Rice in Manipur during 1972–2004

Year	Area (100 ha)	Production (1000 tonnes)	Yield (kg/ha)
1972–73	146.60	152.20	1038.00
1975–76	177.20	267.40	1560.00
1980–81	188 60	273.00	1447.00
1990–91	157.41	274.17	1741.76
1995–96	134.93	338.05	2505.37

Sources: Government of Manipur. Various issues. *Statistical Abstract of Manipur*. Imphal: Directorate of Economic and Statistics.

Table 4.4 : Estimate Requirement of Household Consumption of Foodgrain in Manipur

(*'0000 tonnes*)

Year	Production	Requirement	Shortfall
1995–96	347.58	404.3	56.72
1996–97	393.31	413.76	20.45
1997–98	368.02	423.33	55.31
1998–99	395.06	433.01	37.95
1999–00	378.92	442.80	63.88
2000–01	395.75	448.34	52.62
2001–02	400.39	458.01	57.28
2002–03	347.07	467.35	120.28
2003–04	392.01	477.02	85.01

Sources: Government of Manipur. 2007. *Economic Survey of Manipur: 2006–07*. Imphal: Directorate of Economic and Statistics.

Agriculture in the State is still at subsistence level and remains stagnant. The problem surrounding it is more of institutional rather than technological. Inadequate irrigation facilities, demographic pressure, unavailability of credit and land reforms are some of the major hurdles in agricultural development in the State. As potential for expanding arable land in the State is limited, the main thrust for increasing production should be intensive use of the available land resources. In this regard importance of irrigation assumes crucial proportions. However, in reality the existing scene is quite different.

Rice is the most important crop and occupies 82 per cent of the total cultivated land area. The scope of diversification of other crops is limited due to inadequate irrigation. By the end of the Ninth Plan, the irrigation potential from the completed or partly completed projects was 28,500 ha with a utilization of only 20,910 ha. Unfortunately the problem of irrigation is more of a problem of administration and implementation failure (Yumnam, 1999). It discourages the practice of double cropping except for few pockets in the valley where double cropping is practiced. There is hardly any crop diversification such as the practice of *rabi* cropping. Demographic pressure has a brutal impact on agriculture especially diversification of crops. Annual growth in cropped area for the period 1982–1992 was 1.43 per cent whereas the annual growth rate in population for the same period was 2.93 per cent. During the decade 1991–2001, the net area sown, in fact, declined whereas population recorded growth at an annual rate of 3 per cent. As a result of this asymmetric growth in cropped area and population, which leads to stagnant yield, the State is facing an increasing deficit in cereal production (Institute for Human Development, 2006, 109).

Though hills occupy majority of geographical area of the State, agriculture scenario in hill is worse owing to institutional, technological and geographical factors and contribution to the State's agricultural land area is only 26.82 per cent. Land people ratio in the hills is substantially higher than the valley. Yet agriculture in the hills continues to be marked by low productivity because of the prevailing land ownership system (Singh, 2005b, 161). Though cereal production in the hill is not conducive, there is tremendous potential for horticulture and plantation. Lack of clarity in the land right system has also created bottleneck for the development of these activities. So financial institutions, people of the hills with capital and entrepreneurs in the valley are hesitant to invest in land development and agriculture due to lack of collateral and existing land right system (Singh, 2005b, 162).

Agriculture in the State has failed to perform satisfactorily its two most important roles in the economy, i.e. supply for foodgrain and raw materials for industry. Subsistence level of agriculture is so high that it has become a secondary occupation for many part time farmers. With massive population growth (primarily because of large scale influx of outsiders), urbanization and government development programmes, agriculture is at the receiving end. Only 6.73 per cent of the total geographical area of the State is clarified as agricultural land (Institute for Human Development, 2006, 107).

Industrialization

Industrialization in the real sense of the term was initiated only after the attainment of statehood. In the pre-statehood period, village and small scale industry was the focal point for industrial development. The process of State-backed industrialization emerged only statehood with the incorporation of the Manipur Spinning Mill in 1974. It was followed by the establishment of a number of Public Sector Undertakings (PSUs). Notable ones include Manipur Cycle Corporation Ltd., Manipur Cement Ltd., Manipur Pulps and Allied Products Ltd., Manipur Food Industries Corporation Ltd., Manipur State Drugs and Pharmaceuticals Ltd., Manipur Vanaspati and Allied Industries Ltd., Manipur Handloom and Handicraft Development Corporation Ltd., Manipur Electronics Development Corporation Ltd., and Manipur Industrial Development Corporation Ltd. From its inception the public sector undertakings have been surrounded by plethora of problems, viz. infrastructural bottlenecks, low level of entrepreneurial and technical skills, limited size of local market, inadequate supply of raw materials, financial paucity and most importantly the virtual absence of necessary State support mechanisms like market protection and trade restrictions on similar products from other industrialised States of India. In spite of these problems public sector undertaking was able to generate handful of employment and output for local consumption. Not only this, the early 80's to the early 90's was marked by increased manufacturing units in the State (See Table 4.5).

Table 4.5 : Production and Employment of Manufacturing Industries (1980–1999)

Year	*No. of unit*	*Total investment*	*Total employment*	*Total production*
1980–81	156	60.63	726	116.14
1985–86	559	207.12	2,573	705.82
1990–91	293	73.10	1,445	530.71
1991–92	253	193.00	3,523	870.00
1993–94	400	113.00	1,280	980.00
1994–95	245	167.00	3,040	646.00

Sources: Government of Manipur. 2006. *Statistical Abstract of Manipur: 2005*. Imphal: Directorate of Economics and Statistics.

During the period a number of industrial policies were framed. For example, the Industrial Policy of Manipur 1982, which laid primary emphasis on development of large and medium scale industry, was followed by the Industrial Policy of Manipur 1989 and 1990. These policies had limited impact on the process of industrialization and were also not complemented by the Five Year Plans; only 5.98 per cent of the total plan outlay was allocated to industry during 1974–90.

India's economic liberalization of the late 80s and early 90s turned out to be the last nail on the coffin for the already ailing PSUs of the State. Liberalization subserved the interest of advanced capitalism of the core economy of the mainland against underdeveloped peripheral economies like Manipur. Though the PSUs of the State were suffering from endogenous factors like infrastructural bottlenecks, the deathblow was given by the strong exogenous factor of economic liberalization. Huge influx of cheap products from mainland India and South East Asia in the post-liberalization period virtually led to the closure of many manufacturing units, ranging from large to small, due to their inability to withstand competition.

Following the national trend of closing down of PSUs and disinvestment, the State Government adopted the ideology of privatization without taking into account the reality of the State's economy in keeping with the policy prescriptions of New Delhi under the plea of fiscal streamlining. With the advent of the ideology of privatization and the virtual withdrawal of industrial entrepreneurial support systems, Manipur is far away from real industrial development (Singh, 2005a). The State Government has shut down most of the PSUs established during the pre-liberalization period. The vacuum left by the State own industrialization is not backed up by the private sector owing to a number of socio-politico and economic factors. Deindustrialization rather than industrialization is the current trend in Manipur. The State is nowhere on the industrial map of India. The State remains as an industrially backward State with all the districts under the category of "no industry district" by all India standards. Appropriate State intervention in the nick of time would have produced a different story in the industrialization process of the State.

Infrastructure Bottleneck

Lack of proper infrastructure has been the biggest hurdle to all-round development of the State. Throughout the Five Year Plans, infrastructural development has been given the maximum thrust. In spite of this, Manipur still faces the challenge of providing infrastructural facilities conducive to social and economic development. According to the Eleventh Finance Commission, Manipur's index of relative development of infrastructure for 1991–92 shows that it is lagging far behind the national average by one-fifth (Institute for Human Development, 2006, 125). Surface transport is the most important means of transport in Manipur. However, connectivity is pathetic, as even district headquarters are not connected. The total road mileage increased more than three-fold from 2,107 km in 1973 to 7,172 km in 2002. While the mileage of State highways remain stagnant, i.e. from 650 km in 1973 to 675 km in 2002 that of national highways increased more than four-fold from 212 km in 1973 to 957 km in 2002. The phenomenal increase in national highway mileage is a clear indication of privileging inter-State trade rather than intra-State trade.

Leaving aside the horrible condition of the roads, density ranges from 120 to 143 km per 100 sq. km in the valley. Road density in the hill as compared to the valley is worse. In the hill districts, road density ranges from 19 km to 24 km per 100 sq. km. Inadequate all-weather road connectivity between hill and valley has, to a large extent, contributed to the weak hill-valley linkage, which in turn leads to economic dichotomization of hill and valley. Emphasis on inter-State connectivity with other States and neglect of intra-State connectivity, smoothen the influx of cheap products manufactured in industrialized mainland India resulting in the tapering down of hill-valley interdependence. Over the years, the traditional symbiotic relationship between hill and valley has drastically changed. Both hill and valley are made to look for their basic requirements to the mainland. Dependency of both hill and valley to the mainland has outranked interdependency between them. The earlier hill-valley relationship is being replaced by two relationships hill-mainland and valley-mainland (Singh, 2005b, 165).

Power represents another important infrastructural base for economic development; its shortage in Manipur is so acute that it cannot even cater to domestic requirements. The per capita power consumption of the State declined from 120 kWh in 1995–96 to 72 kWh in 2002–03, which is very low compared to the national average of 355 kWh. In Manipur domestic consumption (55%) dominates the power sector whereas the share of industries (6.4%), irrigation and agriculture (0.23%) remain stagnant. The power sector has to go a long way in fulfilling the demands of domestic consumption as well as for the important sectors like industry and agriculture.

Banking services in the State has failed to cater to the requirements for bank credit of the people. Although there are large number of branches of the nationalised banks in Manipur bank credit is the scarcest commodity in the State (Singh, 2005*c*). Banking services remain inaccessible to majority of the rural population whose genuine needs for agricultural credits are neglected by the nationalised banks in their interest to confine themselves to the economically well-off traders, business community and government transactions.

From NEC to DoNER: Agents of Development

With persisting backwardness of the North East region in the first four Five Year Plans in comparison to the rest of the country and particularly with the reorganization of the region, the North East Council came into existence by an Act of Parliament as a Regional Advisory Body in 1971. The NEC began functioning in 1972 covering the States of Assam, Mizoram, Meghalaya, Tripura, Arunachal Pradesh, Manipur and Nagaland. In December 2002, the NEC Act was amended in order to bring Sikkim under the purview and was subsequently upgraded to a Regional Planning Body. However, even after 30 years of its inception, the NEC has failed to perform its role of a catalyst for development of the region. Efforts from the Central Government witnessed the establishment of the Department of North East Region (DoNER) in September 2001 in addition to the NEC. It was accorded the status of a Ministry on May 27, 2004. Crores of rupees have been poured in the region through NEC and DoNER, in addition to the Prime Minister's Special Packages. Even all the eight constituent States of the region are treated as Special Category States outside the Gadgil formula and 90 per cent of their plan allocations are treated as grant

(Government of India 2007, 2). However, the ultimate result is not in the expected line. The region is the most backward region of the country and is lagging behind in every economic indicators of development.

The sector-wise plan investment of NEC depicts a tragic scene in the development drama of the North East. From 1972 up to the Tenth Plan, Rs. 9,651.63 crores have been invested, of which 36.10 per cent has been spent on water and power development projects and 41.27 per cent on transport and communication. A critical examination of the investment in other sectors reveals that investment in other equally important sectors such as agriculture and industries was marginal (see Table 4.6).

NEC spends major portion of its plan outlay in developing infrastructure. Not only this, other funds meant for North East such as Non-Lapsable Central Pool of Resources (NLCPR) are channelised for infrastructural development. NLCPR was created in 1998 from the unspent balance of 10 per cent provisioning in the Budget by Central Ministries/DoNER. The Ministry of DoNER sanctions infrastructural development project for the North East region out of the allocation made through normal budgetary route from NLCPR. The approved cost under NLCPR as on December 31, 2006 for the sole purpose of infrastructural development was Rs. 5,823 crores (Government of India, 2007, 9). In a region where majority of the area is covered by hills the concern about infrastructural development is understandable. But the sheer neglect of important sectors like agriculture and industry reflects

Table 4.6 : Sector-wise investment by NEC since its inception in 1972 up to Tenth Plan

Sectors	*Rupees (in crores)*	*Percentage*
Agriculture and allied programmes	324.42	3.37
Water and power	3483.82	36.10
Industry and mining	233.13	2.41
Transport and communication	3983.82	41.27
Manpower development	448.09	4.64
Social and community service	734.31	7.60
General services	88.55	0.92
External aided project	183.49	1.90
Science and technology	172.00	1.78
Total	**9651.63**	**100.00**

Source: www.necouncil.nic.in. Accessed on August 20, 2007.

the Central Government's intention for nurturing the region into a dependent economy. The neglect of agriculture, where more than 60 per cent of the population is dependent for their livelihood, and industry, even though the region has huge potential for industrialization (Ahmed and Biswas, 2003, 55) resulted in acute dependence of the region on the mainland economy. The Shukla Commission (1997) estimated that about Rs. 2,500 crores worth of consumables are imported from mainland India.

From the initial stage of its inception, NEC has been focusing on development projects, which benefits not only the host State but also other States of the region. The generally backward economic condition of the region supplies the element of homogeneity while the physical features strengthen the need for interdependence. Except for a patch of plain land in Tripura, the region is locked in by the surrounding hills. Further, the 4,000 km long boundaries make it impossible for any State to be economically developed independently of the others (Munshi *et. al.* 1978, 7). NEC's policy has strengthen the interdependence among the North Eastern States in terms of education, health, water, power, transport and communication, and dependence of the whole region on the mainland India for day-to-day requirement of consumer goods ranging from foodgrains to manufactured goods. The logic is simple: strengthening interdependence among the North Eastern States and dependency of the region on mainland India.

Owing to its geo-strategic location, as the region shares 98 per cent of its borders with the neighbouring countries and a miniscule 22 km. wide connection with the Indian heartland through the Siliguri Corridor coupled with the problem of insurgency, dependency is seen as a process of strengthening integration with the Indian Union (Sharma, 2006). Overemphasis on infrastructural development and neglect of strengthening the productive base of the region has failed to accomplish the much-cherished dream of balanced regional development. Moreover, infrastructural indices associated with modernization have no correlation with actual growth indices in the units of the North East region (Munshi *et al.*, 1978, 16). From administration point of view, NEC adopted a highly bureaucratic and technological approach in its pursuit for finding regional policies for the region (Ahmed and Biswas, 2003, 55) exclusive of people's participation and involvement.

Conclusion

The productive base of the economy was not given its due attention during the centralised planning in the pre-statehood period. Commitment from the State Government in the post-statehood for strengthening the productive base was also lacking though half-hearted efforts for industrialization was initiated in the late 1970's. The effort was too late as it fails to lay down a strong foundation to withstand the forces of liberalization. Stress on unsustainable infrastructure and simultaneous neglect of agriculture and industry both by State Government and NEC is fallout of politician-bureaucratic-contractor nexus. Double trouble befell on the feeble economy of the State with huge influx of cheap products from mainland Indian and more from the South East Asian countries in the post Indo-Myanmar Border Trade Agreement phase. Heightened tertiarization is the order of the day in the State. The so-called catalyst of development, NEC and the new protean incarnation, DoNER failed to revitalise the economy of the trouble prone North East.

Massive inflow of fund in the region for infrastructural development have made the region's economy purely a monetary phenomenon which in reality turns out to be just an eyewash as it has failed to make the economy stand on its own legs. In the immediate years following statehood, the government both at the State and Centre was obsessed with the "geographical isolation" syndrome in explaining the underdevelopment of the region. But in the recent times, there has been a paradigm shift in their approach; it is the "insurgency" syndrome that currently grips the mind of the policy-makers. The Central Government's attitude in dealing with the problems of the State is more alarming. By turning a blind eye, if not completely, to economic causes of underdevelopment of the region and elevating insurgency as the main cause for underdevelopment reflect its hypocrisy. The myopic approach to a political and socio-economic problem is wrecking havoc to the State's economy. It is crucial to remember that insurgency was a fringe phenomenon in the early years as dissent was articulated peacefully in moderate terms. Rather than a security or law and order approach, the government should address the underlying problem with sensitivity and alacrity (Institute for Human Development, 2006, IV). The State is highly dependent on financial assistance from the Centre. Resource mobilization is negligible. It is high time that both the State and Central Government start acting sincerely with commitment. Both the State Government and agencies of the Central Government like the NEC and DoNER should focus on accelerating the local forces of production so that a self-perpetuating economy is nurtured in lieu of a dependent economy persisting till date.

CITED WORKS

Ahmad, Raiful and Biswas, Prasenjit. 2004. *Political Economy of the Underdevelopment of North East India*. New Delhi: Akansha Publishing House.

Chandrasekhar, C.P. and Ghosh, Jayati. 2004. *The Market that Failed: Neoliberal Reforms in India*. New Delhi: Leftward.

Government of India. 2007. *Annual Report 2006–07*. New Delhi: Ministry of Development of North Eastern Region.

Government of Manipur. 2006. *Statistical Abstract of Manipur: 2005*. Imphal: Directorate of Economics and Statistics.

Government of Manipur. 2007. *Economic Survey of Manipur: 2006–07*. Imphal: Directorate of Economics and Statistics.

Government of Manipur. Various issues. *Statistical Abstract of Manipur*. Imphal: Directorate of Statistics and Economics.

Institute for Human Development. 2006. *Manipur State Development Report*. New Delhi: Planning Commission.

Munshi, S., *et. al.* 1978. Regionalisation and Integrated Economic Development in North East India. In *Social and Economic Project of North East India*, edited by B. Dutta Ray, 6–17. New Delhi: B.R. Publishing House.

Sharma, Hanjabam Isworchandra. 2006. Manipur's economy from 1949 to 1972: Birth and nurturing of dependent economy. *Alternative Perspective* II, I, October–December: 21–33.

Singh, Ch. Priyoranjan. 1985. *Aspects of the State Economy and Planning for 2000 AD*. Seminar Paper Presented at Manipur 2000 AD, October, in Manipur University, Imphal.

Singh, Ch. Priyoranjan. 2005a. Manipur's Economy, Historical Roots and Structural Evaluation. *Eastern Quarterly* 3, III, October–December: 149–59.

Singh, E. Bijoykumar. 2005b. Development discourse in Manipur: Hills *vs.* Valley. *Eastern Quarterly*, Vol. 3, Issue III, October–December: 160–69.

Singh, Loitongbam Udhop. 1989. *A Brief History of Agricultural Development in Manipur.* Imphal: L. Saratkumar Singh & Brothers.

Singh, M. Iboton. 2005c. *Political Economy of Manipur*: Transformation within the Mixed Economy Paradigm. *Eastern Quarterly* 3, III, Oct.–Dec.: 170–79.

www.necouncil.nic.in. Accessed on August 20, 2007.

www.northeast.nic.in. Accessed on August 20, 2007.

www.northeast.nic.in/writoreaddata/sublinkimages.AREng 06074449976817.pdf. Accessed on August 20, 2007.

Yumnam, Amar. 1997. Socio-Economic Profile of Manipur. *Economy of Manipur Series* No. 7, September. Department of Economics. Manipur University, Imphal.

SECTION-II

Problems and Prioritizations

5

Foodgrain Economy and Food Security

N. Manichandra Singh

Introduction

The economy of Manipur is characterised by an ever-increasing service sector (which comes from an inflated government service sector) on the one hand and the industrial sector (without much scope for expansion at a large scale) on the other. In between, agriculture sector continues to support the people. The share of agriculture sector in employment and income has decreased over the years. However, it continues to play many vital roles in the economy of Manipur. By 2001, agriculture sector (cultivator and agricultural labourer only) provides 49.69 per cent of the employment to the State's workforce as main workers, which is still significantly large, though lower than 68.45 per cent in 1991 or the employment percentage in the earlier decades of 1970s and 1980s.

The sector also shares 23.32 per cent, out of 26.82 per cent for total primary sector, of the State's Gross Domestic Product in 2006–07, which is greater than the total primary sector's share of 20.55 per cent to total GDP at the all-India level (see Table 5.1). If one considers food processing, trading services in agricultural inputs and produces, etc., the contribution and role of agriculture in the economy is predominant.

Diversification of Agricultural Crops

One of the important features of the agriculture sector is the lack of diversification and heavily preponderance of food over non-

Table 5.1: Sectoral Distribution of GSDP and Percentage Share of Primary Sector (All India Level) at 1993–94* and 1999–00** Prices

(Area in '000 ha)

Year	Manipur			All India
	Primary sector total	Secondary sector total	Tertiary sector total	Primary sector total
1993–94*	35.49	18.61	45.90	33.54
1994–95*	33.97	18.83	47.20	32.94
1995–96*	32.68	20.05	47.27	30.59
1996–97*	31.78	20.76	47.46	30.87
1997–98*	32.53	19.83	47.64	29.02
1998–99^	32.62	21.16	46.22	28.86
1999–00**	26.91 (23.09)	22.29	50.80	27.32
2000–01**	29.94 (25.69)	21.25	48.81	26.18
2001–02**	29.03 (25.11)	21.66	49.31	26.19
2002–03**	28.17 (24.23)	23.82	48.01	23.73
2003-04**	29.21 (25.40)	26.55	44.24	23.90
2004-05**	29.16 (25.66)	27.81	43.03	22.40
2005-06**	25.98 (22.46)	30.03	43.99	21.67P
2006-07**	26.82 (23.32)Q	29.64Q	43.54Q	20.55Q

Sources: Various issues of *Economic Survey of Manipur* and *Economic Survey 2002–03 and 2007–08.*

Note: Figures within brackets are the percentage shares of agriculture sector including livestock and Q – quick estimate.

food crops (*Economic Survey of Manipur*, 2002–03). The preponderance is seen in terms of both absolute and percentage of cropped area. By 1990–91 and 1991–92, cereal crops (i.e., Rice, Wheat, Maize and other Coarse Cereals) comprised 80.08 per cent and 82.02 per cent respectively of the total cropped area in the State. It decreased below 80 per cent, with fluctuation, in the following years of 1990s and in the early 2000s. Yet, it still comprised more than 76 per cent of cropped area by 2006–07. On the other hand, the percentage of area under non-cereal crops more or less remained around 20 per cent even in the mid of 1990s. Only by 1998–99, some positive changes have taken place and its percentage of area increased briefly to 25.86 per cent in 2002–03 only to come down to around 23 per cent in the succeeding years (see Fig. 5.1).

The percentage of area of cereal and non-cereal show opposite trends with a slight decreasing in the former and an increasing in the latter respectively in the period between 1990–91 and 2006–07.

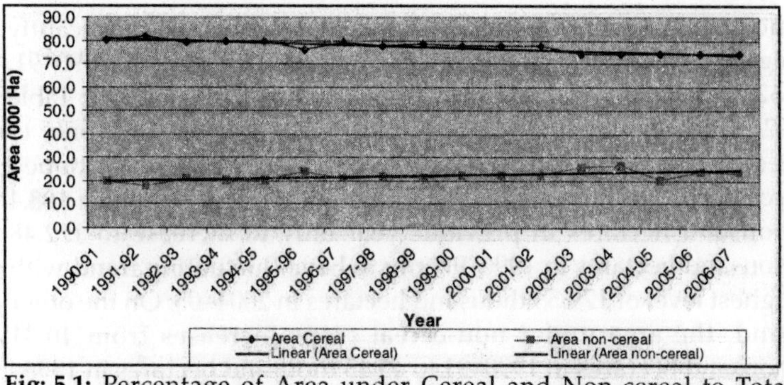

Fig: 5.1: Percentage of Area under Cereal and Non-cereal to Total Cropped Area

(Area in '000 hectares)

Table 5.2: Estimated Area and Percentage of Area under Cereal and Non-Cereal Crops in Manipur

Year	Area		Total area	Percentage of Area	
	Cereal	Non-cereal		Cereal	Non-cereal
1990–91	162.02	40.31	202.33	80.08	19.92
1991–92	164.29	36.01	200.30	82.02	17.98
1992–93	153.99	40.70	194.69	79.09	20.91
1993–94	164.59	41.74	206.33	79.77	20.23
1994–95	168.40	43.22	211.62	79.58	20.42
1995–96	137.48	43.17	180.65	76.10	23.90
1996–97	172.48	45.45	217.93	79.14	20.86
1997–98	161.47	45.92	207.39	77.86	22.14
1998–99	169.85	46.29	216.14	78.58	21.42
1999–00	161.39	46.25	207.64	77.73	22.27
2000–01	161.63	46.84	208.47	77.53	22.47
2001–02	167.63	48.53	216.16	77.55	22.45
2002–03	156.65	54.65	211.30	74.14	25.86
2003–04	160.17	58.74	218.91	73.17	26.83
2004–05	179.53	45.90	225.43	79.64	20.36
2005–06	169.11	54.04	223.15	75.78	24.22
2006–07	168.71	51.60	220.31	76.58	23.42

Source: Government of Manipur. 2004 and 2007. *Statistical Abstracts of Manipur,* Imphal: Directorate of Economic and Statistics.

However, these are not of very clear reflections of their respective absolute areas in the period under consideration. The area under cereal more or less remained stagnant with fluctuation between 1990–91 and 2006–07. Whereas, the area under non-cereal crop increased until 2003–04 then followed by fluctuation in the succeeding years until 2006–07, yet it remained at significantly higher level in the decade of 2000s compared to 1990s. In 1990–91, 162.02 thousand hectares was under cereal crops (Fig. 5.1; Table 5.2). It increased to 164.29 thousand hectares in 1991–92 only to decrease in the subsequent year. In 1995–96, the cereal cropped area decreases drastically to 137.48 thousand hectares from 168.4 thousand hectares in previous year only to increase to 172.48 thousand hectares in 1996–97only to have fluctuating trend with highest level of 179.53 thousand hectares in 2004–05. On the other hand, the area under non-cereal crops increases from 40.31 thousand hectares in 1990–91 to 45.45 thousand hectares in 1996–97 and further to 58.74 thousand hectares in 2003–04 but decreased later and it could not follow the increasing trend. However, the changes still indicate the diversification that is being taking place at a slow pace in agriculture sector.

Rice in Foodgrain Economy

Rice is the staple diet in the State and it contributes an overwhelming share to both total foodgrain (it is comprised of Cereals, Pulses and Gram) area and output. It contributes more than 96 per cent and 93 per cent of total foodgrain production and area respectively in 1990–91 to early 2000s and their respective figures remain around 98 per cent since 2003–04 (Fig. 5.2; Table 5.3). In 1990–91, 97.15 per cent of the total foodgrain area comprised of rice and was continuously increasing to 98.35 per cent in

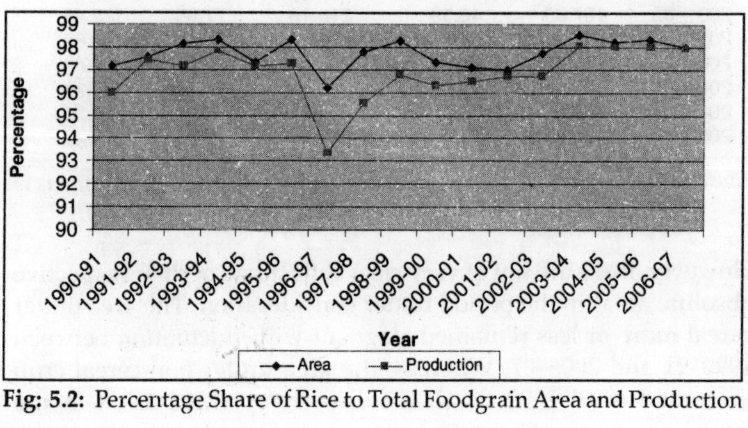

Fig: 5.2: Percentage Share of Rice to Total Foodgrain Area and Production

Table 5.3: Total Production and Area under Rice and the Respective percentage Shares to Total Foodgrain Production and Area in Manipur

(Production in '000 MT and Area in '000 Ha)

Years	Area under Rice	Total Area under foodgrain	% share of rice to total area under foodgrain	Rice Production	Total foodgrain production	% share to total foodgrain production
1990–91	157.41	162.02	97.15	274.17	285.60	96.00
1991–92	160.30	164.29	97.57	340.45	349.50	97.41
1992–93	151.19	153.99	98.18	273.12	281.18	97.13
1993–94	161.87	164.59	98.35	348.82	356.62	97.81
1994–95	163.93	168.40	97.35	358.51	368.93	97.18
1995–96	151.19	153.74	98.34	338.05	347.58	97.26
1996–97	161.87	168.25	96.21	367.28	393.31	93.38
1997–98	157.90	161.47	97.79	351.67	368.02	95.56
1998–99	166.89	169.85	98.26	382.19	395.06	96.74
1999–00	157.05	161.39	97.31	364.98	378.92	96.32
2000–01	156.96	161.63	97.11	381.73	395.75	96.46
2001–02	162.57	167.63	96.98	387.26	400.39	96.72
2002–03	153.11	156.65	97.74	335.67	347.07	96.72
2003–04	157.83	160.20	98.54	381.24	388.77	98.06
2004–05	176.31	197.50	98.21	435.93	444.83	98.00
2005–06	166.23	169.10	98.31	386.07	394.01	97.98
2006–07	165.37	168.70	98.02	389.17	397.44	97.92

Sources: Government of Manipur. (various Issues). *Statistical Abstracts of Manipur*. Imphal: Directorate of Economic and Statistics.

1993–94, only to decrease in the latter part of 1990s. However, the percentage kept on increasing until it reached the highest level of 98.54 per cent in 2003–04 and it remained above 98 per cent. It follows a fluctuating trend between 98.54 per cent and 96.21 per cent of the total foodgrain area in the period 1993–94 and 2006–07 (see Table 5.3).

Rice also shared 94.95 per cent of total foodgrain output in the State in 1990–91. Its share increased to more than 97 per cent in the subsequent years of 1990s until it decreased to lowest level of 93.38 per cent in 1996–97, but it bounced back to more than 96 percentages in the last years of 1990s and further to around 98 percentages since 2003–04 in the period. In 1997–98 to 2002–03, somehow the percentage share of rice remained lower than its earlier level in the first-half of 1990s. However, in 2003–04 to 2006–07, the percentage maintained at higher level than either early 1990s or in 1997–98 to 2002–03.

The year-to-year changes in the percentage shares of area and production of rice can also observe in their respective absolute figures. In 1990–91, 157.41 thousand ha was under rice cultivation; it increased to 160.3 thousand ha in the next year, 1991–92 but decreased at 151.19 thousand ha in the following year only to increase in the subsequent year (Fig. 5.3; Table 5.3). The fluctuating trend continues during the entire period of 1990–91 to 2006–07, between the lowest of 151.19 thousand ha in 1992–93 with the highest of 176.31 thousand ha in 2004–05.

In the case of production, it was 274.17 thousand MT in 1990–91, which has increased to 340.45 thousand MT in the following year 1991–92, but attained at lower level of production in the subsequent year. The fluctuating trend continues in the entire period, 1990–91 to 2006–07, with the highest level of production, i.e., 435.93 thousand MT in 2004–05. The period ends with more or less a higher-level of rice production. Yet, this positive change is not free from the question on its sustainability.

The above analysis shows that rice does dominate in foodgrain scenario, both in terms of area and production, in the State and subjected to fluctuations from year to year. One of the principal causes for the fluctuation in production is generally pointed to forces of nature such as failure of monsoon and flood. Dependence on rainfed cultivation points out weak irrigation facilities in the State, and devastation of crop on account of flood highlights inadequate flood control mechanism in the State by concerned

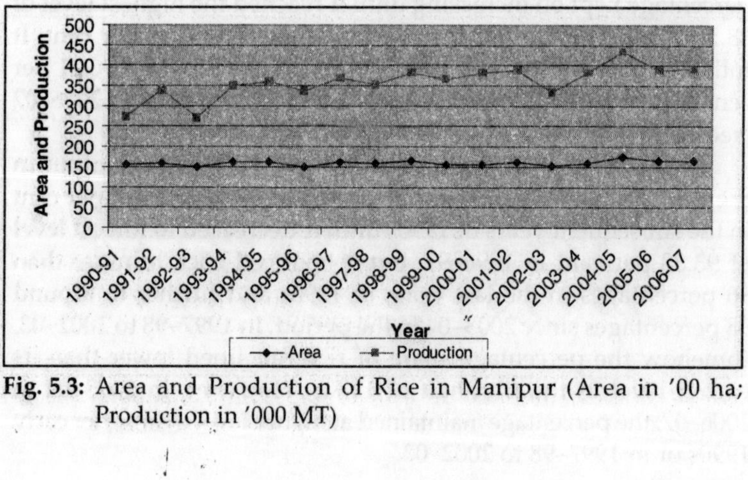

Fig. 5.3: Area and Production of Rice in Manipur (Area in '00 ha; Production in '000 MT)

authorities. In addition to these factors, other causal linkages should be located in socio-economic factors. However, it is beyond the scope of this chapter to analyse such factors.

Foodgrain Situation

Though agricultural economy of Manipur is preponderance on food economy, the State has been facing the problem of foodgrain deficit that emerged in the drought years of 1978 and 1979 (Singh, 1987 and Sachdev, 2000) (see Table 5.4).

As the data in Table 5.4 indicates that by 1995–96, proportions of deficits to production in cereal and foodgrain were respectively 13.54 per cent and 16.32 per cent respectively. The deficits were at lower levels of 2.64 per cent and 5.20 per cent respectively in 1996–97, only to come back with larger magnitudes. The instability continued with a clear sign of increasing trend, with an abrupt sharp fluctuation in the first half of 2000s, over the years under study (Fig. 5.4). However, the production deficit remained below 15 per cent for cereal and 17 per cent for foodgrain as a whole in the following years of 1995–96 until 2002–03. By 2002–03, the

Table 5.4: Total and Percentage of Cereal and Foodgrain Production, Requirement and Deficit in Manipur

Year	*Production ('000 MT)*		*Requirement ('000 MT)*		*% of production deficit*		*Deficit ('000 MT)*	
	Cereal	*Food-grain*	*Cereal*	*Food-grain*	*Cereal*	*Food-grain*	*Cereal*	*Food-grain*
1995–96	345.10	347.58	391.83	404.30	13.54	16.32	46.73	56.72
1996–97	390.69	393.31	401.00	413.76	2.64	5.20	10.31	20.45
1997–98	364.76	368.02	410.27	423.33	12.48	15.03	45.51	55.31
1998–99	392.29	395.06	419.65	433.01	6.97	9.61	27.36	37.95
1999–00	375.90	378.92	429.13	442.80	14.16	16.86	53.23	63.88
2000–01	392.59	395.75	434.51	448.34	10.68	13.29	41.92	52.59
2001–02	397.35	400.39	443.89	458.01	11.71	14.39	46.54	57.62
2002–03	343.94	347.07	452.94	467.35	31.69	34.66	109.00	120.28
2003–04	388.77	392.01	462.31	477.02	18.92	21.69	73.54	85.01
2004–05	444.83	449.32	471.73	486.74	6.05	8.33	26.90	37.42
2005–06	394.01	398.39	481.22	496.54	22.13	24.64	87.21	98.15
2006–07	397.44	402.68	490.76	506.38	23.48	25.75	93.32	103.70
2007–08	414.59	419.23	500.36	516.29	20.69	23.15	85.77	97.06

Sources: Government of Manipur. *Economic Survey, Manipur*, 2002–03 and 2008–09. Imphal: Directorate of Economics and Statistics.

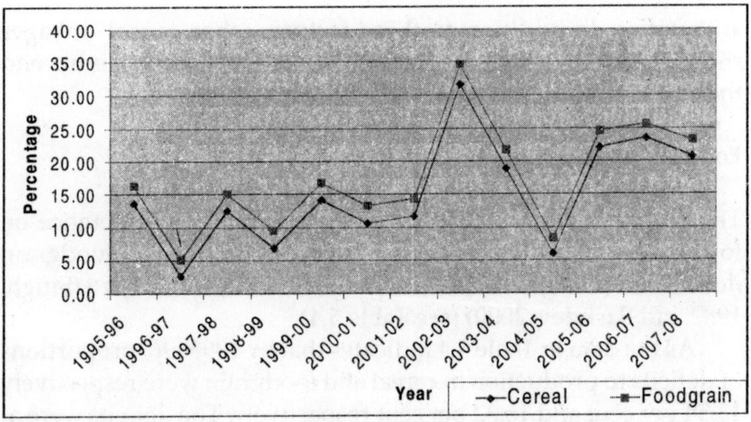

Fig. 5.4: Percentage of Cereal and Foodgrain Deficit to their respective Total Production in Manipur

Source: Government of Manipur. *Economic Survey of Manipur*, 2002–03 and 2008–09. Imphal: Directorate of Economics and Statistics.

deficits were as large as 109 thousand MT and 120.28 thousand MT for cereal and foodgrain respectively, which comprised 31.69 per cent and 34.66 per cent of their respective productions in that year. It was followed by an abrupt sharp decline in the deficit for two years only to increase at a high level of more than 20 per cent and 23 per cent for cereal and foodgrain respectively in the second half.

The scenario of foodgrain in the State can observe better by looking into both demand and supply sides of these essential goods. In those years with relatively good productions, either of cereals or of all foodgrain, deficit was relatively low (Table 5.4). In the years 1996–97 and 1998–99, the cereal production was 390.69 thousand MT and 392.29 thousand MT and the foodgrain production was 393.31 thousand MT and 395.06 thousand MT in the respective years. In these years, the cereal and foodgrain production were higher than their respective past years and hence the deficits were comparatively low. However, it is not true in 2000–01 and 2001–02. In these years, the cereal and foodgrain production were higher than either that of 1996–97 or 1998–99, but demand were comparatively higher and, therefore, higher deficits (Fig. 5.5).

Contrary to the production side, demand side shows a

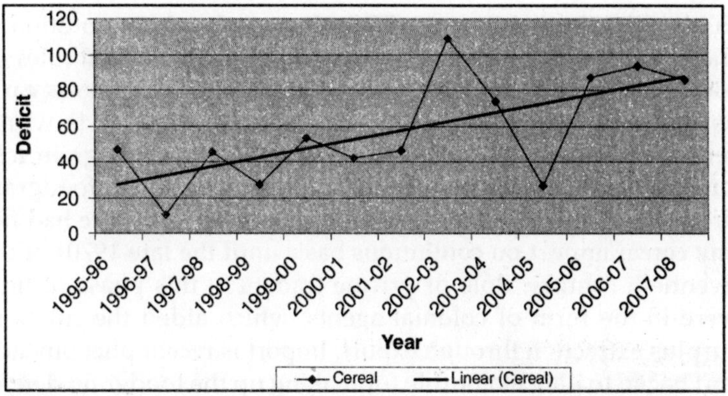

Fig. 5.5: Estimated Cereal Deficit in Manipur (*in '000 Tonnes*)

continuously increasing trend both for cereal and foodgrain. It will be continuing so even with assumptions of some pulling down effect on demand side due changes in consumption pattern of households, which are brought about by mainly changes in their per capita income level and lifestyle. The decadal growth rate of population in the State is still at a high rate of 30.04 per cent during the decade of 1991–2001 (Census of India, 2001) and there may not be any drastic decline of the growth rate in the present decade either.

The foodgrain supply-demand scenario is very disturbing given the predominance of foodgrain sector in the overall economy of the State. In fact, one needs to remind that the objective of self-sufficiency in foodgrain production finds a place in successive plan documents of Manipur Government. However, a clear-cut agriculture or foodgrain policy has not been formulated as of now. There is no long-term strategy to make the State self-sufficient in foodgrain or at least to reduce the deficit at a manageable level. The problem of deficit in foodgrain production is continuing and has ever been increasing over the years. Lack of will and commitment on the part of State Government will only have negative bearing on the food security situation of the State.

Making Up Production Deficit

Production deficit of foodgrain in the State is made up by two ways. First, through private trade and second by government's

Public Distribution System (PDS) through Food Corporation of India (FCI). Private traders have been plying influential roles on foodgrain trade in the State, which can be traced back to as early as the first part of the previous century. Here, it is worth remembering that Manipur did have a history of foodgrain self-sufficiency. The State had remained comfortable on foodgrain production during the British colonial period and there had not any cereal import on continuous basis until the late 1970s of the twentieth century. Role of private traders in this phase of time were in the form of colonial agents, which aided the rulers in surplus extraction through export. Import is recent phenomenon and began to play major role for making up the foodgrain deficit. The problem of foodgrain deficit has to be located within the framework of development strategy being pursued and pushed by the government. Analysis of development strategy would entail, first of all, to understand the concept of land-lock economy and linkages with the larger market, and if at all, due consideration has been given to this specificity while framing a development framework for Manipur.

Traders import foodgrain from the rest of India and across the Indo-Myanmar border. Availability of foodgrain in the State is principally overdriven by price differences and hence, profit.

From the State's foodgrain security point of view (short and long-term), two concerned cannot be neglected. Growth rate of foodgrain production in India stands at 1.2 per cent; lower than the annual population growth rate of 1.9 per cent during 1990–2007 (*Economic Survey 2007–08*). The total rice production also remained stagnant at 80 thousand million MT since 1999–2000, with a marginal increase in 2005–06 and 2006–07 (Fig. 5.6). Over and above, there is little scope for expanding cultivated area of rice and no technological breakthrough foreseeable in near future to increase production. This would certainly affect availability and price of foodgrain, including rice in India as well as in Manipur.

The import from across the Myanmar border has suffered setback as a result of recent cyclone (Nargis) that hampered its foodgrain production. Recuperation from the havoc of cyclone to earlier level of production will certainly take time.

Looking at the other option for making up deficit, it should be noted that foodgrain brought in for PDS through FCI is meant for carrying out targeted programmes, not for filling up foodgrain

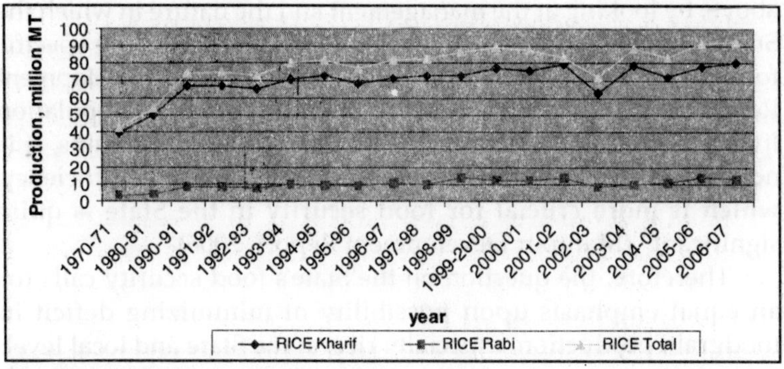

Fig. 5.6: Production of Rice in India

Source: Government of India. (Various issues). *Economic Survey*. New Delhi: Ministry of Finance.

deficit. Since the year 2002, 35 kg of cereal has been provided to each of the households Below the Poverty Line (BPL) under TPDS.

There is already an all round sustained increase in the prices of essential commodities, across the world. In the case of Manipur, retail price of rice increased by almost double within the first-six months of 2008. To make the situation worst, there were instances of non-availability of rice to meet day-to-day requirements in different parts of the State. The increase in prices cannot be explained purely by economic factors as high prices ensued on account of lack of price control mechanism and manipulation by traders. Thus, there is a need for effective mechanism of price control, distribution system and clear-cut foodgrain policy on the part of the State Government.

Food Security in Manipur

According to the Food and Agricultural Organization (FAO), food security is defined as a situation in which, "all people, at all times, have physical and economic access to sufficient, safe and nutritious food to meet their dietary needs and food preferences for an active and healthy life". The question of food security has become a serious issue and challenge before the global community. Its relevance and importance is even more increasing for a tiny State like Manipur, which has a small area of arable land. The State is in the midst of a serious food crisis which is evident as elaborated above, by looking at the management and the nature in which the State's production deficit is filled up and absence of any specific foodgrain policy in the State. In this context, Manipur Development Report states, "In the case of Manipur with a dispersed population living in remote, intractable and poorly connected terrains, it is not the self-sufficiency in foodgrain *per se* but local self-sufficiency, which is more crucial for food security in the State is quite significant" (Manipur Development Report, 2006).

Therefore, the question on the State's food security calls for an equal emphasis upon possibility of minimizing deficit in foodgrain production, especially rice, at the State and local level. It becomes more urgent now to ease than ever before because danger of food crisis is hanging like the Sword of Damocles upon the State. The crux issue here is on exploring the possibilities and scope of increasing foodgrain production without negative environmental and consequences.

Generally, economists and agronomists for enhancing production of agricultural crops are highlighting three main options or ways. They pertain to expansion of net sown area, enhancement of intensity of land use (through adoption of double and triple cropping systems) and improvement of land productivity through adoption of new technology. In the case of Manipur, scope for expansion of net sown area under rice cultivation in the valley areas is insignificant. We witness a reverse trend, where arable lands are being aggressively used for various projects and schemes of both the State and Central Governments. By 2000–01, only 200 ha of fallow land and 740 hectares of cultivable wasteland were available in the valley areas of the State (*Statistical Abstracts of Manipur*, 2004).

In 1985–86, the net sown area under rice had been estimated at 164.6 thousand ha for the State as a whole and it followed a fluctuating trend over the years under study. It increased to 176.31 thousand ha by 2004–05, though declined later it still maintained at a higher level than any of years 1985–86 to 2003–04 (see Table 5.5).

In fact, the fluctuating trend is a reflection of the changes both in the valley and hill areas. However, valley area experienced a slight declining trend, which is opposite to increasing trend in hill area (Fig. 5.7). The net sown area under rice in valley declined from 98.15 thousand ha in 1985–86 or from the high level of 101.34

Table 5.5 : Total Estimated Area and Percentage Share of Area under Rice in Hill and Valley of Manipur

Year	*Percentage*		*Area ('000, hectares)*		
	Hill	*Valley*	*Hill*	*Valley*	*Total Manipur*
1985–86	40.37	59.63	66.45	98.15	164.6
1990–91	35.62	64.38	56.07	101.34	157.41
1995–96	42.55	57.45	57.41	77.52	134.93
1999–00	43.18	56.82	67.81	89.24	157.05
2000–01	43.3	56.7	67.96	89.00	156.96
2001–02	44.05	55.95	71.62	90.95	162.57
2002–03	47.5	52.5	72.73	80.38	153.11
2003–04	48.82	51.18	77.05	80.78	157.83
2004–05	42.81	57.19	75.48	100.83	176.31
2005–06	49.72	50.28	82.67	83.59	166.26
2006–07	48.27	51.73	79.83	85.54	165.37
2007–08	43.56	56.44	72.37	93.78	166.15

Sources: Government of Manipur. Various issues. *Statistical Abstracts of Manipur* and *Economic Survey of Manipur*. Imphal: Directorate of Economics and Statistics.

thousand ha in 1990–91 to around 90 thousand ha in 2001–02 or to the significantly low level of 80.38 thousand ha in 2002–03. Though it was increased to 100.83 thousand ha in 2004–05, declined in subsequent years. The negative impact is mainly caused by population pressure along with other factors, such as submersion, conversion of prime agricultural land into brickfields, educational and other institutional and facility areas.

On the contrary, the net sown area has increased in hill areas from 66.45 thousand ha in 1985–86 to 77.05 thousand ha and further

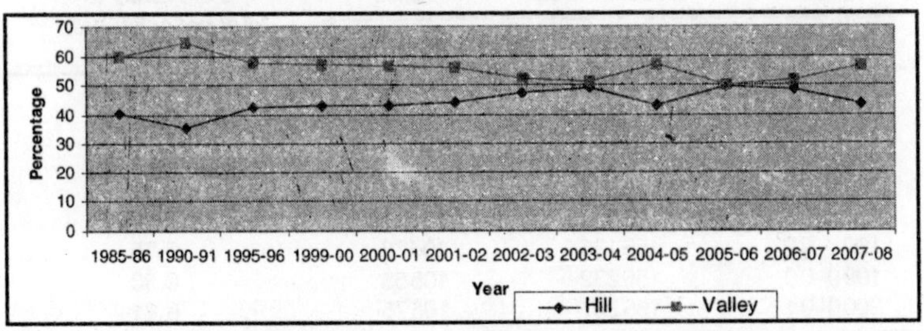

Fig. 5.7 : Percentage Share of Area by Hill and Valley in Rice Production

Sources: Government of Manipur. Various issues. *Statistical Abstracts of Manipur* and *Economic Survey of Manipur*. Imphal: Directorate of Economics and Statistics.

to 82.67 thousand ha in 2003–04 and 2005–06 respectively (Fig. 5.8; Table 5.6). Despite its decline in subsequent years of 2004–05, it is still higher than any of the years before 2002–03. It still can increase to some extent by expanding the net sown area. However, the cereal productivity in the hills is not only comparatively low but also production generally comes with a price-negative environmental and ecological consequence.

Therefore, preservation of existing valuable agricultural land in the valley of Manipur should be the focal point of any agrarian

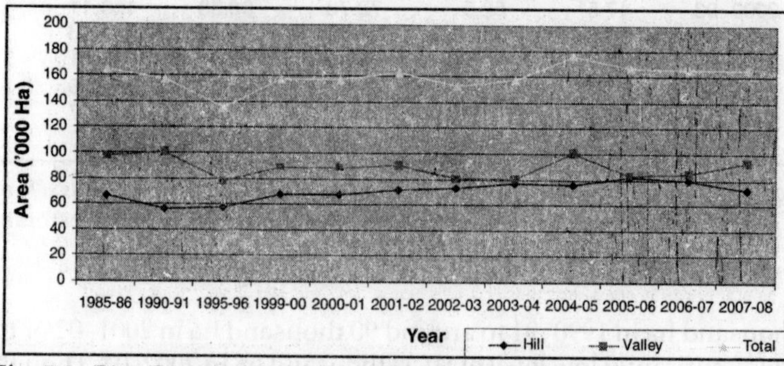

Fig. 5.8: Rice Cropped Area in Hill and Valley, Manipur

Sources: Government of Manipur. various issues. *Statistical Abstracts of Manipur* and *Economic Survey of Manipur*. Imphal: Directorate of Economics and Statistics.

Table 5.6 : Net Sown Area, Area Sown more than once (ASMO) and Percentage of ASMO to Net Sown Area in Manipur Valley

Year	*Net sown area (in ha)*	*ASMO (in ha)*	*% of ASMO to total net sown area*
1990–91	146693	5765	3.93
1994–95	154031	6235	4.05
1995–96	160524	6752	4.21
1996–97	154966	9013	5.82
1997–98	154981	10387	6.70
1998–99	155136	10478	6.75
1999–00	155232	10555	6.80
2000–01	155287	10575	6.81

Sources: Government of Manipur. *Statistical Abstracts of Manipur* (various issues). Imphal: Directorate of Economics and Statistics.

Note : Figures for later years are not available even in the Statistical Report 2007.

policy. In order to restrain the declining prime agriculture land area in the valley on the one hand, and to minimize the negative environmental consequences in the hill areas, on the other, the State Government, civil society organizations and other local bodies should develop critical dialogue on the matters concerning agricultural policies and practices in the State. Government should create the necessary conditions where civil society and local bodies can intervene in policy formation and implementation. There is also an urgent need on the part of civil society and local bodies to pressurise the government for enacting a clear-cut policy for agriculture through democratic process.

Increasing Intensity of Land Use

Mono cropping is the dominant pattern of cultivation for sedentary or permanent (including terrace) type of cultivation in the State of Manipur. Under *jhum* cultivation, the cultivators often adopt mixed cropping pattern. In the method of mixed crop cultivation, both cereal and non-cereal crops planted together on the same field in such a way that the crops can be harvested in a phase-by-phase manner. This method not only increases total production for a given *jhuming* area but also increases the productivity of the land. However, unavailability of appropriate data on *jhum* cultivation and terraced cultivation has constrained the analysis of intensity of land-use in the hill areas of Manipur.

In the valley area, regarded as the rice bowel of the State, mono (single) cropping still remains the dominant pattern of cultivation.

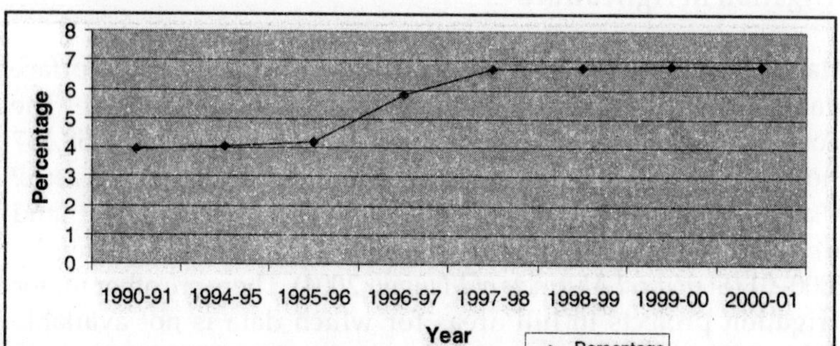

Fig. 5.9 : Percentage of Area Sown more than once to Total Net Sown Area, Valley Manipur

By 2000–01, only 6.81 per cent of total net sown area was adopting either double or multiple cropping systems (Fig. 5.9; Table 5.6). During 1990–91 and 2000–01, ASMO showed an increasing trend, especially in the last half of 1990s, both in absolute and percentage terms (Table 5.6 and Fig. 5.9). In 1990–91, only 5,765 ha comprising just 3.93 per cent of net sown area were cropped more than once. It increased to 6,235 ha in 1994–95 and further increased in the following years. ASMO increased to 10,575 ha, which is 6.81 per cent of total net sown area by 2000–01.

This shows, the net area sown more than once has made almost doubled either in absolute or percentage terms, but remained at a very low level. The dynamics between expansion of area sown more than once and of the area under foodgrain crop has the probability of crop diversification. If this dynamic is set aside for once lies on more than one factor. Among these factors, availability of irrigation facilities is one of the most significant factors required for adoption of double or multiple cropping patterns in Manipur. Besides, availability of suitable technology is also very important. For example, if a new variety of rice is available—requiring only a certain level of soil moisture (as the rice which grows at *jhum* land), cold resistant, high yield and which does not compromise on taste—it will help expand ASMO under rice in the State and hence, will increase cereal and foodgrain production. In the present scenario, positive roles in the form of active participation, engagement and persuasion from agriculture universities, research and development and technological institutions become a *sine qua non*.

Irrigation in Agriculture

Manipur is comparatively rich in water resources especially surface water. Canals are the major source of irrigation in the State. The Command Area Development Projects target to irrigate 58,137 thousand ha of agricultural land by 2001–02 (*Economic Survey of Manipur 2002–03*, 141). Another 1,465.00 ha of agricultural land are to be irrigated by minor irrigation system in the valley by 2000–01 (*Statistical Abstracts of Manipur* 2004). There are other minor irrigation projects in hill areas for which data is not available (Table 5.7).

The agricultural land, which comes under the Command Area Development Project, is quite large as compared to the availability

Table 5.7: Net Area Irrigated by Source*

Year	*Govt. canal*	*Private canal*	*Tubewell & other well*	*Tanks*	*Other sources*	*Total*
1985–86	1209.60	–	–	–	–	1209.60
1986–87	1530.00	–	–	–	–	1530.00
1987–88	1440.00	–	50	–	–	1490.00
1988–89	1460.00	–	20	–	–	1480.00
1989–90	1305.00	–	100	–	–	1405.00
1990–91	1100.00	–	100	–	–	1200.00
1991–92	1400.00	–	100	–	–	1500.00
1992–93	1450.00	–	100	–	–	1550.00
1993–94	1900.00	–	80	–	–	1980.00
1994–95	2300.00	–	100	–	–	2400.00
1995–96	2300.00	–	100	–	–	2400.00
1996–97	2400.00	–	100	–	–	2500.00
1997–98	1940.00	–	60	–	–	2000.00
1998–99	2200.00	–	100	–	–	2300.00
1999–00	2370.00	–	30	–	–	2400.00
2000–01	1465.00	–	–	–	–	1465.00

Source: Government of Manipur. 2004. *Statistical Abstracts of Manipur*. Imphal: Directorate of Economics and Statistics

Note: Figures for later years are not available even in the Statistical Report 2007.

of net sown area. However, in reality, the State remains more or less dependent on rain. Thus, a critical examination of the targeted objectives while realization of the potentials as well as expansion of irrigated area. Then one can find out the possible ways to tackle the problems of irrigation in Manipur.

High Yielding Varieties (HYV)/IV Technology in the State

In Manipur, HYV crops technology (fertilizer-pesticides-irrigation) was introduced under HYV programme in the late 1960s. One of the drawbacks of the programme was over emphasis on use of HYV and use of fertilizers such as urea and DAP, etc. In the absence of soil profiled by soil testing agencies in the State, there is dearth of use of micronutrients and other complex fertilizers. Moreover, proper and timely use of pesticides needs a critical look in the State.

HYV/IV seeds were initially confined to a small area of 400 ha in 1968–69 in Manipur. The programme spread at a very slow pace but significantly progressed by mid-1980s. HYV/IV seeds spreads to 37.55 thousand ha by 1985–86 (Table 5.8). The area increased to 71.83 thousand ha in 1997–98 and further to 90.95 thousand ha by 1998–99. However, there was a sharp decline in 1999–2000 to 72.02 thousand ha and could not increase to 1998–99 level until 2004–05 when the area was increased to 101.32 thousand ha. The area under HYV/IV has been subjected to sharp fluctuation from year-to-year. In the year 2002–03, the area under HYV/IV was as low as 47.36 thousand ha. It recovered in 2003–04, and further increased to the highest level, in the years under study, in 2004–05. Fluctuations can be explained in terms of weather conditions, decrease in prime agricultural land, etc. The fluctuation, which undermines any effort for increasing foodgrain production, was witnessed in area under HYV/IV seeds both in the hill and valley of Manipur during the late 1990s to most of the years in the decade of 2000s (Table 5.8; Fig. 5.10).

As far as valley and hill differences are concerned, there is a wide gap. In the hill area, at maximum of only 21.66 per cent of the rice cultivated area was under HYV seed in 1997–98 (Fig. 5.11; Table 5.8). In any other years during 1997–98 to 2006–07, the percentage was less than 20 per cent. In the year 2000–01, it was just 9.37 per cent of the rice cultivated area in the hill.

On the other hand, more than 63 per cent was under HYV in the valley area, except in the year 2002–03 and 2003–04, with only 48.08 per cent and 57.46 per cent respectively. In some years, say in 2004–05, it was as high as 87.89 per cent. The area under HYV underwent fluctuation. In the first two-three years of the present

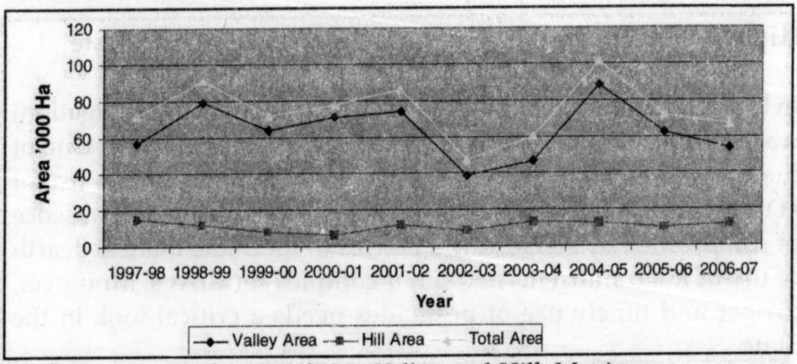

Fig. 5.10: Area Under HYV/IV in Valley and Hill, Manipur

Source: Government of Manipur. 2004. *Statistical Abstracts of Manipur*. Imphal: Directorate of Economics and Statistics.

Table 5.8 : Area under Rice by Variety of Seeds

Year	*Area under HYV/ Improved variety*		*Area under other variety*		*Total area (HYV & other varieties)*		*Total area under HYV/IV (valley & hill)*	*% of area under HYV/IV*		*% of HYV/IV area to total rice cropped area*
	Valley	*Hill*	*Valley*	*Hill*	*Valley*	*Hill*		*Valley*	*Hill*	
1997–98	56.78	15.05	31.64	54.43	88.42	69.48	71.83	64.22	21.66	45.49
1998–99	79.05	11.90	18.88	57.06	97.93	68.96	90.95	80.72	17.26	54.50
1999–00	64.22	7.80	25.02	60.01	89.24	67.81	72.02	71.96	11.50	45.86
2000–01	70.92	6.37	18.11	61.59	89.03	67.96	77.65	79.66	9.37	49.23
2001–02	74.04	12.12	16.91	59.50	90.95	71.62	86.16	81.41	16.92	53.00
2002–03	38.65	8.71	41.73	64.02	80.38	72.73	47.36	48.08	11.98	30.93
2003–04	46.42	13.86	34.36	63.19	80.78	77.05	60.28	57.46	17.99	38.19
2004–05	88.62	12.70	12.21	62.78	100.83	75.48	101.32	87.89	16.83	57.47
2005–06	62.39	9.71	21.20	72.96	83.59	82.67	72.10	74.64	11.75	43.37
2006–07	54.10	12.56	31.44	67.27	85.54	79.83	66.66	63.25	15.73	40.30

Sources: Government of Manipur. Various issues. *Statistical Abstracts of Manipur*. Imphal: Directorate of Economics and Statistics.

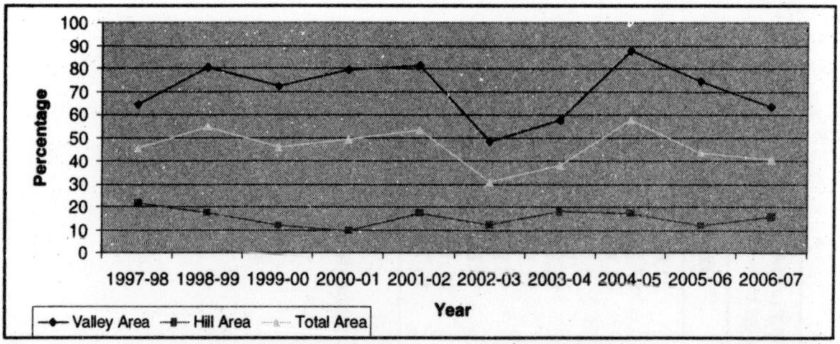

Fig. 5.11: Percentage of HYV/IV Rice Area to Total Rice Area was in Valley, Hill and Aggregate, Manipur

Source: Government of Manipur. 2004. *Statistical Abstracts of Manipur*. Imphal: Directorate of Economics and Statistics. Fertilizer Association of India. 2004. *Fertilizer Statistics*. New Delhi: FAI.

decade, there has been a sharp decline in the proportion in the valley area but recovered in subsequent years. In fact, similar pattern is visible at the State as a whole. This trend has put serious question mark upon the reliability of HYV/IV Programme in the State.

Productivity of Rice

Considering the share of rice crop both in production and area to total foodgrain, one needs to give due attention to its productivity. An interesting aspect emerges while looking at the yield rate of rice in the State. The yield rate of rice in Manipur has been higher than either any of the north eastern states (Assam, Arunachal Pradesh, Meghalaya, Mizoram, Nagaland, Sikkim and Tripura) or that of all India average in 1980's and early 1990's (Singh, 1993 and Sachdev, 2000). In 1996–97, the yield rate was 2211 kg/ha, which was higher than 1879 kg/ha of all India level average. But it was lower than Punjab which recorded a yield of 3397 kg/ha (Table 5.9; Fig. 5.12).

Momentum of high yield rate in Manipur sustained and witnessed steep rise in the years between 1996–97 and 2000–01. It reached 2431 kg/ha in the latter year. Nevertheless, productivity of rice declined in successive years to 2192 kg/ha in 2002–03 and then increased to follow a fluctuating trend. At the all India level, also it follows a fluctuating trend with an increase until 2000–01

Table 5.9: Yield Rate of Rice

[Yield rate (Kg./ha)]

Year	*Manipur*	*Punjab*	*All India*
1996–97	2211	3397	1879
1997–98	2227	3465	1895
1998–99	2290	3152	1928
1999–00	2324	3346	1990
2000–01	2432	3506	1961
2001–02	2382	3545	2078
2002–03	2192	3510	1804
2003–04	2416	–	2078
2004–05	2473	–	1984
2005–06	2322	–	2102
2006–07	2353	–	2127

Source : Government of Manipur. 2004. *Statistical Abstracts of Manipur*. Imphal: Directorate of Economics and Statistics. Fertilizer Association of India. 2004. *Fertilizer Statistics*. New Delhi: FAI.

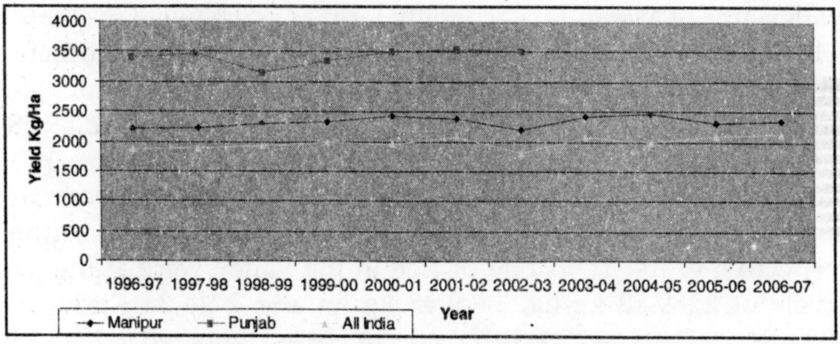

Fig. 5.12 : Yield Rate of Rice for Manipur, Punjab and All India

Source: Government of Manipur. 2004. *Statistical Abstracts of Manipur*. Imphal: Directorate of Economics and Statistics. Fertilizer Association of India. 2004. *Fertilizer Statistics*. New Delhi: FAI.

and then increased again to 2127 kg/ha in 2006–07. In the ensuing years, productivity remained higher in Manipur as compared to the all India average. However, compared to the Punjab's experience, the yield rate of rice in Manipur remained at substantially low level. In Punjab, yield rate is as high as 3545 kg/ha in 2001–02. whereas it was only 2473 kg/ha in 2004–05, in the case of Manipur.

Better productivity of rice in Punjab as compared to Manipur can be explained by considering the differences in irrigation facilities, availability and use of inputs, price support system and other incentives. Punjab being the nerve centre of green revolution in India, benefited in terms of agricultural infrastructure development such as power and irrigation facilities, and a regulatory policy on the part of the government. These conducive factors are conspicuous by their absence in Manipur. Geographical factors also put a limitation to Manipur's productivity in rice. In fact, it has been explained earlier that the yield rate of rice in the hills, which comprised more than two-fifth of the total rice cropped area in Manipur, is substantially lower than that of the valley areas. However, explanations of the relationship between land productivity and its explanatory factors lies beyond the scope of this chapter.

Hill and Valley Differences

Valley area of Manipur is generally term as rice bowl of the State, which contributes around two-third of rice production in the State. In 2000–01, the area contributed 65.43 per cent of total rice production and a slightly lower level of 59.53 per cent and 59.68 per cent in 2003–04 and 2006–07 respectively (Table 5.10). However, the valley area shared only 56.82 per cent, 51.18 per cent and 51.72 per cent of total area under rice cultivation in the respective years. Yield rate of rice in the valley were at higher levels of 2289.82 kg/ha, 2809.48 kg/ha and 2715.34 Kg/ha in 2000–01, 2003–04 and 2006–07 respectively, as compared to 1942.73 kg/ha, 2002.34 kg/ha and 1965.43 kg/ha in the respective years in

Table 5.10 : Total Production, Percentage Share in Total Production and Total Area and Yield Rate of Rice in the Valley and Hill Districts of Manipur

(Production in '000 MT, yield in kg/ha)

Year	Production		% share to total production		% share to total area		Yield rate	
	Valley	*Hill*	*Valley*	*Hill*	*Valley*	*Hill*	*Valley*	*Hill*
2000–01	249.73	131.96	65.43	34.57	56.82	43.18	2289.82	1941.73
2003–04	226.95	154.29	59.53	40.47	51.18	48.82	2809.48	2002.34
2006–07	232.27	156.90	59.68	40.32	51.72	48.27	2715.34	1965.43

Source: Government of Manipur. 2001, 2004 and 2007. *Statistical Abstracts of Manipur*. Imphal: Directorate of Economic and Statistics.

the hill areas. This difference is due to geographical conditions along with other factors, which are conducive for enhancing productivity in the hill areas. In fact, many economists and agronomists identified horticultural crops to be more suitable in hill areas as compared to rice. However, increasing rice production and productivity, both in the hill and valley areas of the State without negative consequences remain a major challenge that needs to be overcome.

Conclusion

It is needless to emphasise the role of agriculture and its relevance in the economic development of the State. One cannot imagine any kind of development without developing the agriculture sector on account of the fact that various sectors of a country's or State's economy are directly or indirectly dependent upon it. In the case of Manipur, too, agriculture sector plays vital roles in its economy. It not only provides an important source of livelihood but also serves as a source of employment.

The sector also contributes around one-fourth of the State's GSDP. However, the shares of agriculture sector and primary sector to GSDP have decreased, though not smoothly, during the period 1993–94 to 2006–07. As at the all India level, agriculture sector supports large shares of the workforce in Manipur, either as cultivator or agriculture labour. But, over the last decades, the employment share of agriculture sector has been decreasing in the State and remained lower than all India level. If one considers food processing, trading services in agricultural inputs and produces, etc., the contribution and role of agriculture in the economy is still predominant.

In spite of the diverse role played by agriculture in the State, it lacks diversification and heavily preponderance of food over non-food crops. In terms of both area and output, foodgrain, especially cereal crops, dominates the agriculture landscape in the State. Among the cereal rice contributes more than 90 per cent of the total foodgrain output. Despite its dominance in agriculture sector, deficit in foodgrain has become a grotesque reality in the State since late 1970s and it has been increasing during 1990s. The production remained saturated with sharp fluctuations at times. In spite of the downward effect of per capita income and lifestyle changes, demand is rising, as population is growing as high as 30 per cent decadal growth rate. As far as high decadal population growth rate in the State is concerned, the share of migrant workers is substantial. Therefore, the question of food security has become a vexing issue now. The State needs to put sustain effort and consistent policy to enhance foodgrain production along with a check on unwarranted population growth to prevent itself from grim reality of foodgrain crisis.

So far foodgrain deficit in the State is filled up through private trade and the PDS. Traders import foodgrain from the rest of India and from Myanmar and distribution of the same hinges on profit. Thus, availability of food in the State is theoretically ensured as long as conditions are favourable to traders. But these options also have serious limitation on account of frequent economic blockades and land slides on the national highways (NH 39, NH 53 and NH 150), which connect Manipur with the rest of India as well as Myanmar.

Two important concerns cannot be neglected from the State's foodgrain security point of view. First, the growth rate of foodgrain production in India was lower than annual population growth rate during 1990–2007. Besides, there is no scope of large-scale increase in rice cropped area and technological breakthrough is unlikely to happen in near future. Therefore, a quantum jump in the production in India may not be possible at least in near future. Such a situation is bound to affect foodgrain availability and their price, including rice in India.

Secondly, the import from Myanmar does not have a good prospect. The country's foodgrain production capability was severely affected by the recent cyclone. Recovery from the devastation of the cyclone may take some years. The situation has affected the business of foodgrain specially rice import, which in turn, affected foodgrain availability in the State. Moreover, one has to understand that foodgrain brought in for PDS through FCI is meant for carrying out targeted programme and not meant for filling up the entire foodgrain deficit. At the same time, it will not be enough for the latter. Thus, both the options have certain inherent limitation. Hence, the State cannot rely entirely upon these options for its food security.

There is a real threat of food security in the State. Within the first six months of 2008, in the State has witness almost a double increase in the retail price of rice and other essential commodities. Moreover, a famine like situation prevails in the south west Manipur (Churachandpur District) due to rodents attacked. The State clearly lacks capability to face such circumstances. However, the need of the hour is to come out of the dependency mentality on the part of ruling political class and set out State's own plan for food self-security. More particularly, food security has to be sought not as foodgrain self-sufficiency *per se* but local/regional level self-sufficiency. The focal point of policy pertaining to the State's food security calls for an equal emphasis upon possibility of minimizing deficit in foodgrain production, especially of rice, at the State and local/regional level on the one hand, and finding out lasting solutions to the problem of the absence of any clear-cut foodgrain policy on the other.

Given the fact that there is no more scope of increasing net sown area in the valley, and expanding net sown area comes with a price in terms of ecological and environmental consequences emphasis should be given on restraining the declining prime agriculture land area in the valley and minimization of the negative consequences in the hill areas. The State Government and Civil Society Organizations can play critical roles to adopt a clear policy guidelines and peaceful approach with a long-term vision for sustainable development in the State. Hence, decentralization and democratization is the key to the harmonious growth of development in both the hill and the valley of Manipur. Enhancement of gross cropped area can also be simultaneously consider through adoption of double and multiple cropping method of irrigation facilities in the State. Besides, undue delay in the completion of major, medium and minor irrigation projects due to lack of political will and inefficient administration seriously hinder the growth of agriculture sector. Critical evaluation, reassessment and review of various irrigation projects being taken up in the State should be initiated promptly. Such endeavour will certainly help in fixing the constraints on the realization of the potentials on the one hand, and expansion of irrigated area on the other hand for better production and productivity of foodgrain. Only then, one can visualize the possibilities of tackling foodgrain crisis in Manipur.

CITED WORKS

Aggarwal, A.K. 1987. *Economic Problems and Planning in the North-East India*. New Delhi: Sterling Publishers.

Bhalla, G.S. and G.K. Chadha. 1982. Green Revolution and small peasant: A study of income distribution in Punjab. *Economic and Political Weekly*, XVII, 20 and 21, May 15–22.

Bhalla, G.S. and Gurmail Singh. 2001. *Indian Agriculture: Four Decades of Development*. New Delhi: Sage Publications.

Bhalla, G.S. 2007. *Indian Agriculture since Independence*. New Delhi: National Book Trust.

Dutta, B.B. and M.N. Karna. ed. 1987. *Agricultural Development in North-East India*. New Delhi: Deep and Deep Publications.

Fertilizer Association of India. *Fertilizer Statistics* (various issues). New Delhi: FAI.

Government of India. 2006. *Manipur Development Report Draft*. Sponsored by Planning Commission. New Delhi: Institute for Human Development. http://manipur.nic.in/planning/DraftMSDR/DefaultDraftMSDR.html.

Government of Manipur. *Statistical Abstracts of Manipur* (various issues). Imphal: Directorate of Economics and Statistics.

Government of India. *Economic Survey* (various issues). New Delhi: Ministry of Finance. Government of India. 1981. General Economic Tables, Part III—A and B Manipur. In *Census of India: 1981*. New Delhi: Registrar General and Census Commissioner.

Government of India. 2003. Seasonal variation in the operational land holdings in India: 2002–03. *NSSO* 56th Round. January–December. New Delhi: Ministry of Statistics and Programme Implementation.

Government of India. 2001. Series 15, Manipur, Provisional Population Totals, paper 3. In *Census of India: 2001*. New Delhi: Registrar General and Census Commissioner.

Government of India. *Statistical Abstracts of India* (various issues). New Delhi: Central Statistical Organisation.

Sachdev, Gulshan. 2000. *Economy of the North-East*. New Delhi: Konark Publishers.

Sharma, R.K.; Brij Bala and H.R. Sharma. 1997. Regional disparities in agriculture development: A study of mountainous states. *Indian Journal of Agricultural Economics*, 52, 3. July–September.

Sharma, U.C. and R.N. Prasad. 1994. Socio-economic considerations in enhancing agricultural productivity in North East States. *IASSI Quarterly*, 12, 3 and 4.

Shukla Committee Report. 1997. *Transforming the Northeast*. High Level Commission Report to the Prime Minister, New Delhi.

Shukla, S.P. and A.K. Aggarwal. 1986. *Agriculture in North-East Region.* New Delhi: National Publishing House.

Singh, N.R. 1987. *Agricultural Development in the North-Eastern Region of India.* Ph.D. Thesis, Manipur University.

Singh, T.B. 1993. A Perspective of Agricultural and Horticultural Development in Manipur during the Plan Period. Ph.D. Thesis, Manipur University.

6

Industrialization in Manipur: Retrospect and Prospect

Lourembam Sanatomba Meetei

Introduction

Even after 55 years of economic planning and having put into practice various development programmes, Manipur still remains industrially backward. She is one of the least industrially developed States of India. All the nine districts of the State have been categorised as "no industries districts" by the all India standard (Government of Manipur, 1997b, 82). Manufacturing sector contributes hardly 9 per cent of the State Domestic Product and a mere 10 per cent of the total working population is found to be engaged in this sector. There is no large and medium industry in the State. The only industries existing in the State are in the form of small and village industries of which handlooms and handicrafts are worth mentioning.

The story of industrialization in Manipur can be traced back as far as 1074 A.D. During his regime, the King of Manipur, Loiyamba, introduced a"division of labour" system by assigning different names in respect of the particular mode of occupation of the people (Sanajaoba, 1993, 3–6). For instance, the blacksmiths were given the surname Thangjam; Phuritsabam to the tailors; Samjetsabam to the comb makers and the utensil makers were assigned the surname Aheibam, etc. So, it is an indication that the occupations of pottery, comb-making, blacksmith, goldsmith, leather manufacturing, fine arts, dyeing and handloom, etc. existed before and after the reign of King Loiyamba.

In the early part of the twentieth century, there was again a short burst of industrial development in the State. The important industries that existed during the period included carpentry, minting, silk dyeing, weaving, salt making, cotton dyeing, cloth dyeing, etc. out of which the silk industry was in almost every household (Laiba, 2002, 234).

With the development of the present Imphal-Dimapur Road (NH-39) during the Second World War, there also came in an unlimited inflow of a large amount of cheaper goods from British India to the state. The few indigenous industries of the state could not face the tough competition with those cheaper goods of British India and it led to their gradual extinction automatically. After becoming a full-fledged State of the Indian union, the effort to initiate the process of industrialization in the State in the early 1970s was again hampered by the opening up of the Indo-Myanmar Border Trade. This time, the competition was with those cheaper products which have come in from the South East Asian countries. While previously the industries that had closed down included iron, glass, paper, salt making, etc., this time industries such as batteries, candle manufacturing, polythene bag industry, soap manufacturing, etc. all died gradually because of the tough competition with goods of the South East Asian countries. Thus, Manipur's history of industrialization would have been different, had these two stages been taken care of properly. So it can be rightly said that Manipur's story of industrialization is a story of missed opportunities (Institute for Human Development, 2006, 147).

Contribution of Industry in NSDP

Table 6.1 gives the contribution of the real secondary sector in general and real manufacturing sector in particular to the total real NSDP of Manipur. It can be seen from the Table that the share of the secondary sector in the NSDP of the State increased from 7.64 per cent in 1980–81 to 32.87 per cent in 2008–09. It means that the share of the secondary sector in the NSDP has increased by more than 300 per cent during the decade.

As far as the manufacturing sector is concerned, its share in the NSDP has also increased but the increase has been very marginal. In 1980–81, the share of the manufacturing sector in the

Table 6.1 : Contribution of the Secondary Sector to the Total NSDP of Manipur at Constant Prices

(in Percentage)

Year/Sector	*1980–81*	*1985–86*	*1990–91*	*1995–96*	*2000–01*	*2005–06*	*2008–09*
Secondary	7.64	9.04	10.20	16.62	19.92	29.59	32.87
Manufacturing	4.60	5.10	5.99	7.44	6.75	5.99	5.88
Registered manufacturing	0.30	0.34	0.17	0.28	0.07	0.13	0.16
Unregistered manufacturing	4.30	4.76	5.82	7.16	6.68	5.86	5.72
Construction	6.55	7.09	8.11	10.17	10.67	21.79	25.39
Electricity, gas & water supply	–3.50	–3.16	–3.90	–1.05	0.02	1.82	1.60

Source: EPW Research Foundation, 2003. *Domestic Product of States of India, 1960–61 to 2000–01*. Mumbai, p. 205.

Note:
1. The period from 1980–81 with 1980–81 prices;
2. The period from 1995–96 with 1993–94 prices;
3. The period from 2000–01 onwards with 1999–00 prices.

total NSDP was only 4.60 per cent, which has increased to 5.88 per cent in 2008–09. Within the manufacturing sector itself, it is the unregistered manufacturing units, which are dominating the scene. The proportion of the registered units has been very negligible. This can be seen from the Table that in 1980–81, registered units accounted for only 6.52 per cent of output of the total manufacturing sector while the unregistered units formed a huge 93.48 per cent. This trend continued in 2008–09 also when out of the total manufacturing sector, a mere 2.72 per cent was contributed by the registered manufacturing sector and the rest was contributed by the unregistered sector.

Another important observation is the high proportion of the construction sub-sector in the secondary sector. This sub-sector contributed as high as 85.73 per cent of the total secondary sector in 1980–81. It was 77.26 per cent in 2008–09.

A comparative profile of the share of the manufacturing sector in the total NSDP of the States in the North Eastern Region has also been shown in Table 6.2. The table shows that Manipur emerged as the most industrialised State in the region in terms of the contribution of the manufacturing sector to the real NSDP in

Table 6.2 : Share of the Manufacturing Sector in the Real NSDP in the North Eastern Region

(in Percentage)

State	1980–81	1985–86	1990–91	1995–96	2000–01	2004–05	2008–09
Arunachal Pradesh	6.51	6.84	6.04	3.36	2.64	2.26	2.64**
Assam	6.52	7.10	6.47	8.54	7.45	7.80	7.43
Meghalaya	3.22	3.30	4.15	2.81	2.09	2.65	3.06**
Mizoram	2.52*	1.12*	5.78*	3.13*	1.02	0.77	1.64
Nagaland	2.14	1.73	8.01	5.58	0.65	1.28	1.48
Tripura	4.59	4.55	3.31	2.98	3.65	2.06	3.71***
Manipur	4.60	5.10	5.99	7.44	7.50	8.87	5.88

Source: Same as above Table 6.1, pp. 192–214.

Note: * At current prices; ** Value at 2007–08; *** Value at 2006–07.

2004–05. But in 2008–09, she has come down to second position next to Assam. In 1980–81, she was placed at third position behind Arunachal Pradesh and Assam. A sharp decline of the manufacturing sector's share in four years during 2004 to 2008 is a matter of great concern.

Contribution of Industries in Workforce

Females dominate the employment structure of the manufacturing sector in Manipur. Tables 6.3 and 6.4 shows per 1000 distribution of usually working persons by PS + SS in different sub-sectors in Manipur based on the various rounds of the NSSO. It can be seen from the Tables 6.3 and 6.4 that working females in the manufacturing sector has been always more than male working population throughout the various rounds of the NSSO in both the rural and urban areas. Considering the rural areas, the proportion of working female population in this sector was 239 per 1000 as against a mere 20 per 1000 of the males in the 32nd round. Though, the proportion of female workers has declined over the years, it was still as high as 172 per 1000 as compared to males at 31 per 1000 according to the latest 61st round of the NSSO. In the urban areas also, the proportion of females working in the manufacturing sector was 394 per 1000 as against 64 per 1000 of the males in the 32nd round. Here also, the proportion of females working in the manufacturing sector has decreased over the years.

Table 6.3 : Per 1000 Distribution of Usually Working Persons by PS + SS by Broad Industry Division in Manipur (Rural)

NSS Rounds	Agriculture		Mining & Quarrying		Manufacturing		Construction		Trade		Transport		Services	
	M	F	M	F	M	F	M	F	M	F	M	F	M	F
32	871	666	–	–	20	239	3	–	14	84	2	–	90	10
38	850	767	–	–	24	167	5	–	31	49	3	–	88	17
43	692	799	–	–	31	101	14	–	29	35	16	1	217	64
50	660	603	1		37	262	41	6	38	56	24	–	196	70
55	780	696	1	18	22	186	13	–	27	58	20	–	137	42
61	694	691	5	6	31	172	50	1	53	87	34	–	132	44

Source: Reports of various Rounds of NSSO.

Table 6.4 : Per 1000 Distribution of Usually Working Persons by PS + SS by Broad Industry Division in Manipur (Urban)

NSS Rounds	Agriculture		Mining & Quarrying		Manufacturing		Construction		Trade		Transport		Services	
	M	F	M	F	M	F	M	F	M	F	M	F	M	F
32	256	272	–	4	64	394	21	–	236	224	12	–	411	106
38	513	609	9	–	71	228	30	–	51	79	40	–	272	85
43	323	289	1	11	77	196	29	–	151	203	21	–	398	301
50	309	261	–	–	44	342	38	3	108	195	46	2	437	196
55	293	263	13	–	55	215	60	3	164	274	44	19	371	225
61	313	215	–	–	78	290	65	–	170	261	60	–	310	234

Source: Same as Table 6.3.

It was 196 per 1000 in the 43rd round which got improved to 342 per 1000 in the 50th round, but again decreased to 290 in the latest 61st round. As for the males working in this sector, their proportion has remained more or less stable in both the rural and urban areas throughout the NSSO rounds. It can also be seen that the proportion of working population in the manufacturing sector is higher in the urban areas than in the rural areas for all rounds of the NSSO.

Another important aspect is the study of the job-creating capability the various sub-sectors in the State. Singh (2007) applied the concept of "employment elasticity" to work out the job creating ability of the various sub-sectors in Manipur. The sectoral employment elasticities are derived by dividing the percentage change in employment by the percentage change in real NSDP at 1993–94 prices originating in that sector. Table 6.5 shows the employment elasticities of the various sub-sectors in Manipur during 1987–88 to 2004–05.

We can see from Table 6.5 that for the two sub-periods, i.e. from 1987–88 to 1993–94 and 1993–94 to 1999–2000, it was the manufacturing sector, which had the least job-creating ability out of all the sectors with employment elasticities of 0.296 and –0.42 respectively. The employment elasticity of the sector improved to 1.437 during 1999–00 to 2004–05 becoming one of

Table 6.5 : Sectoral Employment Elasticities in Manipur

Sector	*1987–88 to 1993–94*	*1993–94 to 1999–2000*	*1999–2000 to 2004–05*	*1987–88 to 2004–05*
Agriculture	1.057	1.93 (0.0)	1.589	1.34
Manufacturing	0.296 (0.4)	–0.42 (0.3)	1.437	0.189
Construction	3.66 (0.9)	–0.282 (0.8)	2.078	0.839
Transport	1.15 (0.6)	0.25 (0.6)	0.85	0.734
Trade	1.785 (0.7)	0.943 (0.6)	1.661	1.508
Services	0.758	–0.189	0.209	0.133
All	0.794 (0.5)	0.303 (0.2)	1.322	0.67

Source: Same as above Table 6.3.
Note: Figures in parenthesis are employment elasticities for all India.

the highest in that sub-period. If we look at the whole time period i.e. from 1987–88 to 2004–05, we see that services had the least elasticity followed by the manufacturing sector. Trade was the most elastic sub-sector followed by agriculture.

Impediments to Industrialization

A healthy process of industrialization in Manipur has been restricted by a number of factors. First of all and the most important, there is the acute infrastructure bottleneck in the State such as shortage of power, inadequate and high cost of transportation, underdeveloped money and capital markets, etc. It is said that infrastructure is the prerequisite for industrial development and it is true in the case of small scale and cottage industries. In the case of large scale industries, they may be able to spend on items such as power generation, factory sheds and labour housing, etc. The small scale units with limited resources may not act like this. So for the development of industries in general and small scale industries in particular, possessing a sound infrastructural base is a must. Another factor that hinders the process of industrialization in the State is the nature of shyness of capital and the underdeveloped nature of entrepreneurial activity and technical skill. Manipur at present lacks in entrepreneurial skill and talent and as a result the majority of the trading activities are being done by the outsiders. Small population with a low level of income and the consequent limited demand and lack of access to markets outside the State are further concerns for the slow pace of industrialization in the State. Handloom and handicraft products of Manipur are famous for their artistic nature and beautiful designs and are widely demanded abroad. But there have been no rigid efforts on the part of the entrepreneurs as well as the State government to exploit that advantage on a bigger scale. Another major issue that has constrained the industrial development in the State, especially on the last few years, is the prevailing law and order situation in the State and the problem of insurgency. There have been frequent killings, bandhs, blockades, strikes, etc. relating to the various social issues. In such an unstable situation, the entrepreneurs of this State are also affected. The various incentives offered in the industrial policies of the State to fasten the level of industrialization such as transport subsidy, capital subsidy, etc. have become ineffective and there is an overall apprehension to invest in industry.

State Public Sector Undertakings

There was hardly any industry in Manipur before the beginning of the Five Year Plans. The only visible form of industry in the State was handlooms and handicrafts. But with the beginning of the Five Year Plans, the State government has been making vigorous efforts for rapid industrialization in the State. Direct government participation in the process of industrialization in the State began with the incorporation of the Manipur Spinning Mill in 1974. The corporation started its commercial production in 1980. The Manipur Small Industries Corporation was set up in 1969 for facilitating the growth of industries in the State and the corporation was finally upgraded to Manipur Industrial Development Corporation Limited (MANIDCO) in 1987. To directly help the production and marketing of handloom and handicraft products in the State, the Government of Manipur set up the Manipur Handloom and Handicrafts Development Corporation Limited in 1976. Subsequently, a number of State

Table 6.6 : Public Sector Undertakings in Manipur

Sl. No.	*Name of the corporation*	*Year of incorporation*
1.	Manipur Spinning Mills Corporation Ltd.	1974
2.	Manipur State Road Transport Corporation	1949***
3.	Manipur Handloom and Handicraft Development Corporation Ltd.	1976
4.	Manipur Tribal Development Corporation Ltd.	1979
5.	Manipur Plantation Crops Corporation Ltd.	1980
6.	Manipur Agro Industries Corporation Ltd.	1982
7.	Manipur Industrial Development Corporation	1969**
8.	Manipur Police Housing Corporation Ltd.	1986
9.	Manipur Electronics Development Corporation Ltd.	1987
10.	Manipur Film Development Corporation Ltd.	1987
11.	Manipur Cement Ltd.	1988
12.	Manipur Cycle Corporation Ltd.	1985*

Source: Singh 2002, 149.

Note: * Incorporated in 1985 as a Public Ltd. But the Company became a government undertaking in 1989; ** Registered under the Companies Act in 1969 and upgraded as MANIDCO in 1987; *** Established in 1949, converted into a corporation in 1976.

sponsored undertakings came into existence in the State. The following Table 6.6 lists some of the major State owned corporations in Manipur along with their year of incorporation.

Thus, we can say that some developments have taken place in the field of medium and large sized industries in the State with the State government leading from the front. However, the performance of these public sector undertakings was such that all of them faced financial problems and there was paucity of funds for maintenance. During the decade from 1988–89 to 1992–93, the rate of return of the major public sector undertakings became increasingly negative from –3.03 per cent in 1988–89 to –26.98 per cent in 1992–93. This compelled the State government to wind up all the corporations except three. The corporations which have been revitalized at present are:

(i) Manipur Handloom and Handicraft Development Corporation (MHHDC);
(ii) Manipur Electronics Development Corporation (MANITRON); and
(iii) Manipur Industrial Development Corporation (MANIDCO).

The return on investment during the period 1988–89 to 1992–93 of some of the major State owned corporations is shown in Table 6.7. Out of the 12 major public sector undertakings in 1988–89, only five undertakings, i.e. Manipur Police Housing Corporation, Manipur Film Development Corporation, Manipur Electronics Development Corporation and Manipur Agro Industries Corporation had positive returns on investment. The main earner was the Manipur Electronics Development Corporation with a net return of 119.66 per cent. On the other hand, the main loser was the Manipur Plantations Crop Corporation with a return on investment of –90.55 per cent. In 1992–93, the number of corporations with a positive return was reduced to four. The biggest loss was found in the case of Manipur Handloom and Handicraft Development Corporation with a negative rate of return of –107.73 per cent. Manipur State Road Transport Corporation and the Manipur Tribal Development Corporation were other big losers with rate of returns of –90.34 per cent and –98.12 per cent respectively. Manipur Industrial

Table 6.7 : Return on Investment in Major PSUs in Manipur

Sl. No.	*Name of the Corporations*	*1988–89*	*1992–93*
1.	Manipur State Road Transport Corporation	–6.52	–90.34
2.	Manipur Police Housing Corporation Ltd.	37.13	2.76
3.	Manipur Tribal Development Corporation Ltd.	–35.84	–98.12
4.	Manipur Industrial Development Corporation	30.31	90.77
5.	Manipur Plantation Crops Corporation	–90.55	–6.05
6.	Manipur Film Development Corporation Ltd.	–2.86	–43.46
7.	Manipur Spinning Mills Corporation Ltd.	–52.50	–84.63
8.	Manipur Cycle Corporation Ltd.	–29.25	–38.21
9.	Manipur Cement Ltd.	0.00	–11.01
10.	Manipur Electronics Development Corporation	119.66	16.93
11.	Manipur Agro Industries Corporation Ltd.	6.67	45.30
12.	Manipur Handloom and Handicraft Development Corporation	–18.44	—

Source: Singh, 2003, 56.

Development Corporation earned the highest with 90.77 per cent rate of return.

Small Scale Industries in Manipur

There is no medium and large industry in Manipur. All the industrial units existing in the State except those of the cottage and village industries belong to the category of the small scale industries (Government of Manipur 2007, 112). So the significance of the small scale industries in the process of industrialization cannot be ignored. There has been a phenomenon growth of small scale industries in the State over the years. In 1975, there were only 304 small scale industrial units in the State which included among others 175 rice mills, 41 oil mills and 18 saw mills (Government of Manipur, 1985, 31). The number of small scale units in the State has increased to 9,993 as on 31st March 2003–04 with an investment in plant and machinery of Rs. 39.47 crores employing 51,842 persons with an annual production of Rs. 173.08 crores. The growth of employment, investment and production of small scale industries in the State over the decade are shown in Table 6.8.

It is clear from Table 6.8 that employment in small scale industries has increased from 19,900 persons engaged in 3,996 units in 1987–88 to 51,842 persons engaged in 9,993 units in 2004–05. It

Table 6.8 : Small Scale Industries in Manipur

Year	*No. of units*	*No. of employment*	*Average no. of employment*	*Investment (Rs. in Cr.)*	*Avg. investment per unit (Rs. in '000)*	*Production (Rs. in Cr.)*	*Avg. production (Rs. in Lakh)*	*Percentage of growth of production*
1987–88	3996	19900	5.0	12.30	30.78	67.26	1.68	–
1988–89	5417	27000	5.0	16.31	30.11	80.26	1.48	19.33
1989–90	6319	31500	5.0	19.20	30.38	89.11	1.41	11.03
1990–91	6788	33390	5.0	20.70	30.49	94.81	1.40	6.40
1991–92	7392	36910	4.9	22.63	30.61	101.45	1.37	7.00
1992–93	7696	38400	5.0	23.61	30.68	106.90	1.39	5.67
1993–94	8096	39680	4.9	24.74	30.56	116.70	1.44	9.17
1994–95	8341	42613	5.1	26.41	31.66	123.16	1.48	5.54
1995–96	8612	43842	5.1	28.23	32.78	127.05	1.48	3.16
1996–97	8910	45460	5.1	29.51	33.12	133.90	1.50	5.39
1997–98	9088	46464	5.1	30.72	33.80	139.39	1.53	4.10
1998–99	9040	47388	5.1	31.53	34.12	143.33	1.55	2.83
1999–00	9415	48514	5.2	33.19	35.25	150.69	1.60	5.13
2000–01	9635	49792	5.2	35.05	36.38	157.66	1.64	4.62
2001–02	9744	50364	5.2	36.07	37.02	162.30	1.67	2.94
2002–03	9876	51123	5.2	37.70	38.21	168.80	1.71	4.00
2003–04	9993	51842	5.2	39.37	39.39	173.08	1.73	2.54
2004–05	10151	52857	5.2	41.38	40.76	177.79	1.75	2.72
2005–06	10264	53719	5.2	43.27	42.16	183.72	1.79	3.33

Source: Government of Manipur. *Industrial Policy of Manipur*. Imphal: Department of Commerce and Industries.

means that employment per unit has increased slightly from 5.0 persons to 5.2 persons in 2003–04 signifying that the erstwhile labour-intensive small scale units have tended to become more capital intensive over the years. Correspondingly, the investment per unit has also increased from Rs. 30.78 thousands in 1987–88 to Rs. 39.39 thousands in 2003–04. As regards production in these units, the figure has increased from Rs. 67.26 crores in 1987–88 to Rs. 173.08 crores in 2003–04. There has been a decline in the growth rate of production of these units. The growth of production has declined from 19.33 per cent in 1988–89 to 2.54 per cent in 2003–04. During the last ten years or so, the pattern of growth of production of these units has been fluctuating. This pattern of growth of small scale enterprises can be attributed to the State's existing poor infrastructural facilities like shortage of power, inadequacy of transport system, etc.

Another feature of industrial structure of the State is that there exists a wide level of disparity among the districts regarding the distribution of the registered small scale units. In 2003–04, as many as 126 industrial units were found registered in the State. Out of these, a total of 113 units were found registered in the State's four valley districts only. Imphal East and Imphal West accorded the highest number of registered units with 37 each while the lowest was accorded in Senapati district with only one industrial unit.

Another attempt has also been made to compare the industrial status of Manipur with that of some of the selected States of India based on the results of the Annual Survey of Industries, 2004–05 in Table 6.9. We find that in terms of the net value added in the factory sector, the share of Manipur in the all India value added is practically negligible and is at the lowest position ranked at 30th out of 32 States and union territories of India under the survey.

Planning and Industrialization in Manipur

There was hardly any process of industrialization in Manipur in the immediate pre-plan period. The only noticeable form of industry that existed during the period was handlooms and handicrafts. With the commencement of the Five Year Plans, efforts have been made for rapid industrialization in the State. But efforts for industrialization were very slow in the State during the first-three Five Year Plans. The shares of the industrial sector in the

Table 6.9 : Net Value Added in Factory Sector

States	*No. of factories*	*Net value added (Rs.)*	*% of NVA*	*Rank at the all India level*
Maharashtra	18,912	5,130,921	19.74	1
Gujarat	13,603	3,601,558	13.86	2
Tamil Nadu	21,053	2,156,743	8.30	3
Rajasthan	5,740	658,264	2.53	11
Assam	1,710	372,082	1.43	17
Bihar	1,674	24,398	0.09	24
Tripura	275	23,124	0.08	26
Meghalaya	58	9,212	0.03	28
Nagaland	113	1,995	–	29
Manipur	55	575	–	30
All India	136,353	25,990,686	–	–

Source: CSO. 2004–05. Annual Survey of Industries, Factory Sector.

total plan expenditure during these three plans were only in the tune of 0.66 per cent, 0.02 per cent and 1.49 per cent respectively. With the attainment of statehood and in the fourth plan, due importance was given in the industrial sector. The total outlay was substantially increased to Rs. 1.17 crores. Thus, with the Fourth Five Year Plan, the process of industrialization can be said to have been initiated in the State. Table 6.10 gives a picture of share of industry and mining in total Five Year Plan expenditures.

Table 6.10 shows that the Plan expenditure in industry and mining has been rising in Manipur in absolute terms but in terms of the percentage of the total plan expenditure, it has been very erratic. This suggests that this sector has not emerged as a priority sector at any point of time during the entire planning era in the beginning from 1951–52. The State government has outlined the following as the main thrust areas in its Tenth Five Year Plan (Government of Manipur, 2002, 40).

(i) Infrastructure development projects like Industrial Growth Centre, Integrated Infrastructural Development Centre, Export Promotion and Industrial Parks, etc.
(ii) Agro based industries such as food processing industries.
(iii) Development of handloom industries.
(iv) Intensification and augmentation of mineral exploration.
(v) Revitalization of Industrial Corporations, etc.

Table 6.10 : Plan Expenditure in Industry and Mining in Five Year Plans of Manipur

Plan	*Total expenditure (Rs. in lakhs)*	*Expenditure on Industry & Mining (Rs. in lakhs)*	*% of total expenditure*
1st Plan (1951–56)	102.56	0.68	0.66
2nd Plan (1956–61)	596.93	12.08	2.02
3rd Plan (1961–66)	1,281.28	35.28	2.75
Annual Plan (1966–69)	719.89	18.90	2.63
4th Plan (1969–74)	3100.00	215.00	6.93
5th Plan(1974–78)	6,661.91	474.76	7.13
6th Plan (1980–85)	24,312.32	1,352.44	5.56
7th Plan (1985–90)	51,732.77	27,744.08	5.36
8th Plan (1992–97)	122,450.97	5,281.11	4.31
9th Plan (1997–02)	184,865.10	9,406.86	5.09
10th Plan (2002–07)	274,142.00	16,484.00	6.01
11th Plan (2007–12)*	815,400.00	65,614.00	8.05

Source: Government of Manipur. *Statistical Abstract of Manipur*. Imphal: Directorate of Economics and Statistics. Various issues.

Note: *Outlay projected.

In the State's Eleventh Five Year Plan, the following objectives have been emphasised (Government of Manipur, 2007, XXIX).

(i) To create agro-industrial growth centres.
(ii) To create and promote entrepreneurship and self-employment opportunities.
(iii) To generate large scale direct and indirect rural based employment through sericulture.
(iv) To intensify mineral survey for exploration.
(v) To set up Special Economic Zones (SEZ) at the border town of Moreh.

Industrial Potential in Manipur

Nature has endowed Manipur with a rich and wide variety of resources. Following is the list of industries which have a high chance of success and can sustain in the long run in the State. These industries, if developed and nurtured properly, will be able to transform the economic structure of the State and face competition in today's global market.

Bamboo Based Industries

Manipur is a land of bamboos. Bamboo forest covers a total area of 3,268 sq. km. and in Jiribam alone, it covers an area of 387 sq. km. The annual potential yield of bamboo in Manipur is estimated to be around 14.48 lakh tonnes (Laiba, 2000, 327). Varieties of bamboo grown in Manipur are: Saneibi (*Bambusa Arundinacea*), Kal Sundi (*Bambusa Pallida*), Meiribob (*Dendrocalamus Giganteus*), Wanap, Unap, Pecha (*Dendrocalamus Hamiltonii*), Manbi (*Melocana Bambusoides*), Dulu (*Teinostachya Dulooca*), Utang (*Bambusa Tulda*), etc. Out of these, Muli bamboo can be used to make high quality paper. Based on the availability of the vast bamboo resources, paper and pulp industry of a large scale can be developed in the State. Moreover, bamboo shoots have a high demand in the foreign countries, viz. Japan, China, Thailand, Hong Kong and United Kingdom, etc. Since, the local demand for the shoots is high as well, there is the possibility that the vast bamboo resources can be processed into a variety of products such as canned bamboo shoots, bamboo shoot chutney, bamboo shoot pickles, fermented bamboo shoots locally known as *soibum* and bamboo shoot powder, etc.

Tea Industry

Manipur is one of those areas where tea plantation can be taken up on a large scale. The State possesses all the essential requisites of growing tea such as climate, soil, etc. The climate and soil of the State are suitable for growing tea on hill slopes. Availability of cheap unskilled labour, a moderate rainfall, etc. call for a bright prospect of setting up tea industry in the State.

Sericulture

Sericulture has a long tradition and has been practised from time immemorial in the State. The State has a high potential for the development of tasar culture. The quality of tasar silk found in Manipur is better than that are found in the mainland India. The State also has the privilege of being the first State in India to produce oak tasar of unique quality. During the Ninth Five Year Plan, the State government took up a project called "Manipur Sericulture Project" with the assistance from OECF (Overseas

Economic Co-operation Fund) now renamed as JBIC, Japan in order to increase the annual production of silk yarn to the tune of 328 MT (Government of Manipur 2004, 123).

Horticulture Industry

Horticulture is another area where Manipur has got immense industrial potentiality. Because of varied agro climatic conditions, there is a great scope for commercial plantation of various fruits like lemons, orange, grapes, pineapple, banana and passion fruits, etc. Pineapples of Manipur are of superior quality and can compete with those available in countries like Singapore. The identified potential area under horticulture in the State is estimated at around 2,77,000 hectares (Government of Manipur, 2004, 18). The Table 6.11 shows some of the existing small scale horticulture units in the State both under public and private sectors.

The North Eastern Industrial Consultants (NECON) has identified the following food processing industries (Table 6.12) in the State based on locally available raw materials.

Handloom

Handloom industry is the largest cottage industry in Manipur. It is a traditional cottage industry in which most of the weavers are self-employed artisans who are carrying on their profession in their own homes. As per the National Handloom Census Report, 1996–97, there were 3.39 lakh weavers with 2.77 lakh looms in the

Table 6.11 : Horticulture Industries in Manipur

Sl. No.	*Unit*	*Sector*	*Capacity (MT per annum)*
1.	Magfruit	Public	240
2.	Heirang	Co-operative	240
3.	Waifru	Private	240
4.	Ratna Fruits	Private	50
5.	Likla	Private	50
6.	Sana	Private	50
7.	Manifru	Private	50
8.	Hill Fruits	Private	50

Source: Government of Manipur. 2002. *Investment Potentials in Manipur.* Imphal: Department of Commerce & Industries.

Table 6.12 : Feasible Food Processing Industries in Manipur

Sl. No.	Projects	Input raw materials
1.	Fruit juice concentration	Pineapple, orange, lemon
2.	Pectin and allied citrus products	Peels of orange, lemon
3.	Consumers pack of fruit juice	Any fruit
4.	Tomato paste	Tomato
5.	Banana/Guava pulp	Banana, guava
6.	Canned fruits, slices, peach, plum, etc.	Pear, peach, plum, pineapple, orange
7.	Potato chips	Potato
8.	Papain	Papaya
9.	Ginger oil extraction	Ginger
10.	Mushroom processing	Mushroom
11.	Canned bamboo shoots	Bamboo shoots
12.	Dry fish fermentation	Dry fish

Source: Same as above Table 6.11.

State. Manipuri clothes with picturesque and indigenous designs are in great demand throughout India and even outside the country. This inherent skill can develop a thriving industry in the State. The following Table 6.13 gives a picture of the population of looms and weavers in Manipur according to the National Handloom and Powerloom Census, 1996–97.

So far, we have mentioned some industries, which have tremendous scope and potential for development in the State. Following are the industries in the State which are compatible with the optimum utilization of locally available resources:

Table 6.13 : Handloom Production and Population in Manipur, 1996–97

Sl. No.	District	No. of weavers	No. of looms	Consumption of yarn per month (kg.)	Consumption of cloth per month (M)
1.	Imphal *	91,820	68,273	5,01,936.10	44,26,402.00
2.	Thoubal	37,835	26,586	1,60,334.50	19,33,600.00
3.	Bishnupur	53,069	31,420	1,86,294.70	13,25,974.00
4.	Churachandpur	39,294	43,847	56,502.10	3,61,953.60
5.	Ukhrul	24,233	22,629	23,567.00	1,98,933.50
6.	Senapati	44,250	35,443	12,763.80	92,901.12
7.	Chandel	13,554	11,639	26,204.70	71,615.00
Total		**339,632**	**276,755**	**10,70,557.00**	**86,40,814.00**

Source: Same as above Table 6.11.

Note: Combined Imphal West and Imphal East.

(i) Dehydration plant, (ii) Ginger oil, (iii) Pineapple fibre, (iv) Citronella oil, (v) Spinning mill, (vi) Sugar mill, (vii) Herbal medicine, and (viii) Brick field.

Over and above these industries, there are also some demand based industries in the State which are listed below:

(i) Backery,
(ii) Hosiery,
(iii) Plastic goods industries,
(iv) Water filter,
(v) Mineral water,
(vi) Tyre retreading,
(vii) Manufacturing of soaps,
(viii) Wooden furniture
(ix) Construction firms.

Conclusion

Industry is yet to get its due share in plan allocation. Though medium and large industries have been taken up since the Fourth Five Year Plan in the right earnest, the performance has been unsatisfactory. The share of manufacturing in the real NSDP has been increasing gradually mainly due to the growth of unregistered segment. It endorses the finding that the proportion of female workers in manufacturing has been higher than male workers both in rural and urban Manipur. However, the industrial potential of the State has not been realized as is evident from the list of feasible industries. Given the market and abundance of raw materials, industrialization of Manipur need not be an unrealizable dream.

CITED WORKS

EPW Research Foundation. 2003. "Domestic Product of States of India: 1960–61 to 2000–01". Mumbai: *EPW*.

Government of Manipur. 1985. *Economic Review of Manipur: 1984–85*. Imphal: Directorate of Economics and Statistics.

Government of India. 1997. *Ninth Five Year Plan, 1997–2002 and Annual Plan: 1997–98*. Imphal: Planning Department.

Government of India. 2002. *Draft Tenth Five Year Plan: 2002–07 and Annual Plan 2002–03, Proposals, Vol. 1*. Imphal: Planning Department.

Government of India. 2002. Investment Potential in Manipur. Paper presented at North East Business Summit, Mumbai. Imphal: Department of Commerce and Industries.

Government of Manipur. 2004. *Economic Survey of Manipur 2003–04*. Imphal: Department of Economics and Statistics.

Government of Manipur. Various issues. *Statistical Abstract of Manipur*. Imphal: Department of Economics and Statistics.

Institute for Human Development. 2006. *Manipur State Development Report*. New Delhi: Planning Commission.

Laiba, M.T. 2000. *Geography of Manipur*. Imphal: Public Book Store.

Sanajaoba, N. (ed.) 1980. *Manipur Treaties and Documents: 1110–1971, Vol. 1*. New Delhi: Mittal Publications.

Singh, Elangbam Bijoykumar. 2007. *Nature of unemployment and employment in the North East: A Case Study of Manipur*. ICSSR Sponsored Project.

Singh, Kh. Tomba. 2002. Industrial Sickness in Manipur. Ph.D. Thesis, Manipur University.

Singh, S. Brajamani. 2003. *Economic Growth in Manipur: An Empirical Analysis*. Imphal: N. Romesh Singh.

7

Educated Youths and Issues of Unemployment

Th. Joychandra Singh

Education is one of the most important necessities of human society. It is an important indicator of social and economic status of the society. Education is an important component for the formation of human capital and thus, contributes towards uplifting the quality of life of the people. Being so, it forms an indispensable part of the social sector. Recognising the importance of education has led the Indian Government to declare "Education for All" as a national agenda whereby universalization of primary education for children in the age group of 6 to 14 years has been made compulsory (NSSO Report, 2007–08). A cursory look at available data can illustrate literacy rate of India as well as Manipur in the year 2001. Census of India 2001 puts the literary rate of India at 64.84 per cent of the total population. In the case of Manipur, overall literacy rate is 70.5 per cent, in which female accounts for 60.5 and male accounts for 80.3. The rural and urban literacy rates are 67.3 and 79.3 per cent, respectively, in Manipur. Manipur has a higher rate of literacy than all India average according to the 2001 Census.

However, the qualitative uplifting factor needs to be translated in terms of giving an opportunity to earn a livelihood whereby the contributory role (empowerment) becomes more meaningful. In the face of rising educated people in India as well Manipur, an appalling situation is the corollary rise in the number of unemployed educated person. The accommodative power of the job market remains low. In such a situation, educated persons remain an unproductive human capital.

In this chapter, an attempt is made to highlight the depth of educated unemployment in Manipur based on the number of persons registered in various employment exchanges in the State. The examination will be at the backdrop of an increasing number of educated youths located in an environment of shrinking job opportunities in an economy characterised by the absence of industry, lack of expansion and diversification.

In order to highlight the problem, the author takes into account methodology of estimation of unemployment recommended by the Committee of Experts on Unemployment Estimates set by Planning Commission in the 27th Round of NSS, which is given below:

(a) Chronic unemployment or usual principal status employment is measured in number of persons, i.e. persons who remained unemployed for a major part of the year. This measure is more appropriate to those in search of regular employment, e.g. educated and skilled persons who may not accept casual work. This is also referred to as unemployment.
(b) Weekly status unemployment (measured in number of persons), i.e. persons who did not find even an hour of work during the survey week.
(c) Daily status unemployment (measured in person-days or person-years), i.e. persons who did not find work on a day or some days during the survey week.

Rising Number of Unemployed Educated Youths

There has been an increasing trend in the number of job-seekers registered with employment exchanges in Manipur. In year 2006, the total number of registered job-seekers stood at 5.8 lakhs. The percentage break-up in terms of valley and hill areas are 73 per cent and 27 per cent, respectively.

Table 7.1 gives the details of job-seekers registered with employment exchanges by sex from year 2001 to 2006. From Table 7.1, it is evident that the overall number of job-seekers registered with employment exchanges in Manipur has been growing at a Compund Annual Growth Rate (CAGR) of 7.39 per cent in the period of time given in Table 7.1. This symptom does not represent a sign of a good and vibrant economy in the State of Manipur.

At the same time, the percentage share of female job-seekers has been steadily increasing in the given period of time, from close to 26 per cent in 2001 to around 28 per cent by 2006 of the respective overall number of job-seekers (except for years 2004 and 2005). In the case of the male job-seekers, highest percentage was visible in the year 2004 and lowest observed in the year 2006. But in absolute terms, we witness an ever increasing trend in both the sex groups.

Category-wise number of educated job-seekers in Manipur is given in Table 7.2. As Table 7.2 shows, there are numerous categories of job-seekers with different qualifications. Under-Matric and Matriculation constitutes the highest number of job-seekers, followed by intermediate, graduates (social sciences and humanities) and post graduates, with respective percentages of close to 73, 15, 9 and 1.5.

There is an ever increasing number of job-seekers including technical and professional job-seekers. The given data may be inadequate as there may be large number of educated unemployed persons who are not registered with the employment exchanges. At the same time, Table 7.2 also shows level of human resources

Table 7.1 : Job-seekers Registered with Employment Exchanges by Sex in Manipur in lakhs (as on December 31 of given respective years)

Year	*Female*	*Male*	*Person*
2001	1.05 (25.86)	3.01 (74.14)	4.06
2002	1.08 (26.02)	3.07 (73.98)	4.15
2003	1.09 (26.14)	3.08 (73.86)	4.17
2004	1.18 (25.64)	3.41 (74.36)	4.59
2005	1.26 (25.66)	3.65 (73.34)	4.91
2006	1.6 (27.59)	4.2 (72.41)	5.8

Note: Figures in parentheses indicate percentage contribution to the respective total.

Sources: (i) Directorate General of Employment and Training. 2006. Ministry of Labour selected Socio-Economic Statistics, India.

(ii) Gender Statistics Manipur, 2006. Directorate of Economic and Statistics, Government of Manipur, 2006.

Table 7.2 : Category-wise Number of Educated Job-seekers in Manipur (as on December 31, 2004)

	Job-seekers			
Category	*Male*	*Female*	*Total*	*% to the Total*
Under Matric and Matriculates	261,635	71,864	333,499	72.7
Intermediates	45,936	23,455	69,391	15.1
Graduates (arts, science & commerce)	24,589	16,345	40,934	8.9
Technical (graduates)	1,883	561	2,444	0.5
Law Graduates	189	68	257	0.1
Other Graduates	218	246	464	0.1
Post Graduates	3,773	2,809	6,582	1.4
Technical Post Graduates	22	11	33	0.0
Law Graduates	11	1	12	0.0
Others Post Graduates	122	112	234	0.1
Diploma Holders	1,821	367	2,188	0.5
Others	953	1,783	2,736	0.6
Total	**341,152**	**117,622**	**458,774**	**100**

Source: (i) Directorate of Employment, Government of Manipur.
(ii) Economic Survey of Manipur 2006-07. Imphal: Directorate of Economic and Statistics.

possessed by Manipur, which if meaningfully utilised/employed can contribute to the development of the State. However, such a postulation remains a wish owing to the financial constraints faced by the State.

Moreover, in order to cut down the administrative expenditure of the State, appointment of personnel to various departments of the government has been stopped from the early part of the 2000s. Simultaneously, following the same logic, the State pursued a policy of downsizing, in which many employees of different departments were discharged from their services to the government.

To illustrate the dismal picture of job opportunity in the State, let us consider the case of job appointments to government services in the period 1992–93 to 2002–03. A total number of 4,174 persons were appointed to various positions in the government services during the given period of time (*Economic Survey of Manipur, 2006–07*). Thereafter, the State witnessed a reducing trend. This situation highlights a gloomy picture of widening gap between the number of able-bodied persons and job available to them. In this gloomy atmosphere, getting a white-collar job remains a privilege for a few influential groups of the society. It can be said that there is a wide gulf between supply and demand for educated manpower in terms of seeking a job. Supply of educated manpower is much higher than the demand for educated manpower in Manipur. This indicates the inability of State economy to generate and multiply job opportunities. In turn, perpetuates to a great extent in deepening an imbalance social condition.

Unemployed Educated Youth in the North East India

Unemployment is a social reality in the rest of India, too. However, the level and degree is higher in the case of the North East region, as absence of secondary manufacturing units as well as service oriented sectors are comparatively in nascent stages. Service oriented sectors such as information technology, hospitality and tourism have not taken a firm root on account of prevailing armed conflict witnessed in the region. And where armed-conflict is absent, such as in the case of Arunachal Pradesh, low development of infrastructure poses as a deterring factor.

Table 7.3 shows the number of job-seekers registered with respective employment exchanges in seven States of North East. The total number of job-seekers registered with employment exchanges in the seven States of North East India for the year 2001 and 2002 stood at around 2,402 lakhs and 2,452 lakhs respectively. Percentage of women job seekers in both the years were 25 per cent each.

Assam has the largest number of job-seekers followed by Manipur, Tripura, Mizoram, Meghalaya, Nagaland and Arunachal Pradesh in the year 2001. The same ranking is visible in the year 2002, also. Assam had total registered job seekers of 1,487 lakhs in 2001. Percentage break-up between female and male registered job-seekers, stood at 24 and 78, respectively. Manipur had 406 lakhs registered job-seekers, out of which female and male accounted for 26 and 74 per cent, respectively. Tripura had 326 lakhs registered job-seekers, in which female comprised of 37 per cent. Mizoram has 85 lakhs job-seekers out of which female and male accounted for 29 and 71 per cent, respectively. Meghalaya had 38 lakhs registered job-seekers, out of which female and male accounted for 40 and 60 per cent, respectively. Nagaland had 38 lakhs registered job-seekers with female accounting for 23 per cent. Arunachal Pradesh had 23 lakhs registered job-seekers, in which female constituted 34 per cent.

Table 7.3 : Job-seekers Registered with Employment Exchanges (*in lakhs*)

State	2001			2002		
	Female	Male	Total	Female	Male	Total
Arunachal Pradesh	8	15	23	8	15	23
Assam	321	1,166	1,487	328	1,220	1,548
Manipur	105	301	406	108	307	415
Meghalaya	15	23	38	14	22	36
Mizoram	25	60	85	12	29	41
Nagaland	9	29	38	9	27	36
Tripura	122	204	326	132	221	353
Total	**604**	**1,798**	**2,402**	**610**	**1,841**	**2,452**

Source: (1) Directorate General of Employment and Training.
(2) Gender Statistics Manipur 2006. Imphal: Directorate of Economic and Statistics.

The unemployment rates for the seven North East States by sex and sector during 1999–2000 can be observed from Table 7.4.

Table 7.4 : Size of Unemployment as Percentage of Labour Force during 1999-2000

State	Rural		Urban	
	Female	Male	Female	Male
Arunachal Pradesh	0.1	0.9	10.0	1.4
Assam	11.9	4.7	22.3	9.1
Manipur	2.5	2.4	10.3	7.4
Meghalaya	0.3	0.5	6.8	3.4
Mizoram	0.5	2.1	2.6	4.4
Nagaland	3.8	3.0	10.8	9.3
Tripura	4.6	0.8	8.8	5.5

Source: (1) Women and Men in India, 2004.
(2) Gender Statistics of Manipur 2006. Imphal: Directorate of Economic and Statistics.

Factors Responsible for Increasing Number of Educated Unemployed Youths

There are many reasons for increasing number of educated employed youths in Manipur. Some of the important reasons are enumerated here. Majority of the educated youths aim for white-collar jobs in Manipur. Lower and manual works are considered to be of lower status harming their esteem and unsuited to their educational qualifications. The situation is similar to what Mark Blang had observed nearly four and half decades ago in his study of unemployment in Europe and United States. Blang observed, "Manual job may be available, the employed even who have been through secondary school as well as college and university experiences will not take, as being beneath their dignity. Graduate of urban schools and colleges are unemployed because they refuse to get their hands dirty" (Blang, 1964).

In similar fashion, educated unemployed youths in Manipur do not want to indulge in low paid services such as furniture and carpentry works, taxi plying, and building construction work and so on. Entrepreneurship in poultry and fish farming, candle and soap making works, etc.

The liberation of women from their traditional domestic confines as a result of modern education and changed attitude of society towards women's education and employment can also be cited as one of the main reasons for increasing number of educated unemployed youths in the State and elsewhere. In the last 10 years the number of educated women has increased significantly. However, absorption capacity of the State is low in terms of gainfully employing them.

Another reason for the increasing number of educated unemployed youth in the State is on account of absence of industries and a stagnant tertiary sector. In Manipur, one can hardly find any meaningful large and medium scale industries. But in addition to this, lack of entrepreneurship and weak government support aggravates the situation.

Middle class in Manipur usually confines their activities to construction works, trade and to the most extent, occupying a white-collar job. This limited vision has resulted in non-indigenous/locals holding key positions in trade and commerce of the State, wherein locals end up with the role of middlemen traders. Failure of the government, which is supposed to play a critical role in inspiring and instilling a spirit of entrepreneurship among the educated youths, accentuates the already existing problem. In this context it is worthwhile to mention that if young people have an early discouraging labour market experiences, this will have long term consequences on their attitudes towards works and their assimilation into labour market (Lisa, 1983).

The above-mentioned factors should also be seen in the context of various programmes sponsored by Central Government for removing unemployment problems and poverty. Mention can be made of programmes such as Indira Aawas Yojana (IAW), Swarnajayanti Gram Swarozgar Yojana (SGSY) and Sampoorna Grameen Rozgar Yojana (SGRY) for the rural employment generation and Swarna Jayanti Sahakari Rozgar Yojana (SJSRY) and the Urban Wage Employment Programme (UWEP), etc. for the urban self-employment programme. However, these programmes have failed to solve the problems of educated unemployment or contain the numbers of unemployed youths in Manipur. Obvious reason is limited scope and funding of the programmes in the face of rising number of educated youths. There has to be a larger mechanism to provide solutions to the problem of unemployment of uneducated youths.

Suggestions

Some of the remedial measures to contain the problem of educated unemployment in Manipur are enumerated below:

(a) Developing agriculture sector and thus enlarging the scope of trade of the produce where the youths can take an active role and gainfully use their knowledge.
(b) Setting up of industries such as cane and bamboo based industries, food processing and so on. In this context, one should invite investment in Manipur from private players. At the same time, encourage entrepreneurship from the educated youths.
(c) Finally, as Nehru asserted, "If educated young men do not accept manual work, our responsibility of providing to them 'ceases' (Nehru quoted in Puri, 1989). Thus, educated youths should be willing to engage themselves in every form of work to sustain livelihood.

CITED WORKS

Blaug, Mark *et al.*, 1964. *The Causes of Graduate Unemployment in India.* London.

Government of Manipur. 2006. *Gender Statistics Manipur*. Imphal: Directorate of Economic and Statistics.

Government of Manipur. 2007. *Economic Survey 2006-07*. Imphal: Directorate of Economic and Statistics.

Government of India. 2008. *Economic Survey 2007-08*. New Delhi: Oxford University Press.

Lynch, M. Lisa. 1983. Job Search and Youth Unemployment. *Oxford Economic Papers* 35.

Puri, Mishra. 1989. *Development and Planning Theory and Practice*. Delhi: Himalaya Publishing House.

8

Invisible Workforce: Role of Women in Economy

Soibam Haripriya

The Romanticised "Empowered Women"

The place and role of women in economy in most of the societies largely tell a similar kind of experience and story as they have historically remained a compliant subject. The case of Manipuri women is not different. Presence of Manipuri women in the daily economic affairs poses an interesting point of debate on the issue of women's status in the society. A take off point for this debate can be from two existing dominant forms of narratives. One school of thought gives a comfortable perspective on the historicity of women's effective presence in the economy of Manipur. The second school of thought critiques the first perspective as a cosmetic simplification and insensitive to women's invisibility in the economic realm. This article engages with these two perspectives but more emphatically explores the second approach in order to critically examine the historicity and invisibility of women in the economic affairs of the State.

The first perspective largely sees a distinctive and strong participation of women in the economy of Manipur and thus, romanticises empowerment of Manipuri women. Such understanding is informed by images of *Nupi keithels* (women's markets) located across the valley and colonial historiography. To cite one of the verbatim of colonial writers such as E.W. Dun:

> All the marketing is done by the women, all the works of

> buying and selling in public, carrying to and fro of articles to be sold, whilst at home, they are busy employed in weaving and spinning (Dun, 1886, 37).

Women would have exercised extensive role in the economy of Manipur, however, one cannot conclude if they were equally empowered as their male counterparts. One should resist entrapment of such simplified romanticizations but take cognizance of the historicity under which women started to appear in the public space with regard to analysis of women's status, participation and role in the economic realm of the State.

Historically, *Lallup* system (royalty labour that forced male folks in the service of Kings in the nineteenth century) is considered to have increased the proactive role of women in the economy of Manipur. Moreover, constant war with Burma (now Myanmar) during Manipur's existence as a kingdom prior to British colonial rule is also cited as viable causality for increasing women's economic role. However, it should be noted that assertion of Manipuri women in the economic sphere in particular and public domain in general was accompanied and entrenched by its constant encounter and resistance to colonial impositions. For example, in the year 1904, thousands of women demonstrated in Imphal to protest and disobey the order of the British Superintendent who declared to compel the general public to supply bamboo, cane and so on, at free of cost (Singh, 1963). *Nupi-lan* of 1939 (popularly known as Women's War) is another illustration, when women revolted against the King and British authority to stop the export of rice from Manipur. It can be argued that growth of women's participation in the economic activities of Manipur was historically enhanced in the wake of movement and resistance that women had to pose against colonial policies.

Claim and demand for justice in the two above cited instances and others were not specific to the needs and rights of women but for the larger good. Despite evident historical assertions, including prominent ones in contemporary times, social status and political representation have been rather subservient to male dominance. Over and above, in the present scenario, one cannot find a parallel women's movement juxtaposed against movements demanding for self-determination in the State. There seems to be a tacit understanding that self-determination can engender a gender sensitive society in Manipur. An *a priori* judgement would also indicate the need for political emancipation for the common populace, which should not be devoid of functional equality among genders.

Manipur women's encounter with modern political economy, similar to other women's across the globe, reflect some of the contradictions inherent in finance capitalism under the prevailing system of neo-liberal economic policy and ensuing structural violence. As a result of the Structural Adjustment Programme (SAP) initiated since the early 1990s in India, women have started to face displacement and deprivation. Displacement can be visibly observed over the North East India as the forces of globalization, privatization and liberalization acting through public and private corporations, backed by the Indian State's overt nation building exercise and its encroaching hegemony over local economy are ousting indigenous women's markets and production centres. Poverty is being created, intensified and deliberately entrenched. In its new *avatar*, State seeks to perpetrate feminised poverty (Barua and Devi, 2004). Bulldozing of *Sana Keithel* or *Khwairamband Bazar* in recent times to construct a multi-storeyed market building is a case in point that explicates how neo-liberal forces have cordoned off the hitherto accessible place to all classes of women (petty traders).

Another important issue that challenges the existing romanticised understanding of empowered Manipuri women comes from the fact that women continue to be either silenced or deprived in terms of political representation and economic entrepreneurship. While historical legacies promise a fertile environment for women's participation in the modern representative form of politics, women's role is negligible other than exercising their periodic franchise. Present prevailing patriarchal social structure do not encourage women to be active in electoral politics. So far, not more than ten women have been elected in the State legislative assembly. On the other hand, ironically, one would witness women's active role at the grassroot level as "regular" activists as far as human security and human rights protection is concerned. Institution of *Meira Paibi* (women torch bearers) is an illustrative example. Prevalence of similar anomaly has led scholars to question the status of women in Manipur and if they are mere cultural symbols used to sustain patriarchy in Manipur.

With regard to entrepreneurship, the issue remains to be

controversial as existing data does not reflect prevalent social reality. In other words, high prevalence of women entrepreneurs cannot be equated with possessing a high social status. The second all India census of small-scale industries units conducted in 1990 reveals that 12.5 per cent of the units in the North East India are controlled and managed by women as against 7.7 per cent in the country. There is a state-wise variation. Women entrepreneurs account for 35.4 per cent in Manipur followed by 23.6 per cent in Mizoram and 18.7 per cent in Assam. Nagaland accounts for a mere 0.3 per cent. According to the National Sample Survey Organisation (NSSO), against the national average of women entrepreneurs at 31.6 per cent, the percentage of women entrepreneurs in Manipur is 82.8 per cent in year 2003 (*India Business Insight*, 2003).

Claim made on increasing entrepreneurship among the women in Manipur carries the danger of negating existing low social status in terms of domestic violence, conflict-related trauma, low literacy, political representation, underemployment and gendered role in work, *etc*. For the purpose of illustration, let us examine the sexual division of labour as prevalent in Manipur. Women continue to perform expressive gender roles as housewife, nurturer of children and various domestic chores at homes. Home is separated from workplace and women's labour goes unpaid. Under prevailing framework of dominant economic norms women's domestic labour does not get any recognition. In terms of contribution as a labour force in agriculture, women continue to perform traditionally assigned gendered role such as weeding and transplantation, which are labour intensive. The social and economic deprivation of women in Manipur has to be seen in linkage with the existing patriarchal structure of the society. And thus, the question of women's entrepreneurship has to be situated in the larger matrix of women's existential reality.

Against the backdrop of the issues raised above, the essay explores the presence and role of women in few select economic sectors of Manipur. First section deals with women in the organised and unorganised sector. Second section discusses few select sectors of the economy where presence of women is high. Overall, the essay seeks to critically analyse women's contribution to the economy and their invisibility in terms of local economic system and decision-making power.

Women in the Organised and Unorganised Sector

In a State like Manipur, options of being gainfully employed in the organised sector are quite low. Organised sector, here, is understood as those parts of the economy which operate through institutions which feed figures into official statistics, details of which are accessible. This includes firms organised as companies, payments made via the banking system, incomes reported to the tax authorities, sales reported to the value added tax authorities and so on. The organised sector offers secure and relatively well paid jobs. Manipur is an economically backward State and private investors shy away; being so, existence of companies with potentials of job creation is low. Thus, opportunity of working in the organised private sector is less in the State.

Only 5 per cent of women are recorded to be working in the organised private sector as opposed to 95 per cent of women working in organised public sector in the years 2000 and 2001 (Table 8.1). One can also compare with other North Eastern States and draw inferences on the options that are available in the organised sector for women.

In 2000, there was a total of 28,57,000 women working in the organised public sector in India out of which only 17,700 is contributed by the women workforce in Manipur. There has been a marginal increase in the year 2001 with the national figure standing at 28,59,200, of which the figure in Manipur is 18,000. At all India level, the organised private sector also showed an increase from 20,65,800 in 2000 to 20,90,100 in 2001. However, the figure in Manipur remains stagnant at a dismal 1,000 for both the years. In terms of percentage changes, Manipur recorded a positive change of 1.5 per cent over the two years, while national figure was 0.5 per cent only. Within the North East region, Manipur is next only to Assam in terms of percentage increase in the workforce with Assam recording an increase of 1.7 per cent.

As against the organised sector, a huge percentage of women's workforce is engaged in the unorganised sector.[1] According to the 62nd Round of NSSO, a total of 36,442,799 workers in India are estimated to be working in the unorganised sector during the year 2005–06. Close to 38 per cent of the total unorganised workers in India are female workers.

At the State level, Manipur has the highest percentage (74.4%)

Table 8.1 : Women Employed in Organised Sector in North East India

State/Zone	As on 31-3-2000			As on 31-3-2001			% Change		
	Public Sector	Private Sector	Total	Public Sector	Private Sector	Total	Public Sector	Private Sector	Total
Assam	77.2	271.6	348.8	79.1	275.6	354.7	2.5	1.5	1.7
Meghalaya	15.0	4.4	19.3	15.0	4.4	19.3	0.0	0.0	0.0
Manipur	17.7	1.0	18.7	18.0	1.0	19.3	1.6	–0.6	1.5
Mizoram	10.4	0.6	11.0	10.4	0.6	11.0	0.0	0.0	0.0
Nagaland	11.4	1.2	12.6	11.2	1.4	12.5	–1.9	11.8	–0.6
Tripura	21.0	5.8	26.9	21.0	5.8	26.9	0.0	0.0	0.0
NE Zone	**152.7**	**284.6**	**437.3**	**154.7**	**288.7**	**443.4**	**1.3**	**1.5**	**1.4**
All India	**2,857.0**	**2,065.8**	**4,922.8**	**2,859.2**	**2,090.1**	**4,949.3**	**0.1**	**1.2**	**0.5**

Source: Government of India. 2001. *Quarterly Employment Review.* January–March. New Delhi: Ministry of Labour.

of female workers. Out of the total of 81,370 unorganised workers in the State, 60,539 are women. Men accounted only 25.6 per cent of the total unorganised workforce. Women's engagement in unorganised sector is higher in the rural areas comprising 76.9 per cent as against 69.7 per cent in urban areas (Table 8.2).

The Tribune reported on February 6, 2008 that percentage of women workers in the unorganised sector in India increased from 34 per cent in 2000–01 to 38 per cent in 2005–06. In rural areas, almost 44 per cent of the unorganised workers were women, while the rest were men. However, in case of urban areas, the women accounted for about 27 per cent of the unorganised workforce.

Women in Manipur perform different types of activities under the unorganized sector such as agricultural labour, animal husbandry and livestock rearing. They are also engaged in cottage industries, brick kilns, stone quarries, building and construction and as petty traders/vendors and domestic workers.

The rise of female participation in the unorganised sector is on account of increasing economic compulsions in families. It is observed that more and more women are entering the unorganised sector with the rise of female headed households in the State as a consequence of the conflict situation. Employers' preference for female employees being available as flexible and often pliable labour force is also another factor that promotes entry of women in the unorganised sector.

Half of the State's women workforce is either involved in organised or unorganised sector as their source of living. In rural areas, the work participation rate[2] for male is 50.07 and that of female is 43.20. In urban areas, the work participation rate for male is 45.17 and that of female is 32.28. The difference in work participation of male and female is more marked in urban areas. The combined workforce, however, does not show marked difference in workforce participation of male and female as illustrated in Table 8.3.

As discussed above, one can see that women are largely involved in the unorganised sector, which is characterised by absence of a binding written contract, unspecified hours of work and absence of bargaining power in terms of wages. Women working in such conditions are also at health risk as a consequence of the more strenuous kind of work involved. A lot of women who work in the unorganised sector are also underpaid and devoid of

Table 8.2 : Unorganised Workers by Gender in North East India

State	Percentage of workers by gender								
	Rural			Urban			Rural + Urban		
	Total no. of workers	% of female	% of male	Total no. of workers	% of female	% of male	Total no. of workers	% of female	% of male
Arunachal Pradesh	2,299	4.2	95.8	1,002	18.3	81.8	3,301	8.5	91.5
Assam	535,424	37.4	62.6	97,057	20.6	79.4	632,481	34.8	65.2
Manipur	**52,991**	**76.9**	**23.1**	**28,379**	**69.7**	**30.3**	**81,370**	**74.4**	**25.6**
Meghalaya	83,285	35.2	64.8	7,151	21.8	78.2	90,437	34.1	65.9
Mizoram	4,949	12.4	87.6	4,498	34.4	65.6	9,447	22.9	77.1
Nagaland	10,939	48.8	51.2	5,369	29.6	70.4	16,307	42.5	57.5
Sikkim	6,406	22.4	77.6	1,219	8.4	91.6	7,626	20.1	79.8
Tripura	131,651	20.0	80.0	13,209	19.0	81.0	144,860	19.9	80.1
All-India	**23,458,286**	**43.9**	**56.1**	**12,984,514**	**27.3**	**72.7**	**36,442,799**	**38**	**62**

Source: Government of India. *NSSO* 62nd Round. New Delhi: Ministry of Statistics and Programme Implementation.

Table 8.3 : Workforce Participation Rate in Manipur, 2000

	Rural	*Urban*	*Combined*
Male	50.07	45.17	48.91
Female	43.20	32.28	40.51
Total	46.72	38.71	44.79

Source: Government of India. 2001. *Census 2001*. New Delhi: Registrar General & Census Commissioner.

social security measures such as paid leaves, maternity leaves and wage parity.

Majority of women working in the unorganised sector carry the double burden of poverty and discrimination. Women are confined to "inside" occupation, the invisible and unorganised sector, while men's domain is "outside", the visible world of work. Having to work in the unorganised sector of the economy, women get no recognition as economically active individuals.

Women's Contribution in Select Sectors of Economy

For the purpose of analysing the contribution of women in the economy, the following sectors—agriculture, trade, handloom and handicraft—have been selected. These are sectors where the participation of women is high. Sectors like agriculture and handloom require long hours of work and are mostly subsistence in nature as we shall see in the following paragraphs. Women also contribute to various other sectors. However, the article is not in a position to elaborate/validate their role and contribution in them due to paucity of data.

Agriculture

Agriculture is vital to the economy of the State. It engages about 76 per cent of the total working population. Manipur has two distinct regions—the valley (encompassing around 2,200 sq. km. of fertile land) and the hills (where farming is largely subsistence in nature). The net agricultural area is 2,89,826 ha and the net agricultural area in the hills is 3 per cent as compared to 47 per cent in the valley. Women are a significant contributors to this sector. The traditional job of women in agriculture includes sowing, transplanting, weeding, harvesting and threshing. They are also involved in activities after harvesting. However, the aforementioned activities when performed in household owned field would not be considered as paid activity. The above activities are taken up by group of women as collective daily wage labour. Either paid or unpaid, women's involvement in agriculture outnumber men. The sector absorbs a significant size of rural population as shown in Table 8.4.

As shown in Table 8.4, number of women involved in rural farm employment is ever increasing as compared to men. In India as well as the North East, women outnumber men in rural farm employment. Though the percentage share of both decreased in 2001, percentage share of women is higher as compared to men in Manipur as well as at the all India level. Percentage share for women in Manipur was 63.68 as compared to 59.33 for men. The all India figure also shows a similar trend with women's percentage share at 77.05, while men's share at 68.34. This is to be understood against the fact that women involved in farming in their household farms are not recorded. The same is true for men, too.

It is evident that rural farm hands of the country largely lie with women. As discussed earlier women are involved in more tedious manual labour as compared to men who easily adapt to mechanised farming. There is a need to introduce technology in a way friendly to women so that they could be trained to adapt to it and also become a part of the "skilled" labour force. Moreover, daily wage earning of women is considerably low compared to men. For instance, women involved with rural work in Manipur earn a daily wage of Rs. 114 as compared to Rs. 216 for men (Census

Table 8.4 : Male and Female Rural Farm Employment in the North East

	Gender	*1981*	*1991*	*2001*
All India	Male	81.70	79.70	68.34
	Female	89.70	89.55	77.05
North East	Male	75.66	70.49	59.32
	Female	89.25	75.04	66.53
Manipur	Male	77.82	62.40	59.33
	Female	77.72	80.00	63.68

Source: Government of India. *North East Data Bank* (various issues). Guwahati: North Eastern Development Finance Corporation.

of India 2001; National Sample Survey Organization 2004–05; National Family Health Survey 2005–06). Women are, thus, involved in labour intensive and low paid work. Their involvement in "decision-making" related to the farming process remains relatively low though women get to do the more arduous work as compared to men.

Trade

Role of Manipuri women in the agrarian economy of Manipur is a crucial one to reckon. Their involvement begins right from production to selling and marketing of foodgrains. Women manage most of the internal trade of food and clothing. They are the most important buyers and sellers in the main market (*Khwairamband Bazar*).

Many of the small and big markets in the State have stalls manned primarily by women. Some of the prominent markets include *Ima keithel* (Mothers' market) at *Kwairemband, Singjamei keithel, Khurai keithel, Kwa keithel, Thoubal keithel, Kakching, Nambol keithel* and so on in addition to those in the hill district headquarters. *Ima keithel* is unique in being one of the biggest markets in Asia run solely by women. It consists of the core nucleus of *Nupi keithel* (Women's Market) and other "extensions". One sees women selling and trading in various items such as vegetables, fish, handloom items, hosiery items, jewelleries and so on. Women *seemingly innocuously* man the stall, however, has to negotiate with a number of people. For example, with moneylenders operating the market, night watchmen and nearby shopkeepers where they keep their goods for the night, and also the Imphal Municipal Council where they pay general as well as road tax (road tax are given by women who ply their goods on the road).

A national survey conducted on street hawkers states that women vendors in Imphal contribute on an average 12 hours of work per day. There are more than 350 stalls in the *Khwairamband keithel* with approximately 4,000 women trading therein (Khumancha, 2003). In the *Nupi* market, on an average vegetable vendor earns in the range of Rs. 50 to Rs. 200 per day, depending on the season. But the fish vendors earn more than other vendors. They earn in the range of Rs. 200 to Rs. 500 per day during the festive seasons such as *Ningol Chakkouba* (in October/November).

A network of middlemen operates in the market. There is a system of *sendoichaba* (money lending, for instance the moneylender would lend out a sum of Rs. 100 and collect the principle along with a daily of interest of Rs. 10). This system is quite common in the marketplace. Such money transactions put women vendors in a disadvantaged position; transactions occur in the absence of written agreement.

Women in the market are a conglomeration of various communities from the valley as well as the hills, and collectively play a vital role in the economy of the State. The *Keithels* also become a unique focal point for mobilising women for protest and demonstrations against political actions. Women in the *Keithels* are regarded as active in such actions. However, their participation in decision making and negotiations beyond sporadic protests is yet to be seen.

In addition to the above cited role of women in *Keithels,* women are also involved in trading. Earlier, women were involved in Indo-Nepal trade, trading with Silchar. With the opening of the Indo-Myanmar trade, women are more involved in trade with Myanmar. Though exact figures are not available, a sizable number of women are engaged as petty traders in goods such as clothes, shoes and chappals, dry fruits and vegetables, etc.

Handloom

Handloom industry plays a crucial role in the economy of the State and is considered to be the largest amongst cottage industries. Women play a vital role in this industry as all the weavers are women. Mythology tells that Goddess Chitnu Tamitnu, discovered cotton and produced the yarn. When the threads were ready for weaving she arranged the required equipments and constructed the *Sinnaishang* (work shed). Popular myths also narrate that Goddess Panthoibi learned weaving after observing a spider spinning its web.

Weaving is supposedly a women's task with almost all weaving in the State undertaken by women. Amongst weavers, approximately 70 per cent of the women in the valley and 30 per cent in the hills are involved in full time weaving. Weavers from Wangkhei, Bamon Kampu, Kongba, Khongman, Utlou, etc. are well-known for their skill and intricate designs in fine silk items.

Tribal shawls of various fabrics are renowned for exotic designs and motifs. Fabrics and shawls of Manipur are in great demand in the national as well as the international market.

Population of looms and weavers in Manipur is given in Table 8.5. Main handloom products for the valley (including Imphal, Thoubal and Bishnupur) are cotton and polyester clothes like *saree,* bed sheet, curtain, towel, table cloths, fashion garments with intricate designs, cushion and pillow covers, upholstery, draperies, scarves, terry towels, dressing gown, *lashingphee* (cotton tweed cloth) and so on. The five hill districts mainly produce acrylic/ woollen clothes such as *shawl, sarong,* wall hanging and coverings, upholstery, hanging bags, curtain and so on.

Table 8.5 shows that approximately 3,40,000 weavers exist in the State producing more than 86,00,000 metres of cloths per month. Majority of the weavers are not full time workers as many refrain from full time weaving on account of the fear that the goods will not get sold. Middlemen occupy an important role in the handloom industry in Manipur. They supply yarns/threads and other raw materials to weavers and also procure finished products from the weavers. Majority of the middlemen are non-Manipuris. Women depend on middlemen for design inputs and marketing the finished goods and are often victim of low returns as dictated by middlemen.

Table 8.5 : Population of Looms and Weavers in Manipur (1996–97)

District	*No. of weavers*	*No. of looms*	*Consumption of yarn per month (kg)*	*Production of cloth per month (MT)*
Imphal	91,820	68,273	5,01,936.10	44,26,402.00
Thoubal	37,835	26,586	1,60,334.50	19,33,600.00
Bishnupur	53,069	31,420	1,86,294.70	13,25,974.00
Churachandpur	39,294	43,847	56,502.00	3,61,953.60
Ukhrul	24,233	22,629	23,567.00	1,98,933.50
Tamenglong	35,577	36,918	1,02,953.80	2,29,434.30
Senapati	44,250	35,443	12,764.00	92,901.00
Chandel	13,554	11,639	26,205.00	71,615.00
Total	**339,632**	**276,755**	**10,70,557.00**	**86,40,814.00**

Source: Government of India. 2007. *National Handloom and Powerloom Census*. New Delhi: National Council of Applied Economic Research.

Though there are government run cooperatives and schemes for the weavers under the Ministry of Textiles, there is still dearth of cooperatives providing weavers with working capital and loans. In fact, the present trend of the government policies which encourage public-private partnership (with more onus on private investment) carry the potential of creating conflict of interest between private investors and women weavers. Adequate compensation for women is still an issue in the sector where the middlemen earn a huge portion of the profit.

Handicraft

Women in Manipur also contribute in State economy by engaging themselves in the handicraft sector. Since cane, bamboo and water reeds are abundantly available in the State, basketry is a popular occupation of the people. Variety of baskets with indigenous designs is manufactured for domestic and ritualistic purposes. Women make significant contribution in basketry works, too.

Pottery is another occupation taken up by women in the State unlike in other parts of India. Pottery is an intimate part of Manipuri traditional culture and women's involvement is immense. Based on the types of soil, pots of various colours are made. Major centre of pottery industry in Manipur include Andro, Sekmai, Chairen, Thongjao, Nungbi and parts of Senapati District. Chakpa (a tribe in Manipur) women are famous for their mastery over pottery.

Embroidery is another area of handicraft where women excel in Manipur. Single stitch embroidery is a unique art of Manipur. This is done in dark matching hues with untwisted silk thread on the border of the *phanek* (lower body wrap worn by women). Colours in dark red, plum or chocolate are usually used.

Women as Consumers

While women's contribution in the economy as producer, cultivator, labourer and traders is appreciated, one should also recognise women as important consumers in the State. Women's role as nurturer also means that they play a prominent role in buying essentials for home. Here considering monetary management undertaken to run a family and deciding appropriate items of goods to be purchased is worth mentioning. Largely, familial budget management is considered to be an exercise unworthy of situating within the realm of positive labour spend/contribution, and thus, overlooked. But whether or not it is recognized as work, maintaining budget and shopping is an activity fraught with challenges.

As consumers, women live under a good deal of pressure. Many women must find ways to fend for their families on a limited budget thus having to reconcile with rational spending. Maintaining a balance between affordability, nutrition and availability, countered with personal preferences of family members is a hard unsung task. Women who are working outside of the home face the added problem of time constraints. Certain purchases may be made to save time and energy when women are squeezed between work and family responsibilities. Women are also often responsible for clothing themselves and their families and are faced with similar demands in this task.

Postscript

Understanding the economy of Manipur and women's presence therein cannot be conclusive with a modern sectoral analysis *per se*. There is a need to look into multiple forms of economy available in the State in which women are traditionally deep rooted. Adoption of neo-liberal economic policies has undermined traditional modes of economic institutions. However, indigenous systems of capital management and savings such as *marup*[3] based on mutual trust has continued to remain as viable mode of local economy. *Marups* are largely run by women. Though in recent times, men's participation have increased. In recent times, a notorious form of moneylending known as *shendoi-chaba* has also emerged as a popular way of earning easy money. Run by women, victims are petty women vendors and traders.

Importance of these local systems has grown manifold as public sector (government employees) in the State has not been a dependable source of earning as salaries are dispensed sporadically. The ongoing conflict situation and corrupt systems have also affected the local economy in terms of job opportunities and investment avenues. Thus, the indigenous systems of savings become one of the important alternatives to the existing morbid economic situation in the State. Role of women continues to be significant in these local systems of savings and capital management. Understanding women's role in the economy and sustainable equity based development calls for an approach that would critique the existing oppressive forms of labour. Public policies should be gender sensitive. For example, technology can be introduced in such a way in which opportunity exist where women can adapt and learn.

The non-recognition of women's domestic labour as productive denies the possibility for rightful share of resources and dignity in the society. It is ironical that much has been written about women's contribution but such writings have largely failed to actually deepen the understanding on the needs and deprivation of women. The truth is that dominant framework largely ends up making a passing reference to women and their role. This dominant perspective has also successfully created a romanticised image of Manipuri women which in turn has weakened the possibility of rethinking on the existence of poverty, displacement, trauma and low social status, which are historically embedded in the social structures. One cannot outrightly deny the role of women in the economy of Manipur. However, such a perspective should not be assumed uncritically without questioning the structures of power in the society that defines man-women relationship which ultimately renders women subservient to man.

NOTES

1. Unorganised sector is the sector where workers are not able to formally and legally organise themselves in pursuit of their common interest due to constraints like casual nature of employment, ignorance and illiteracy among workers, and small and scattered size of the establishment, etc.
   The Second Commission on Labour (2002) specifies the characteristics of unorganised labour as: apprentices, casual and contract workers, home based artisans and a section of self-employed persons involved in jobs such as vending, rag picking, rickshaw pulling, agricultural workers, migrant labour and those who perform manual and helper jobs.
2. Work force participation rate is the ratio between the labour force and the overall size of their cohort (total number of people who are in their productive age). It is calculated as: (Labour force/Labour

force population) × 100. Those who have no interest in working are not included in the participation rate.

3. Indigenous system of 'savings' whereby one contributes money on a weekly or monthly basis and the lump sum amount is given on a serialised manner. Women are primarily members of such groups.

CITED WORKS

Barua, Indira and Anita Devi. 2006. Women market of Manipur: An anthropo-historical perspective. *Journal of Human Ecology*.

Bhasin, Kamla. 2000. *What is Patriarchy*. New Delhi: Kali for Women.

Dun, E. 1996. (first edition 1886). *Gazetteer of Manipur*. New Delhi: Manas Publication.

Government of India. 2001. *Census of India 2001*. New Delhi: Registrar General and Census Commissioner.

Government of India. 2007. *National Handloom and Powerloom Census*. New Delhi: National Council of Applied and Economic Research.

Government of India. 1981, 1991 and 2001. *NER Data Bank*. Guwahati: North Eastern Development Finance Corporation.

Government of Manipur. 2001. *Statistical Handbook of Manipur*. Imphal: Directorate of Economics and Statistics.

Kabeer, Naila. 1996. Reversed realities: Gender Hierarchies in Development Thought. *Gender and Society* 10(5).

Khumancha, T. Michael. 2003. An Exploratory study of Khwairamband Women Market in Manipur. http://www.epao.net.

Singh, R.K. Jhalajit. 1965. *A Short History of Manipur*. Imphal: OK Store.

9

Medicinal Plants of Manipur: A Potential Sector of Economy

Potsangbam Kumar Singh

Introduction

Since 1995, there has been an increasing effort, with the declaration of International Decade for the World's Indigenous People, to recognize the contemporary relevance of indigenous knowledge systems. Need to conserve and reward indigenous knowledge systems was articulated in the publication by United Nations Development Programme, "Conserving Indigenous Knowledge Integrating Two Systems of Innovation". It is an attempt to reward the contributions of tribal medicine or traditional medicine which uses indigenous medicinal plants and the conservation of biological diversity by tribal and traditional communities. The attempt also involves recognition of the contribution of herbalists on the value addition they make to such medicinal knowledge. Understanding is, knowledge systems cannot be pigeonholed in watertight compartments. Also that, evolution of knowledge systems has been continuous in its qualitative and quantitative dimensions but discontinuous in their method of preservation. Tribal and indigenous communities have generally preserved their tradition, art, culture and practice of agriculture, although the present information age has tended to disrupt the continuity in their lifestyle and sources of livelihood. The ecological and social problems of the unsustainable lifestyles and consumption patterns associated with modern civilization have resulted in a rekindling of interest in ethno-biology and indigenous knowledge systems.

Increasing health consciousness among the people have also acted as a catalyst for recent resurgence of use of traditional medicine. Holistic approach of medicine has come to be appreciated more and more in the present day as against harmful side effects caused by administration of drugs of the modern system of medicine. Internal and external demands for medicine systems such as Homeopathy, Yunani and Ayurveda, etc., which are primarily dependent on the medicinal plants for drugs and therapies, are increasing enormously. According to an estimate by the WHO in 2003, the global market of traditional therapies and herbal products is estimated to touch US$ 5 trillion by 2050.

At the backdrop of this background, the present essay attempts to highlight medicinal plants in Manipur as a potential sector of economy for the State. Since ancient time, local communities have been using rich biodiversity of the State in two major ways. In the first case, for sustenance, wild edible plants form supplementary/ substitute food for hill and plain communities at the time of scarcity. In the second case, wild plants are used as medicines; a tradition in continuum from the traditional past.

Wild plants either as edibles or medicines have great commercial potential in local, national and international markets. There is a great scope for enhancing the acceptability of wild plants as income generating resource for the hill and plain communities of Manipur. In order to exploit such an opportunity, there is a need for the identification and domestication of wild plants and develop effective strategies for wider consumption.[1]

Traditional System of Medicine in Manipur

Traditional medicine is the sum total of all the knowledge and practices whether explicable or not, prevention and elimination of physical, mental or social imbalance and relying exclusively on practical experiences and observations handed down from generation to generation, whether verbally or in writing. Traditional system of medicine has their roots either in folk medicine or household remedies. Some of the earliest forms of medicine and prescriptions became widespread and were subjected to certain refinements, revisions and improvements through practices by trained medicine-men (*Maibas*, in the case of Manipur) and thus incorporated in organized systems of medicines. But a large number of folk-medicines remain endemic to certain regions, practiced largely in remote areas by tribal societies.

Wild plants are core ingredients of traditional medicine system practised among the Meetei community in Manipur. Preservation of wild plants is an age old tradition of the local inhabitants. Kitchen garden is usually the place where wild edible plants with healing properties are transplanted and nurtured. Royal patronage played an important role towards the recognition and preservation of medicinal plants and usage for treatment of various diseases. Inception of systematic use of folk medicine is credited to King Lairel Naophungba (428–518 AD). However, the preliminary application of herbal medicine was started under the leadership of Meidingu Senbi Kiyangamba Kiyamba (1467–1508 AD). He introduced the use of *Ponheiton* or *Pungdon* (guava) as a medicine for diarrhoea. The use of herbal medicine and application was further strengthened during the reign of Lainingthou Senbi Khagemba (1597–1662 AD) and believed to have reached a genuine scientific form during the reign of Meidingu Chingthangkhomba (1763–1798) (Singh, 1960).

Indigenous knowledge system of medicine, where usage and application of herbal medicine is found, was practiced by the *Maibas*. Appointment of personal *Maiba* to serve the King was a regular feature observed in the kingdom.[2] The institution of *Maiba* survives till today and indigenous herbal medicinal system being practiced in present day in the State is a continuous process inherited from the traditional past in the *Meetei* community. This form of medicine continues to be one of the most popular one in Manipur co-existing with other systems of medicine such as Allopathy, Homeopathy, Ayurvedic and so on.

Maibas in addition to providing medicinal services to the people also recorded their knowledge and personal experiences relating to medicine, which are passed from generation to generation. *Puya* (chronicle relating to a particular discipline or knowledge system recorded during the times of the kings) serve as an important source for understanding the indigenous knowledge system of herbal medicine in Manipur. Some available *Puyas* relating to traditional system of medicine are: (1) *Hidaklon* (Nos. 1–5), (2) *Kanglei Sanglen Puba Puya*, (3) *Shingligi maram*, (4) *Laimuron*, (5) *Taoroinai Yangbi*, (6) *Thepalon*, (7) *Pakhangba Yangbi*,

(8) *Laihatlon Lambuba,* (9) *Paphal Lambuba,* (10) *Wachetlon Nunglon. Pathup,* (11) *Shikaklon Mikouron* and (12) *Woomunglon.*

Puyas are written in Manipuri script and some do not carry the name of the author. In recent years, keen interests have been taken by researchers to unravel the secrets of the *puyas* and recognize the value of traditional knowledge of medicine. Such studies can enhance significance of herbal medicine as an alternative form of medicine.

Plant Diversity of Manipur

According to the World Conservation Monitoring Centre (WCMC), the working figure of species at the global level is around 1,26,50,000 (WCMC, 1993). Biologists estimate that there are at least five million but perhaps as many as 50 million species today on our planet (McNeely *et al.*, 1990). Botanists Alvin Gentry estimates that between 15,000 and 20,000 unknown species of tropical flowering plants exist. At present, probably less than five per cent of the biological diversity of the rain forests is known to science.

India's contribution is 1,26,188 species. Nearly 72 per cent of India's bio-wealth is contributed by fungi (18.23%), insects (40%) and angiosperms (13.5%). Currently, over 9,500 wild plant species are used by tribal for meeting their varied requirements, which are of ethno-botanical value. Only 4,000 of these are commonly known to science and many are unknown (Government of India 1994). Break-up of ethno-botanical plants used by tribal are as follows:

- Edible: 3,900
- Medicinal: 7,500
- Fibre and cordage: 525
- Fodder: 400
- Pesticides: 300
- Gum, resin and dye: 300
- Incence and perfumes: 700
- Other materials and cultural requirements: 700

There are two megacentres of endemism in India, the Western Ghats and the Eastern Himalayas with 26 micro endemic centres.

Manipur incidentally happens to be one of the two bio-diversity hot spots of the country. Geographically, it is a part of the Manipur-Nagaland Organic Belt (MNOB), which in turns forms the northern part of the Indo-Myanmar Range (IMR). IMR is a Vavilovian centre of diversity and origin of a variety of angiospermic plants yielding food. Outflow and inflow of flora and fauna occurs through this region between the South East Asian countries and the Indian subcontinent.

Manipur possesses a unique, diverse and complex forest resource. In comparatively small geographical area, it has distinction of having a wide range of forest types such as the Tropical wet evergreen forest; Tropical moist deciduous forest and Montane wet temperate forest. The valley flora forms a dividing zone between the pine forest of Manipur eastern hills and evergreen mixed forest of Manipur western hills. The forests are home to a wide range of flora and a Vavilovian centre of diversity of various indigenous plant forms.

Pioneer floristic exploration of Manipur was conducted by Watt, member to the Boundary Commission of 1881–82, and reported 143 plant species, among which were 10 monocotyledonous plants (Watt, 1889). Later on, Clarke reported 1,050 flowering plants and ferns under 114 families from Manipur and Nagaland (Clarke, 1889). He claimed to have discovered 87 new species and recorded 422 species from Manipur.

A detailed study was made by Deb (1957,1961) and reported 2,192 plants species distributed over 213 families and 1,012 genera. Close to 1,500 species were deemed new (Deb, 1956). Sukla and Baishya (1982) reported 43 species of flowering plants and 13 cryptogams from the State. They reported *Platecerium Wallichii* from Manipur as a new report from India.

Sinha (1987a) reported 523 plant species under 363 genera as ethno-botanically important plant species. He also reported a new plant species called *I soetes debii* (Sinha, 1987b & 1990). Bikram (Singh, 1987) described 667 plant species including 8 varieties under two new texa, namely *Codonopsis manipurensis* and *Cymbidium manipurianum.* Singh (1990) described 640 species of the flora of Tamenglong district of Manipur including some ethno-botanical aspects; 566 plants were indigenous to the district.

Kumar studied medicinal plants of Manipur and collected about 150 plants (Singh and Singh, 1995). Singh listed 54 medicinal plants according to the phyto-chemical constituents of the plants (*ibid*). Sinha (1996) reported 1,200 species of plants, out of which 430 species have been noted down as being used by the local as edible and medicinal plants.

Many researchers also claimed to have identified indigenous plants of edible and medicinal importance. Singh and Singh (1995) described 18 indigenous plants traditionally used in botanical folklore with reference to *Meetei* culture. Singh *et al.* (1988) reported ethno-botanical uses of some pteridophyte species of Manipur. Singh (1994a) reported 60 medicinal plants, which are used for treatment of dog-bites in Manipur. Singh and Singh (1995) reported 106 plants, which are the medicinal plants of Manipur. Singh (1994b) studied wild edible aquatic plants of Manipur valley and reported 31 wild plants, which are commonly used by the Manipuris as edible plants.

Wild Medicinal Plants

The State ethno-botanical investigation has documented a large number of wild plants used by different ethnic communities for food and medicine. Application of most of the plants recorded are either lesser known or hitherto unknown to the outside world. The State is endowed with a variety of medicinal plants and possesses virgin forests and unexplored ecosystems. Conservation of these plants can benefit human kind.

Popular medicinal plants used in Manipur is as follows. Bamboo (contains Bansloch, an important Ayurvedic drug), *Panax pseudo-ginseng* substitutes of *Panax quinkuifolious* of American ginseng and P. Ginseng of China, *Coptis teeta* Wall. *Taxus baccata* Linn, *Kaemferia rotunda* L., *Goniothalamus sesquipedalis Ihook.* F. and Thoms., *Plectranthus ternifolius* D.Don., *Zizania latifolia* Turcz. Ex Stapf.; *Lemania australis, Dorònicum hookeri* substitute of *Doronicum pardalianches (Darunal aqrabi) of Europe*, and a number of *Polypodium* spp. are substitute of *Polypodium vulgare* (Bisfayaz) of Europe and America; *Ployporous* coniferous plant, substitute of *Polyporous officinalis* (Ghariqoon) of Siberia; *Aconitum ferox* Wall, *A. heterophyllum* Wall and other species; *Rauvolfia serpentina* Benth. ex Kurz., *Aquillaria agallocha* Roxb., etc.

Taxus baccata grows naturally in Ukhrul district. However, it is also planted in Imphal East and West districts. *Aconitum nagarum* is available only in Tamenglong district, *Scirpus lacustris* and *Acronychia pedunculata* grow naturally in Churachandpur and Chandel districts. *Papaver dubium, P. medicaule* and *P. orientale* were found distributed in Chandel district, Churachandpur district, Ukhrul district, Tamenglong district and Senapati district. *Acacia pruinescens, Papaver* spp. and *Arisaema tortuosum* grow in Tamenglong district and Senapati district but are also available in Imphal district. List of medicinal plants of Manipur is given in the Annexure.

Medicinal Plants and Market Opportunity

Production of medicinal plants is directly related to market demand. A steady market is essential for viable cultivation. There should be firm policies for development, preservation, propagation, cultivation, processing and utilization of medicinal plants, which can be translated and implemented in the field. Non-availability of suitable industry in the State or in the country for processing, producing phyto-chemicals, pharmaceuticals, and other ancillary manufacturing units connected with drug industry is a bottleneck in utilization of herbal products in the country. As a result, Indian market remains dependent on foreign markets. This has telling effect on the whole process of medicinal plant production in the country.

Moreover, the whole process of production of herbal medicinal products remains individual concerns on account of lack of concerted efforts in production, co-ordination in collection and transport, deficiency in organization of marketing manufacturing, processing and distribution. This has resulted in wastage of valuable plants, flowers, seeds and roots. Moreover, rapid forest clearing, conversion of rich areas of natural medicinal plants to settlement and *jhum* land have had a disastrous effect. Creation of biospheres, biomes, medicinal plant sanctuary will help preservation and propagation.

Manipur can also take up cultivation of exotic and indigenous medicinal plants at a commercial level. Some important indigenous medicinal plants, which can be grown in different districts of Manipur is given in the Annexure. Cultivation of these plants can conserve the natural biodiversity as well as bring income to the farmers. In this regard, awareness drive has to be initiated

Table 9.1 : Common Income Generating Medicinal Plants

Name of species	*Area (ha)*	*Quantity (kg)*	*Amount (INR)*
Cephaelis ipecacuanha	5	Root = 400	2,00,000
Rauwolfia canescens	15	Root = 1,010 Stem = 1,010	2,16,000
Dioscorea Species	2	Tuber = 8,000	80,000
Costus speciosus	1	Rhizome = 2,000	6,000
Emblica officinalis	4	Fruit = 24,000	6,000
Terminalia citrine	4	Fruit = 8,000	40,000
Terminalia beleriana	4	Fruit = 16,000	64,000
Hydnocarpus kurzil	2	Fruit = 16,000	80,000
Mentha arvensis	1	Plant = 1,200	12,000
Total			**7,70,000**

by knowledgeable people and convince people to save our forest wealth as well as educate people about the potential economic value returns. Since ancient times, medicinal plants have been a part of our socio-religious rituals, and thus, convincing people about its potential economic return should be easy. A model farm run by agronomists and display the result to the farmers would be encouraging.

Currently, *Dalchini, Longpepper* and *Smilax* are the principal medicinal plants commercially exploited at a large scale (Table 9.2) in Manipur. There are reports of collection of other medicinal plants such as Sarpagandha and Agar, *etc.*, for commercial exploitation, too.

At the level of farming, farmers should be educated to adopt a commercially viable and easy method of farming. Traditional method of propagating medicinal plants can be replaced by micro-propagation by tissue culture. This method ensures quality and rapid multiplication of germplasm and can be used to multiply species having demand and market potential *in vitro* conditions in laboratories by experts. Seedlings thus created can be made available to the farmers freely or at affordable prices, who in turn can do large scale cultivation. Such efforts would require development of herbarium, training for cultivators/collectors in tribal and rural areas, development of co-operatives at village/block and district levels for storage and marketing of herbs and so on.

Table 9.2 : Commercially Exploited Medicinal Plants of Manipur

Name of medicinal plant	*2000–01 (kg.)*	*2001–02 (kg.)*	*2002–03 (kg.)*	*2003–04 (kg.)*	*2004–05 (kg.)*
Dalchini	26,519	9,000	83,598	63,588	17,600
Longpepper	17,200	16,600	43,940	2,500	1,400
Smilax	21,955	57,060	52,800	24,595	69,600

Source: Government of Manipur. *Forest Statistics* (various issues). Imphal: Department of Forestry.

Preparation of a *Herbal Atlas* of the different zones of the State showing the population density of the plants grown or found in a particular area can be a first step towards achieving the goal of successful commercial exploitation. In this context, it is worth mentioning the study conducted by Singh *et al*., (Singh *et al*., 1988) regarding the development of sustainable cropping of *Ginseng* and *Thalictrum* (medicinal plants) through habitat preservation and mericlonal micropropagation for regenerative economy of Ukhrul and Senapati districts of Manipur. This type of propagation can be done throughout the year. Also, the cost involved is less expensive as many plants can be produced and propagated from a single plant.

Medicinal plants selected for cultivation mentioned in the Annexure will give good returns to the farmers. Cultivation of the plants under organic farming conditions and methods for quality product of the drugs and raw materials for export is the most viable way in the modern system of cultivation.

Threats to Wild Plant Bio-diversity and Endemism

The tropical Indian sub-continent with an estimated 45,000 species of plants and 68,000 species of animals possessed two of the 16 most-threatened biodiversity hot-spots of the world. In India, out of about 15,000 flowering plants including 5,000 endemic species, more than 2,000 are threatened (Jain and Sastri, 1980). Already, 1,500 of the flowering plants, 856 species of angiosperms and 146 species of mammals, birds and animals have entered the endangered list of the Indian bio-environment (Khoshoo, 1996). The degree of threat for the plant species have also been specified for different categories of rare plants (endangered, vulnerable, rare) as recognised by the IUCN (Meville, 1970).

Various plants in Manipur are listed as threatened. Some endangered species of plants (which are in danger of extinction and whose survival is unlikely) in Manipur are as follows: *Rhus hookeri, Grewia elastica, Flacourtia cataphracta, Butea frondosa, Aphanomixis polystachys, Podocarpus wallichii, Rhododendron ellioti, R. wattii, R. johnstoneanum, Agrostis wardii, Dichanthium planipedicellatum, Bambusa arundinacea, B. khasiana, Dendrocalamus strictus, Sapria hemalayana, Cyathea gigantea.*

Some vulnerable plant species (those believed likely to move into the endangered category in the near future) of Manipur are *Phoebe hainesiana, Juglans regia, Magnolia griffithii, Cycas pectinata, Lilium mackliniae, L. chitrangadae, Arundina graminifolia, Ascocentrum amplleceum, Scheonorchid manipurensis, Vanda coerulea, Aquilaria agallocha, Dioscorea deltoidea, Rauwolfia serpentina, Calamus tenuis, C. leptospadix, C. flagellum, C. erectus, Daemonorops jenkinsianus, Gnetum montanum, Cyathea gigantea, Platycerium wallichii, Lycopodium phragmites.*

Some rare plant species (those with small world populations that are not at present endangered or vulnerable but, are at risk) of Manipur are, *Butea frondosa, Aphanomixis polystachys, Magnolia griffithii, Rhododendron formosum, R. macabeanum, R. manipurense, R. trifolium, Lilium mackliniae, L. chitrangadae, Arachnanthe cacthcartii, Arundina graminifolia, Ascocentrum amplleceum, Acanthephippium sylhetense, Coelogyne griffithii, Galeola lindleyana, Kalimpongea narajitii, Paphiopedilum insigne, P. villosum, Scheonorchid manipurensis, Sphiranthes sp. Vanda coerulea, Calamus tenuis, C. leptospadix, C. flagellum, C. erectus, C. floribundus, C. latifolium, Daemonorops jenkinsianus, Gnetum montanum, Sapria hemalayana, Platycerium wallichii, Lycopodium phragmites.*

Endemic plant species (which are found regularly in a particular place or among a particular group of plants and difficult to rid of) of Manipur are *Rhododendron ellioti, R. formosum, R. macabeanum, R. trifolium, R. johnstoneanum, Lilium mackliniae, L. chitrangadae, Ascocentrum amplleceum, Kalimpongea narajitii, Scheonorchid manipurensis, Agrostis wardii, Dichanthium planipedicellatum.*

According to the IUCN Red list, there are 33,730 threatened plants. Among them, 395 are extinct, 394 are in the category of extinct/endangered, 6,019 are endangered, 7,913 are vulnerable, 14,913 are vulnerable with threat of extinction and 4,241 are indeterminate. From Manipur *Lastreopsis wattii* of the family Aspediaceae was found extinct. This plant is one among the six extinct species of North Eastern India.

Forest Status and Bio-diversity Conservation: Manipur

Recent evidence indicates that tropical deforestation rate is 0.7 per cent per annum and losing 100 species per day (Wilson, 1988). Bio-diversity as a whole is endangered. Conservation biologists warn that 25 per cent of all species could become extinct during the next 20 to 30 years. Estimates show that about 1,700 species out of the total 17,000 flowering species have come under the threatened categories. The red data book provides data on 620 such species and about 1,080 species under threat require enlisting and categorizing.

The present forest coverage of Manipur is in a decreasing trend. Close to 11,000 sq. km is dominated by grasslands with few trees only. Dense true forest is estimated to be around 719.3 sq. km; only 3.2 per cent of the total geographical area. Increase in population and absence of suitable effort of conserving forest has led to deforestation. The rapid depletion of the forest is primarily on account of two reasons: clearance of vast areas in the hills due to shifting cultivation and over extraction of the forest produces. The consequent ecological stress has resulted to ecological backlash, e.g. frequent floods and droughts, which affect the economy of the State.

Need for food especially the staple food, i.e. rice has always dominated the economic activity of the hill people in such a way that clearing the forests has gradually become an almost unavoidable process. Another important factor for the depletion of forest of Manipur is the felling of trees for timber and fuel-wood. Due to the decrease of forest, the fuel-wood production is also decreasing.

Conservation of bio-diversity can be focused on three levels such as ecosystem diversity, species bio-diversity and the genetic diversity. All the three are inextricably inter-linked. Maintenance of ecosystem diversity implies maintenance of species, which constitute that ecosystem. Effective conservation of bio-diversity needs large areas to be included in the protected area network (Sharma, 1996).

In Manipur there are many Wild Life Sanctuaries such as Keibul Lamjao National Park (Bishnupur district), Yaingoupokpi Lokchao Wild Life Sanctuary (Chandel district), Buning (Tamenglong district), Zeliad Lake (Tamenglong district), Kailam (Churachandpur district), Jiri Makru (Imphal East), Siroi National Park (Ukhrul district and Loktak Lake (Bishnupur district). These wild life sanctuaries are the places, where threatened plant species are available. Maintenance of *in situ*, and *ex situ* conservation can be done in these areas. On the other hand, the single most important type of institution involved in *ex situ* conservation of wild plants is the "Botanic Gardens". Bulking up such plants and reintroducing them is essential for saving species reduced to critically low population. Conservation or recovery plans can then be developed for these valuable threatened species, often entailing a combination of *in situ* and *ex situ* management.

Approach of bio-diversity conservation should take due consideration of national and State problems. Priority should be given first to conserve those species, which have vital resource benefit to mankind at shorter duration, and also to conserve threatened, endangered and rare species. Increase in the plantation area of locally suited economic plants, restocking of trees as well as proper management by including more areas in the "working plan" may be helpful in replenishing the forests and their resources.

Manpower of taxonomic research should be developed by various governmental organizations that can do identification of plants in the fields with due consideration of employment for persons discovering new species at national and international levels.

Scientific knowledge of bio-diversity conservation should not be restricted on paper. Knowledge should be spread among the people through mass communication, training and awareness programmes regarding loss of bio-diversity through grazing, *jhuming*, continuous extraction of forest resources and so on. Protected areas should be increased in the State. The focus on preserving bio-diversity should not be just species diversity but emphasis should be given to genetic and landscape diversity (Odum, 1996). A commendable effort towards conservation of bio-diversity in Manipur was started by S.C. Sinha since the early 1980s through "Green Cross", which is a symbol of conservation of natural resources (Sinha, 1986). More researchers should follow suit by taking up field and laboratory research on wild plants for conservation of cultural and bio-diversity.

Conclusion

Medicinal plants have been consumed as food and folk-medicine since pre-historic times in Manipur. Even in this modern world, these plants play an important role during famine and other unfavourable conditions as source of sustenance for a large number of people. Moreover, health conscious people both in the valley and the hills take indigenous wild edible plants as delicacies. Traditional medicine as an alternative system of medicine is gaining popularity in the State.

However, if one looks at medicinal plants as a sector of economy, we can only talk about its potential. The reality is, currently, there is no industry for medicinal plants in Manipur. NMPB is establishing six Medicinal Plants Processing Zones in different parts of the country and one of the zones will be established in Manipur. The processing zone will support cultivation of medicinal plants in 20,000 ha, post-harvest management such as storage, drying, grading, sorting, and marketing including price support, setting up *mandies*, brand promotion and extension activities, etc.

SWOT (Strengths, Weakness, Opportunities and Threats) analysis of medicinal plants revealed the following strengths and weaknesses. In terms of strengths, many medicinal plants can be cultivated due to the diverse and altitudinal variation of the State. There are many research organizations in the State, which may provide required R&D support. Weaknesses include: absence of herbal drug manufacturing units, so the State has to take significant advantage of accelerated growth of AYUSH industries at national level and NMPB scheme and tap the potentiality of the sector.

Opportunities exist for Manipur which is endowed with a rich bio-diversity as highlighted above. Many medicinal plant species and products are available in the State such as Vanslochan, Chirata, Saffron, Ginseng, which are in high demand within herbal industry. Medicinal Plants can provide good livelihood system for large section of rural population. Regarding the issue of threats, the medicinal plants being used locally needs an urgent standardization and validity so as to maintain sustainable resource base harvesting of the medicinal plants.

In addition to the establishment of a medicinal plants processing zone in the State, establishment of State Ayush industry cluster is a must. This can create sustainable livelihood for the people. Manipur can thus exploit the global demand of Ayush and indigenous system of medicine. Accelerated parametric growth in the global market will positively affect medicinal plants industry in the State.

Adoption of market oriented strategy, formulation and implementation of comprehensive action plans and subsequent industrialization along with network of *in situ* and *ex situ* conservation centres will promote enormous viable employment opportunities in the State. Therefore, there is an urgent need to bring medicinal plants sector to the central stage of development planning for the State. Besides, R&D should be promoted so as to improve the yield of medicinal plants especially of those which are in great demand. Main emphasis should be given to the identification of medicinal herbs most commonly available in Manipur. Selection of medicinal plants, preferably the indigenous ones, for cultivation, collection and regeneration, and import substitution and export will be helpful for future development of the sector.

NOTES

1. Government of India has established the National Medicinal Plant Board (NMPB) in 2000 for coordinating all matters relating to medicinal plants. State Medicinal Plants Boards for every State in India were also established accordingly to coordinate with NMPB. Government of India is establishing North Eastern Institute of Ayurveda and Homoeopathy at Shillong and North Eastern Institute of Folk Medicine, at Pasighat, Arunachal Pradesh.
2. For instance, King Meidingu Senbi Mungyamba (1562–1597 AD) appointed Ningthoujam Kiyamba, King Khagemba appointed Konok Thengra and Meidingu Garibniwaj (1709–1748 AD) also appointed Moirang Lalhamba as their royal *Maibas*, respectively.

CITED WORKS

Clarke, C.B. 1889. On the plants of Kohima and Munnepore. *Journal of Zinn. Society* 25:1–107.

Deb, D.B. 1956. Discovery of Sapia Himalayana Greff., from Manipur. *Indian Forestry* 82, 4:510–516.

Deb, D.B. 1957. Study of the flora of Manipur. *Bulletin of Botanical Society of Bengal*. 11, 1:151–224.

Deb, D.B. 1961.Dicotyledonous plants of Manipur. *Indian Forestry* 86, 2.

Jain, S.K. and R.K. Sastry. 1980. Threatened plants of India: A state of art report. *Botanical Survey of India.*

Khoshoo, T.N. 1996. India needs a national bio-diversity conservation board. *Curriculum Science* 71. 7:506–13.

McNeely, J. Miller, K. Reid, W. Mittermeier, and T Werner. 1990. *Conserving the World's Biological Diversity*. Washington: IUCN, WRI, CI, WWF-US and World Bank.

Meville, R. 1970. *Red Data Book*. Morges: IUCN.

Sharma, M. 1996. Current Environment problem and future perspective. *Tropical Ecology* 37, 1:15–20.

Singh, A. 1960. *Amaiba* (Manipuri text). Imphal: Unknown.

Singh, H.B. 1987. Floristic study of Tengnoupal district. Ph.D. Thesis, Manipur University.

Singh, O.K. 1990. Floristic Study of Tamenglong district, Manipur with ethnobotanical notes. Ph.D. Thesis, Manipur University.

Singh, P.K. and T.B. Singh. 1995. Some medicinal plants of Manipur: An ethnic approach. *People Science Network* 2, 1:39–40.

Singh, P.K., N.I. Singh and L.J. Singh. 1988. Ethnobotanical studies on wild edible plants in the markets of Manipur–II. *Journal of Economic Taxonomy and Botany* 12, 1:113–119.

Singh, P.K. 1994a. Ethnomedicine studies on some indigenous medicinal plants of Manipur. *Procedure IV International Congress of Ethnobiology* 56.

Singh, P.K. 1994b. Ethnobotanical studies on Wild edible plants in the Markets of Manipur. *Proc. IV International Congress of Ethnobiology* 242:2–5.

Sinha S.C. 1986. Ethnobotanical plants of Manipur and their conservation "Green Cross" approach. *Regional Seminar on Medicinal Plants (Eastern Region),* at Guwahati. Organised by the Ministry of Health and Family Welfare, New Delhi.

Sinha S.C. 1987a. Ethnobiochemical study of Manipur. Ph.D. Thesis, Manipur University.

Sinha S.C. 1987b. Ethnobotany of Manipur. *Medicinal Plants Frontier Botany* 1: 123–52.

Sinha S.C. 1990. Note on ethnomedical Plant of Manipur (New Report). *Currh Pamlei Letters* 1, 1: 3–7.

Sinha S.C. 1996. *Medicinal Plants of Manipur*. Imphal MASS and Sinha Publication.

Sukla, U. and Baishya, A.K. 1982. A contribution to the flora of Manipur. *Journal of Bombay Natural History Society* 76:224–30.

Watt, G. 1890. The forest of Manipur. *Indian Forest* 14:338–87.

WCMC. 1993. *Global Biodiversity*. London: Chapman Hall.

Wilson, E.O. 1988. The current state of biological diversity. In *Biodiversity*, ed. E.Q. Wilson. Washington: National Academy Press.

ANNEXURE

Distribution of Medicinal Plants in Various Districts of Manipur

Scientific name	*Local name*	*Family*	*Distri-bution*
Abrus precatorius Linn.	Chaning (M)	*Malvaceae*	AD
Acacia pruinescens Kurz	Te-bam (Naga)	*Mimosaceae*	AD
Aconitum nagarum	–	*Helleboraceae*	WD
Acronychia pedunculata Miq.	Khangbailak(Kuki)	*Rutaceae*	WD
Adenium obesum	–	*Lauraceae*	AD
Aegle marmelos Correa ex Roxb.	Heirikhagok (M)	*Rutaceae*	AD
Agave americana Linn	Kewa (M)	*Agavaceae*	AD
Antidesma bunius Spreng	–	*Euphorbiaceae*	AD
Arisaema tortuosum Schott	Lincheishu (M)	*Araceae*	AD
Asclepias curassavica Linn	Krishnachura (M)	*Asclepiadaceae*	AD
Begonia palmata D. Don.	Banhang (Rongmei)	*Begoniaceae*	AD
Begonia picta Smith	Do	*Do*	AD
Blumea balsamifera Linn	Langthrei (M)	*Asteraceae*	AD
Blumea densiflora DC	Karpoor (M)	*Do*	AD
Commelina padulosa Bl.	Wangden khoibi (M)	*Commelinaceae*	AD
Cannabis sativa Linn	Ganja (M)	*Cannabinaceae*	AD
Catharanthus roseus Linn	Kundalei (M)	*Apocynaceae*	AD
Coriaria nepalensis Wall	Guipam (Tangkhul)	*Coriariaceae*	UD
Crotolaria mucronata Desv.	Sen (H)	*Papaveraceae*	AD
Dalbergia stipulacea Roxb.	–	*Papilionaceae*	AD
Datura stramonium Linn	Sagol hidak (M)	*Solanaceae*	AD
Derris ferruginea Benth	Kho (M)	*Papilionaceae*	AD
Jtropha curcas Linn.	Awa–kege	*Euphorbiaceae*	AD

Note: AD = All districts; UD = Ukhrul district; WD West district; TAD = Tamenglong district; SD = Senapati district; (M) = Manipuri; (H) = Hindi.

SECTION-III

Developing the "Development" in Manipur: Towards a Counter Mapping

10

Deconstructing Development Politics

Hanjabam Isworchandra

'Development is a seductive term', writes Gasper (2007, 24). Similarly, the term "development" has been seducing Manipur . It has been extensively propagated by the State to contain boiling public sentiments, or divert the general issue involving the interest of the masses. "Development", it can be argued, had been missing in the policy corridor of the government in the immediate post-British policy; rather landlockedness had been identified as the main cause of underdevelopment of the region in the pre-statehood period. Today insurgency occupies the centre stage of development discourse in Manipur. But the onset of India's Look East Policy (LEP) has added a new dimension to the development debate with regard to the North East region in general and Manipur in particular.

There has been a gradual shift in the formulation of policy planning. Today, "geography as opportunity" has become the password for development in the region. Earlier understanding of the North East inhabiting difficult mountain terrain, which is linked to mainland India *via* "chicken neck", far away from the sea and thus land locked has been nullified through the current mode of understanding. Moreover, construction projects such as dams, roads, highways are promoted as "development" in the State. "Development" has become not only a watchword for the government in the recent times but also a great legitimizing force to suppress people's movement against mega construction projects, which in the ultimate analysis have benefited a few at the cost of the masses. The uncritical acceptance of the statist notion of development without questioning its consequential havoc in the long-term perspective will prove harmful for the State.

This essay seeks to trace the debates and contestations surrounding the meanings and nature of development that has evolved through different stages of history. Finally, the essay endeavours to give a critic of the development politics pursued both by New Delhi and the State Government.

Development of "Development"

The term "development" has evolved through time and carried different meanings as it evolves. Conventionally, "development" connotes improvement in well-being, living standard, and opportunities. It may also refer to a process of commodification, industrialization, modernization or globalization and it can be a legitimization strategy for States (Edelman and Haugard, 2007:86). It synthesises all aspects and components, which implies a favourable change, inferior to superior and worse to better, but development from its very outset have experienced an element of flexibility and approaches to development have witnessed a sea change. Development occupies the centre of an incredibly powerful semantic constellation (Esteva, 1992, 80). Before its entrance into the realm of North-South or developed and underdeveloped countries, enlightenment era – the transformation of feudalism to capitalism in the European society with the advent of industrial revolution is regarded as the pedigree of development. Key theorists like Smith, Malthus, Marx and Engels from the enlightenment to the twentieth century have shaped later development debates in a powerful ways (Edelman and Haugard, 2007, 87). Their main limitation are sometimes relegated to the pre-history of development thought primarily because they concentrated on the economies of Western Europe rather than on the poorer countries of Asia and other continents. Though these theorists had confined to the European context, it has far reaching effect on their colonies through colonial exploitation and imperialism, which later resulted in the debates of underdevelopment of the colonies in the decolonization phase. The era of development (Esteva, 1992, 6) or the age of development (Sachs, 1992, 2) began with the inaugural speech of Truman on 20th January, 1949, where he categorically uses the term "underdeveloped" for the first time to mean former colonies and those countries that did not practice liberal democracy and follow capitalist mode of production. In this way, United States and other Western countries or erstwhile colonisers become developed. The paradigm had been shifted from colonised countries to underdeveloped and the colonisers as developed countries, Truman had only substituted a new word for the enduring problem that had already been there such as backwardness and poverty in order to gain loyalty of the decolonised countries into their fold only to counter the force against their supremacy, the Communist Soviet. The "Truman Show" paved way for the era of American hegemony and Westernization of the World. Post-Truman development discourse have reinforced for an Occidental worldview.

Peiterse (2001) captured the meaning of development over time in a nutshell (see Table 10.1). Classical political economist from Ricardo to Marx, as development thinkers, addressed similar problems of economic development but did not necessarily use the term "development". With the turn of the nineteenth century, late comers to industrialization in Central and Eastern Europe faced basic development questions such as the appropriate relationship between agriculture and industry. In this general context, the general meaning of development was catching up with the industrialised countries (Peiterse, 2001, 5). Colonial economies mark the immediate predecessor to modern development economies. Discourse on colonial economies had been a contentious one and interpreted differently from the colonizer or

Table 10.1 : Trajectory of Development Perspective over time

Period	*Perspectives*	*Meaning of development*
1870	Latecomers	Industrialization, catching up
1850	Colonial economies	Resource management, trusteeship
1940	Development economies	Economic (growth)- industrialization
1950	Modernization theory	Growth, political and social modernization
1960	Dependency theory	Accumulation—national, autocentric
1970	Alternative development	Human flourishing
1980	Human development	Capacitation, enlargement of people's choices
1980	Neo-liberalism	Economic growth—structural reform, deregulation, liberalization, privatization.
1990	Post-development	Authoritarian engineering, disaster

Source : Jan Nederveen Pieterse. 2001. *Development Theory: Deconstruction/ Reconstruction*. New Delhi: Vistaar Publication: 7.

imperialist and the colonised point of view. Colonization took the form of trusteeship assuming to manage colonial economies not merely with a view to their exploitation for metropolitan benefits but allegedly also to develop the economies in the interest of the native population. Development, if the term was used at all, in effect referred mainly to colonial resource management, first to make the colonies cost effective, and later to build up economic resources with a view to national independence (Peiterse, 2001, 5). But writings on colonial exploitation, for instance, by Marx, Dutt and Naoroji on India narrated different perspectives of colonial economies.

The modern development thinking in the immediate post-War II or decolonization process, the central idea of development is economic growth *via* industrialization – still persistent in some of the countries which cannot free themselves from "Western centric" idea of development. The period marks the evolution of many growth theories and big push theory. The pivot of modernization paradigm was the "notorious" work of Rostow titled "The Stages of Growth and Subtitles the Non-communist Manifesto" referring his work as alternative to Karl Marx's theory of human history and denouncing the superiority of socialism. When development thinking broadened to encompass modernization, economic growth was combined with political modernization, i.e. nation building, and social modernization, such as fostering entrepreneurship and achievement orientation. Modernization theory has come under severe criticism for emphasizing on economic measure such as Gross National Product (GNP) which only measures monetised economic activity.

Dependency theory emerges as a criticism of its immediate predecessor development theory, it criticised the modernization theory for its ahistorical approach for keeping the historical relationship between development and underdevelopment. The relationship between developed and underdeveloped has been metaphorically understood as centre-periphery, metropolis-satellite in the hands of its proponents Gunder Frank and Raul Prebisch. According to dependency theory, the core meaning of development likewise was economic growth, under the heading of accumulation. Its distorted form was dependent accumulation, which led to the 'development of underdevelopment' and an intermediate form was 'associated dependent development'. The positive goal was national accumulation or autocentric development (Peiterse, 2001, 6).

The onset of alternative development thinking in 1970s, development comes to be focused on social and community development. Participatory and people centric approach also occupies important space in alternative development thinking. Following the works of Amartya Sen on capacities and entitlements in mid-1980s, capacitating and enlargement of people's choice became the meaning of development. Although the concept of development as enlargement of people's choice comes from Sen, its intellectual genealogy can be traced back to the works of Caribbean economist Arthur Lewis (Des Gasper, 2005, 38). The Human Development Report, 1996, of United Nations Development Programme (UNDP) defines development "as a process of enlarging people's choice'. Neo-liberalism and post-development, two radically different perspectives on development emerge in the development discourse around the same time. Both the perspectives present an anti-development position with divergent approaches. According to neoliberal view, the central objective that is economic growth is to be achieved through structural reform, deregulation, and liberalization, privatization – all of which are to roll back government and reduce market-distorting interventions, and in effect annul "development". In other words, one of the conventional core meanings of development is retained, i.e. economic growth, while the "how to" and agency of development switches from state to market. Accordingly, neoliberalism is an anti-development perspective, not in terms of goals but in terms of means (Pieterse, 2001, 6).

Post-development thinking also puts forth an anti-development position. This is still more radical for it applies not merely to the means (the state is accused of authoritarian engineering) but also to the goals (economic growth is repudiated) and the results (which are deemed a failure or disaster for the majority of the population) (Rahnema and Bawtree, 1997, cited in Pieterse, 2001, 6). Instead of alternative ways of reaching development, post-development upholds the view that it is time to think for alternatives to development. It stigmatises the Eurocentric development discourse and approach such as economic growth, industrialization and modernization, and engrosses with the strategies of those excluded by the western model of development. Escobar (1995), one of the leading post-development protagonists, describes the hallmarks of post-development as an interest not in development alternatives but alternatives to development. Thus, a rejection of the entire paradigm; an interest in local cultures and knowledge; a critical stance towards established scientific discourses and stood for the defence and promotion of localised, pluralistic grassroots movements comes to the fore within the domain of post-development theory. Development theory has evolved through time, manufactured by academia and intellectuals under the influence of political ideology of liberalism, Marxism, post-structuralism, etc. It has also served as mirror for economic and social choices of different times, and tends to be policy oriented and problem driven.

India like other developing countries followed the modernization approach—industrialization, agriculture mechanization, urbanization, modern government—immediately after independence. Planning becomes the vehicle for attaining development goals. Economic planning (read Five Year Plan, FYP) served as a pivot for pursuing different development goals and have been central to development since its inception in the immediate post-independent India. FYP was conceived as the ultimate approach for attaining economic and social goals in the country. In the post-war Third World countries, planning embodies the impression that the economic and social change can be orchestrated and directed. The idea that poor countries could move more or less smoothly along the path of progress through planning has always been held as indubitable truth, an axiomatic belief in need of no demonstration, by development experts of most persuasions (Escobar, 1992). Planning was instrumental in nurturing a domestic capitalist class, with FYP pouring into the industrialization. It had only helped strengthening the base of domestic capitalist class which has already laid their foundation in the colonial period. Neo-colonial direction of the planning was quite evident as the inward looking policy favours the mainland India's capitalist class while peripheral region like Manipur remain isolated from the development matrix of the country in the initial stages of planning. Policy-makers of independent India continued the policy of treating the region as frontier periphery which, in fact, is a British colonial articulation and legacy.

The hegemony of the domestic capitalist class over the economy of the region was established, not by the interplay of market forces, but by coercion and introduction of non-market factors in the direction of the captive economy. Geographical isolation, hostile topography, land lockedness occupied the development approach in the region. This image of being a "landlocked" region was to remain as main anchoring perspectives on the political economy of the region. Maximum attention was paid to more connectivity with the rest of the country. As a consequence, there is a ceaseless dumping of goods from mainland India and neighbouring countries. Investment on infrastructure, government machinery, education, health and other service sectors with total negligence on productive culture had created a class of government officials, contractors, and non-local business professionals in the sphere of economy. This class constitutes the rising ruling class of the post-British society.

The politics of planning for development ingrained in the region with the inception North East Council (NEC) in 1972 was to catch up with the rest of the country. The NEC adopted a highly bureaucratic approach in addressing the regional problems exclusive of people's participation and involvement. NEC only facilitated the ruling class—politicians, bureaucrats and contractors, extensively subverting the producing class. With the coming of NEC, the region has witnessed institutionalization and bureaucratization rather than democratization of development politics. Development of North Eastern Region (DONER) is the latest institution which is being projected by the centre as the saviour of the North East region. The name itself signifies a deep rooted agenda and conveys a strong message that the North East is still shaping development under the mercy of centre. As development funds pour in the region, which comes in the form of grants, development in the region remains donor driven and makes the region dependent. Apart from the contested theories of development mentioned in the essay, even within the present development strategy of neo-liberalism North East region is still in the "embryonic" stage in terms of development. North Eastern Region—Vision 2020 aptly observes that the gap between the region and the rest of the country in terms of various developmental outcomes, productivities and capacities of people and institutions is large and growing, and has to be bridged.

The vision document, the first of its kind concerning the North East region, puts forward a strategy for inclusive development of the region as given below:

> The maximization of self-governance and participatory development, rural development having its focus on improving agricultural productivity; development of agro-processing industries, modernization and development of sericulture, harnessing the large hydroelectric power generation potential, augmenting infrastructure such as rail, road, inland water and air transportation and ensuring adequate flow of resources for public investments, a framework for private participation in infrastructural development (*North Eastern Region Vision* 2020, Vol. I, 3–4).

The vision document also visualizes a catching up strategy for the North East region with that of all India. It hypothetically assumes the continued growth of the Indian economy at 9 per cent per year from 2006–07 to 2020 at the same time expecting the deceleration of population growth over the period. If everything goes as expected or planned, by 2020, per capita income in the Indian economy is expected to be about Rs. 87,459 at the 2006–07 prices or about US$ 2,250 at the prevailing exchange rate. In order to reach this level of income GSDP in the North Eastern region will have to grow at 12.95 per cent per year on an average, or at 11.64 per cent in per capita terms between 2006–07 and 2019–20. For the said period the GSDP of Manipur will have to grow at 13.25 per cent per year on an average in order to reach the projected level of per capita income (*NE Vision* 2020, Vol. I, 9–13). Thus, the vision document has set a great ambition for the North East region. The Vision 2020 document propagates a catching up strategy with the rest of the country.

Catching up strategy is quite significant in view of its application and propagation by the developed countries towards the underdeveloped and developing countries across the continents of ASAFLA (Asia, Africa and Latin America). Such view puts development in a linear continuum wherein certain countries are taken as developed and rest of the countries are expected to catch them up. However, in actual practice such strategy of development has strengthened the hold of so-called developed countries upon the underdeveloped and developing countries because of the reason that the latter is following a "given" model of development wherein the former had the upper hand in various aspects. Given the practical effects resulting from the application of this strategy at the global level and lacunae and exploitative potential inherent in it, its application in the North East region needs to be cautious. Feasibility of achieving expected 13 per cent GSDP on average for the region to abridge the gap with the rest of the country is another challenging aspect which calls for closer scrutiny. There is no denying the fact that Government of India has taken up a vital step for the development of North East by way of a comprehensive vision document even though it is after more than six decades of India's independence. However, it will be too optimistic to expect such a higher growth rate barely within 13 years which India is unable to achieve within 60 years.

Rethinking Development of Manipur

Development approach in Manipur has been largely *ad hoc* in nature and non-durable in terms of impact. For instance, construction works and State service sector have been the site of public experience of development.This narrow and restricted view of development is something which the government constantly propagated, justified, defended and imprinted in the social consciousness of the people. The State is experiencing a "stunted" development, to borrow a word from Marx. Large construction projects such as dams, highways, expansion of roads and railways, government building are showcased as development in the region without actually engaging the deeper issues in development such as equity, social justice, food security, quality health care facility, protection of environment and ecology, indigenous people's rights, human resource development and basic amenities of our social life that constitute the elements of development and its liberating aspect. However, the development scenario resulting from a restricted view depicts a picture similar to the post-World War II European reconstruction programme.

For example, Development was relentlessly pushed by the western liberal countries under the leadership of US to counter and contain the spread of communism, and similarly it is being pushed in the region by the centre to counter and contain insurgency. As Esteva (1992, 4) writes in the global context, by now development has become an amoeba like concept, shapeless but ineradicable. Its contours are also blurred that it denotes nothing while it spreads everywhere because it connotes the best of intentions.

The intensive construction projects and recruitment to government service—particularly in security forces—of the State is manifested in its contribution to the Net State Domestic Product (NSDP) which accounts for more than 30 per cent. Look East Policy (LEP) and urban renewal programme such as JNURM (Jawaharlal Nehru Urban Renewal Mission) seem to have created euphoria among the ruling elites in the State as huge amount of funds are likely to pour into the State. Such large scale construction projects have so far benefited ministers, bureaucrats and contractors at the behest of the people at large. Moreover, most of the construction projects are confined to a small area within the Imphal city. Urban biased approach has generated valley and hills dichotomy, rural and urban disparity debate. In short, urban biased construction works have fragmented the population into various shades and categories on the one hand, and converted the Imphal city as one of the most congested, polluted and disorganised cities on the other hand.

Rapid urbanization and expansion of the so-called development projects have resulted in large scale displacement and many of the mega projects are more in the pipeline. Harmful effects of these projects such as environmental degradation are only a tip of the iceberg; the larger picture is that such displacement has far reaching political, economic and social consequences. Displaced people will not only be displaced from their homes and ancestral lands, but also alienates from their aged old means of livelihoods. As majority of the locals earn their livelihood from their natural surroundings and vegetation or informal sector. Alienation of livelihoods from the local/indigenous people is observable.

Displacement is associated with a radical reduction in economic and social resources and, therefore, increases political vulnerability (Colson, 2007). The whole debate of development and displacement will go on but the displaced people will be sandwiched between political insecurity and loss of livelihoods. Employment generation has become an important ingredient for development politics in developing countries like India. A number of employment generation programmes have been taken up in the country, the latest being National Rural Employment Guarantee Scheme (NREGS). While the effects of this policy at the grassroot level in terms of amelioration of living condition of the masses is yet to be assessed critically, it is being used as a trump card for electoral politics in the country. As the productive sector of the state is stagnant, it is unable to generate gainful employment through backward and forward linkages.

Government in the name of generating employment is making massive recruitment policy of the youths to State security forces with funding from the Centre. "Militarization of employment" is taking place on a war footing. Ironically, government claims such endeavours as a serious means to resolve the problem of unemployment. "Militarization of employment" is the most and popular employment generation scheme in the State of Manipur. The argument put forth by the State government in favour of the policy is to maintain law and order by countering the insurgency on the one hand, and giving employment to the youths on the other hand. In the process State itself gets militarised as it is drifting towards a police State. Diversion of productive youths to military has certain implications—dependency both in real and monetary terms, adverse effect on number of producing base, corruption, and social crisis. Militarization is a tense process which can create conflict between social sectors and most importantly between those who might benefit from militarization and those who might not, but who nonetheless may bear some of its cost (Lutz, 2007).

Redefining Development

Development should be an enabling one. It should not only give the people equal opportunities but also provide equal conditions to enable every individual or group a decent living condition. The notion of development should go beyond economism because development should be holistic. It is as much as political as economic and social. Development is not to be articulated purely in economic terms as it is being witnessed in Manipur, for it involves creation and destruction of complex network of relations which can lead to the exploitation and pauperization on the one hand, and accumulation of wealth on the other hand. Untangling the exploitative networks in any development pattern is a crucial challenge. Any development model or theory bereft of such effort amount to the perpetuation of the existing structure of exploitation. It should provide a wholesome social system encompassing both human and natural environment and their harmonious relationship.

Challenges to development come from two crucial fronts. First, development impacts which is produced by the working of a particular model of development upon the society at various levels. The unequal distribution of wealth and income, environmental degradation and its associated consequences, displacement of human population, etc. are the crucial site of people's engagement by way of resisting development brought to our social lives.

Second challenge comes from the contested nature of the concept of development itself. Development, as argued above, is not a given or fixed one, rather it is a constantly evolving concept having new issues and dimensions. For instance, sustainable development and climate change have become inalienable components of development debate both at global and regional levels. Given the present contextual reality reconstituting and reconceptualising development by accommodating the issues and challenges is of paramount imperative. Therefore, the present mode of development vigorously pursued under neo-liberalism must be subjected to a surgical analysis and try to explore new frontier in the horizon of mind to search an alternative theory, meaning and trajectory of development.

The present development strategy in Manipur is not only top down but also highly bureaucratic in approach. Apart from the undesirable result of disparity in wealth and income, fragmentation of society based on the criteria of wealth, destruction of fertile land and environment, the prevailing development model in the State has led to the shrinking space for engaging the rationale behind so-called development advanced by the State. Ever increasing intolerance of the State in its response towards the plethora of social movements resisting the mega projects such as Tipaimukh dam, Mapithel dam, Tulihal Airport expansion, Capitol project, etc. are testimony to the above-mentioned point.

Such intolerant attitude is reflective of deficit of democracy and representative character on the part of the State. Multiple effects of the existing development strategy can be aptly described as development anarchy—a condition of haphazardness, chaos, unsystematic, undue delay, opaqueness, etc. in the policies formulation and their application. The debate of (under) development in the region in general and Manipur in particular is incomplete without the reference to development strategy of India. Modernization and neo-liberalism are the development approaches which the country has adopted whole-heartedly and unhesitatingly, and the two approaches have complemented each other well. Modernization approach of the post-independent India has significantly engineered "local" capitalist class in North East with an uneven economic development.

The irony of neo-liberalism in the region is that despite the intensified integration into global capitalism there is almost no significant productive base in the State. It can be said that neo-liberalism has brought home more social and economic disparity—de-industrialization, unemployment, inequality, proletarization, etc. Neo-liberal policy of the Indian State has created 'an economic regime that produces some of the world's top billionaires at the one end and thousands of peasants' suicides on the other' (Patnaik, 2009).

What is happening in the North East is not different from the above-mentioned tragedy since India has embarked upon the neo-liberal path of development. Now the Government of India is pursuing a top-down development strategy in the name of catching up with the mainstream. And, the political elites and administrators are hell bent to implement such development policy without any critical evaluations. The North East Region in general and Manipur in particular are in different environmental, cultural and social settings. Therefore, any theory of development must take into account these factors. This strategy is akin to what the developed countries have done to most of the third world countries.

Development discourse in the country has been dominated by 'western' idea of modernization or neo-liberalism that has brought unwanted socio-economic and political consequences. It is time to resist this western idea of development and try to visualise alternative development discourse such as post-development approach, which has challenged the might of western idea. Post-development embraces the revalorization of vernacular cultures, the need to rely less on expert knowledge and more on ordinary people's attempt at constructing more humane and culturally and ecologically sustainable worlds, and the important point of taking seriously social movements and grassroots mobilizations as the basis for moving towards a new era (Escobar, 2007).

CITED WORKS

Colson, Elizabeth. 2007. Displacement. In *A Companion to the Anthropology of Politics,* edited by David Nugent and John Vincent, 107–120. Oxford: Blackwell Publishing.

Edelman, Marc and Angelique Haugerud. 2007. Development. In *A Companion to the Anthropology of Politics,* edited by David Nugent and John Vincent, 86–106. Oxford: Blackwell Publishing.

Escobar, Arturo. 1992. Planning. In *The Development Dictionary: A Guide to Knowledge as Power,* edited by Wolfgang Sachs, 132–145, London and New Jersey: Zed Books.

Escobar, Arturo. 2007. 'Post-Development' as concept and social practices. In *Exploring Post-development: Theory and Practice, Problems and Perspectives,* edited by Aram Ziai, 18–32. New York and London: Routledge.

Escobar, Arturo. 1995. *Encountering Development- The Making and Unmaking of The Third World,* Princeton: Princeton University Press.

Esteva, Gustavo. 1992. Development. In *The Development Dictionary: A Guide to Knowledge as Power,* edited by Wolfgang Sachs, 6–25, London and New Jersey: Zed Books.

Gasper, Des. 2005. *The Ethics of Development.* New Delhi: Vistaar Publication.

Lutz, Catherine. 2007. Militarization. In *A Companion to the Anthropology of Politics,* edited by David Nugent and John Vincent, 318–31. Oxford: Blackwell Publishing.

Patnaik, Prabhat. 2009. Time for Change. *Frontline* 26, 7. March 28–April 10: 21–3.

Pieterse, Jan Nederveen. 2001. *Development Theory: Deconstruction/ Reconstruction.* New Delhi: Vistaar Publication.

Sachs, Wolfgang (ed.). 1992. *The Development Dictionary: A Guide to Knowledge as Power.* London and New Jersey: Zed Books.

11

Democratic Decentralization of Economic Development

Homen Thangjam

Development Discourses on Manipur

Choosing an alternative paradigm of development becomes problematic as Manipur has not really tasted the fruit of success or failed to evaluate the missing components of any policy as a result of administrative lapses and politicizations. Nonetheless, in the wake of fast modernizing economies, the anchoring point of economic planning should be based on democratic decentralization of development with sufficient attention to participation, specificity of culture(s), equity and durability. In addition, development projects should not alter or displace the irreversible relationship between the cultural moorings of a specific society and their needs, and their dependence on natural resources. For, these societies are capable of effecting substantial understanding and knowledge about resource management and draw "local" trajectories of development. With the making of development projects work at such a plank some of the immediate frameworks should be brought back as a major rationale of development discourse. For instance, with the foregrounding of sustainable grassroot developmental economics there is an urgency to stop and reduce pressure on arable land and fragmentation of the same.

In the recent past the stubbornness on the part of the State to surpass these concerns has only resulted in stronger binaries. This binary is manifested in the form of sweeping neo-liberal economic pursuit, on the one hand, and people's resistance movements, on the other hand. Put simply, any serious look out for an alternative politics of an alternative economies should be acquiescent to issues at grassroot and, therefore, sufficiently democratise the perspective of economic development.

Discourses on development on Manipur or the North-East are shaped by people occupying positions of power situated at different centres of power. New Delhi, for example, comfortably views that the region is "the country's pampered child" and disproportionate amounts of Plan funds have flown into the entire North East, considering that only 10 per cent of the Plan funds are loans while the other States receive 70 per cent as loans. Further, 10 per cent of each Ministry's funds are earmarked for the North East where the population criterion is not applied, so that per capita devolution is far higher for the North Eastern States.

The opposite view emanating from the region accuses the Centre that the region is underdeveloped and socio-economically backward, and has been virtually isolated from the mainstream of development in the country and as a result denied the opportunity of exploiting its full potential (Institute for Human Development, 2006, I). In addition to these, a third and newer understanding of the region is that insurgency is a result of underdevelopment and that the situation of conflict has acted as a firewall against all possible remedies for development.

As far as the developmental status of Manipur is concerned, the existing reality presents a gloomy scenario. Manipur Development Report states that economy of Manipur remains largely underdeveloped and agrarian with a weak industrial sector and inflated services sector. The half-hearted attempts at State sponsored industrialization have not been successful in contributing to the economy in any substantive way. On account of the low economic activity, Manipur has a huge developmental and fiscal deficit (Institute for Human Development, 2006, I). This is despite the fact that Manipur is one of the major States in the region, and policy-makers in Delhi regard the State as one having considerable strategic importance for India. Growing interest in the State in the past decade or so has been for varied reasons. "The State is rich in bio-diversity and has the resources to produce exportable goods based on horticulture, floriculture and sericulture. It can serve as a transit for 'facilitating' trade and other contacts with the East and South East Asian countries with which the region has deep-rooted historical and ethnic ties" (Institute for Human Development, 2006, I). But such an ardent interest taken in the recent past gives a missive to the people. Many finds this new found fascination for the State as informed by the unfolding neo-liberal dictates sweeping over India and as a means of investing her capital in the form of Look East Policy. The Policy does not stand to benefit the people of the North East in general or Manipur in particular.

Many authors have propounded corrective measures so that the State can meaningfully come out of the impasse of underdevelopment. Two diametrically opposing views are prevalent in this regard. One view, such as propounded by Gulshan Sachdeva, emphasises upon the creation of market structures, financial institutions, uniform labour law, private investment as found in the Himachal Pradesh, opening up of the region, and so on, in the lines of thinking emanating from institutions of Government of India. He recommends that the region will have to focus on integrating itself with the rest of the country and the world. It has to build hard and soft infrastructure and revitalise its agriculture. Above all, North East has to become investor friendly, and stand on its own feet without excessive dependence on the Centre. To link the region with dynamic East Asia, the book has argued for declaring certain areas as free trade areas as well as developing an aggressive strategy for a growth quadrangle involving the North East of India, Myanmar, South West China, Northern Thailand and Bangladesh (Sachdeva, 2000).

The other opposing view keeps the primacy of the State in undertaking development. For example, Priyoranjan Singh opines that policy-makers should meaningfully address the structural dimension of the State as well as put in the right perspectives. He traces the historical and structural distortions suffered by Manipur's economy as how that had led to the emergence of a political economy with vested interest in the perpetration of a tertiarised economy with a weak productive base. During the pre-colonial period, Manipur had a stable food economy with high surplus of agriculture along with an extremely weak and subsistence manufacturing sector. The colonial rule left an economy with a strong agricultural base. However, instead of capitalizing on further strengthening the agricultural sector, the process of tertiarization was intensified thereafter at the cost of a rapidly marginalized productive base. He argues that the productive base of agriculture and manufacture only can be the springbroad of a resurgent economy (Singh, 2005, 149–60).

In a similar fashion Thingnam Kishan opines that underdevelopment alongside a systematic plundering of the region's (*sic* North East) resources formed the matrix of dependency during British colonial period. Post-British policies failed to transform this dynamics as economic development was reduced to the successful establishment of a market for products manufactured elsewhere. He raises the fundamental issue of production as the basis of meaningful development and argues that unless production assumes centrality, development will remain lopsided. Meaningful utilization of the region's resources by generating production remains the logical way out of the current impasse (Kishan, 2006, 55¬68).

It is worthwhile to recall that way back in 1997, a High Level Commission Report submitted to the Prime Minister of India, pointed out that North East cannot be treated merely as a resource region, market dump and transit yard. 'There is strong resentment over what is seen as an earlier phase of "colonial exploitation" in which its wealth was extracted for others' enrichment' (Shukla, 1997). Thus, initiatives have to be undertaken by the Indian State to shed its cloak of colonial designs of domination and extraction, thereby ushering in era of development for the region.

This article emphasizes the centrality of meaningful utilization of land (agricultural) which is scarce in the State for any developmental purposes. Land shall continue to form as the most valuable asset or capital in any endeavour to bring about development in the State, be it the classical model of development or a model based on post-development theory. This understanding also impinges upon decentralization of development, so that the people of Manipur can be equal partners in a process of culturally friendly, equitable and sustainable development. Read differently, people at the local level can meaningfully exercise ownership rights of the resources, reduce corruption, extract accountability, apply local knowledge for development. Embedded in this perspective is the understanding that manufacturing units should be set up in other areas other than the agricultural land of Greater

Imphal valley, so as to reduce pressure on land and fragmentation, taking into account conduciveness and suitability of available resources. It must be added here that the New Industrial Policy, 1996 of the State has also laid emphasis on creating a strong industrial base and employment opportunities in the State through provision of various growth inducing factors based on locally available resources such as raw materials and minerals. This proposition, however, calls for good governance on the part of the government and determined efforts.

Development Trend : Flawed Utilization of Land

A major factor which has a direct bearing on development in Manipur is the pattern of utilization of land. Two existing Acts, and the manner in which they have been employed, have had a negative impact on arable land. The former pertains to Land Acquisition Act 1894 (extends to the whole of India except the State of Jammu and Kashmir), which has been perpetually (mandatory) used by the State or Central Government to undertake massive development projects for "public purpose". The second pertains to Section 20 of the Manipur Land Revenue and Land Reforms Act 1960, put in place for purpose of revenue collection based on nature of landholding and to avoid diversion of land but hardly given importance in the case of Manipur. If followed in spirit, this Act can act as a deterrent to increasing instances of converting arable land into settlement areas or other purposes in Manipur.

Section 3(a) of the Land Acquisition Act states, "The expression 'land' include benefits to arise out of land, and things attached to the earth or permanently fastened to anything attached to the earth." The Maharashtra Government amended this section in 1964 stating, "The expression 'arable land' means land fit for cultivation whether in fact cultivated or not; and includes garden land". Sections 4(1) and 4(2) are mandatory to be used by any government when any land is intended to be acquired. Section 4(1) reads:

> Whenever it appears to the [appropriate Government] that land in any locality [is needed or] is likely to be needed for any "public purpose" [or for a company], a notification to that effect shall be published in the Official Gazette [and

> in daily newspapers circulating in that locality of which at least one shall be in the regional language] and a Collector shall cause public notice of the substance of such notification to be given at convenient places in the said locality [the last of the dates of such publications and the giving of such public notice, being hereinafter referred to as the date of the publications of the notifications].

Further Section 4(2) reads:

> Thereupon, it shall be lawful for any officer, either generally or especially authorised by such government in this behalf, and for his servants and the workmen,—to enter upon and survey and take levels of any land in such locality; to dig or bore into the sub-soil; to do all other acts necessary to ascertain whether the land is adapted for such purpose; to set out the boundaries of the land proposed to be taken and the intended line of the work [if any] proposed to be made thereon; to mark such levels, boundaries and line by placing marks and cutting trenches; and, where otherwise the survey cannot be completed and the levels taken and boundaries and line marked, to cut down and clear away any part of any standing crop, fence or jungle: provided that no person shall enter into any building or upon any enclosed court or garden attached to a dwelling house [unless with the consent of the occupier thereof] without previously giving such occupier at least seven days' notice in writing of his intention to do so.

Using these rigid Sections, government has been forcibly acquiring lands in the name of "public purpose". An alarming scenario is the acquisition of agricultural lands for development projects. It is a fact that agricultural lands are being aggressively used for various projects and schemes of both the State and Central Governments (Singh, 2007, 4–29). Two issues further arise as a consequence of acquisition of the land for "public purpose". On the one hand is the immediate injury caused to the owners of the land, and second is the damage caused in the aftermath of construction of development projects, both of which lead to destruction of agricultural land. Two illustrative examples are discussed in this regard. One pertains to the recent most case which concerns the acquisition of 519,843 acres of agricultural land for the construction of Industrial Growth Centre at Waiton, Chingarel, Imphal East District (Government of Manipur, 2008, i–xxiv) and the second case relates to the submersion of 27,404.94 acres of agricultural land in three districts of Manipur as a result of commissioning of the Loktak Hydro Project at Komreikap in the year 1994.

It is worthwhile to elaborate here that Growth Centres scheme was initiated in the Eighth Plan by the Government of India with the aim of tackling the problem of regional imbalances in industrial development. As a model, large villages or small towns which have the potential to become the nuclei for the socio-economic development of the surrounding area are identified as Growth Centres. The Growth Centres can be identified by different orders with respect to the quality and the quantity of services and facilities, service area and population. A Growth Centre of lowest order should have services such as agricultural input centre, primary and middle school, maternity and child care centres and daily market. At the highest level, it must have manufacturing industries, hospitals, colleges and so on.

Idea of Growth Centres is situated within the understanding that with the doing away of the system of licensing of industries and coming into play of market forces, the industries tend to gravitate towards already developed areas which provide better infrastructure, easier availability of skilled workforce and forward and backward linkages in terms of availability of raw materials and markets for products. Growth Centres are, therefore, taken as special measures to promote development of industries in backward areas by policy-makers.

Under the Growth Centre Schemes, in year 2008, the Central Government approved an Industrial Growth Centre Project in Manipur at Lamlai, Napet at a project cost of Rs. 30 crores of which Rs. 15 crores will be the Government of India contribution, Rs. 5 crore as State government contribution, Rs. 4 crores as loan and equity contribution from the financial institutions and Rs. 6 crore as loans and equity from other sources. A sum of Rs. 1.50 crore was sanctioned and released by the Government of India. However, there is no official notification defining the nature of the proposed Centre.

As a follow up to this proposal, site of the proposed Centre was shifted. In a notification dated November 18, 2008, the Government of Manipur through the application of Land Acquisition Act 1894, authorised the concerned authority to acquire around 519.843 acres of agricultural land for the construction of Industrial Growth Centre at Waiton, Chingarel, Imphal East District. Ironical issue is that the Government "knows" that the land to be acquired are agricultural land. For example, the same Gazette elaborates the classification of the lands in question into two types such as *Anganphou* and *Phourel*.

A public notice served by the affected farmers read as follows:

> This is a very fertile land giving yield of around 1,000 kg to 1,400 kg per acre. Annual production of rice in this area is around 1,032,000 kg giving an annual income of around Rs. 2.27 crore from rice only. In addition, from associated agricultural works such as weeding, transplantation, cutting and threshing, etc. gives income to agricultural workers, annually, a total sum of around Rs. 6.20 lakhs. Income from hay and straw sums up to around Rs. 6.02 lakhs from this area of agricultural land. Furthermore, seasonal fish, vegetables and herbs are other benefits given to the people by this area of agricultural land (Waiton Mamang Chingarel Loukol Kanba Lup, 2008).

Table 11.1 illustrates the total number area proposed to be acquired by the State government, number of persons likely to be affected by the construction of the proposed Growth Centre.

With regard to the second example, as per a Report conducted by the Committee of Experts, Constituted by the Government of Manipur, *vide* Order No. 25/15/99-Power (HC) dated December 22,

Table 11.1 : Schedule of Land Proposed to be Acquired for Industrial Growth Centre, Chingarel

Area of agricultural land likely to be acquired (in acres)	*No. of pattadars likely to be affected*
519.843	339

Source: Government of Manipur. 2008. *Manipur Gazette*. 2008. No. 309, December 1. 1–26.

1999 submitted to the Gauhati High Court Imphal Bench in connection C.R. No. 32 of 1994, which was duly signed by Chief Engineer (Power), Government of Manipur, Chief Engineer (ICFD), Government of Manipur, Pr. Conservator of Forest, Government of Manipur, Director of Agriculture, Government of Manipur, Deputy Commissioner of Bishnupur, Imphal West and Thoubal, Joint Secretary (Power), Government of Manipur, and Commissioner Revenue, Government of Manipur, respectively, the estimated areas of land affected due to submersion by the Loktak Hydro Electric Project is 27,404.94 acres of 12,129 *pattadars* (approximately). The district-wise affected area due to the commissioning of the Loktak Hydro Project at Komreikap in the year 1994 is given in Table 11.2.

The Committee was of the view that since maintaining Loktak at certain predetermined level and/or in a manner controlled by the National Hydro-Electric Power Corporation (NHPC) in order to enhance retention of water in the reservoir for generation of hydro-electric power largely factored in the submersion of agricultural and other classes of lands around the lake, the Corporation, among others, has the onus to find ways and means to redress the grievances of the affected people on the one hand, and to conserve the Loktak Wetland on the other. The Committee also felt that degradation of the catchment areas resulting in deposit of silt in Loktak over the years is another factor that has contributed to submersion of lands at the periphery of the Lake and loss to a large number of land owners and farmers. But the question is why

Table 11.2 : District-wise Affected Area due to the Commissioning of the Loktak Hydro Project at Komreikap in the Year 1994

District	*Area of land affected (in acres)*	*No. of pattadars affected (as on March 2006)*
Imphal West	8,818.75	3,109
Thoubal	11,989.57	5,978
Bishnupur	6,596.62	3,042
Total	**27,404.94**	**12,129**

Source: Government of Manipur. 2006. *Report of the Committee of Experts constituted by the Government of Manipur (vide Orders No. 25/15/99-power (HC) dated 22-12-1999 in pursuance of the Hon'ble Gauhati High Court's orders passed on 12-11-1999 in R.R. No. 32 of 1994) to examine loss and damage caused by Loktak Hydro-Electric Project.* Imphal: Secretariat (Power Department), April 18: 4.

the stakeholders, especially the NHPC, which has been exploiting the Loktak (reservoir) to generate hydro-electric power for more than two decades at minimum cost, did not invest the resources at their command, for the purpose of conservation/sustainable development of (the catchment areas of) Loktak Wetland—its ecology, bio-diversity, form and character (Government of Manipur, 2006, 5). Tables 11.3 and 11.4 show details of loss suffered by affected land.

Here, it is worthwhile to add that in spite of the visible damages that have come forth with the commissioning of a hydro project, Government of Manipur still has not learnt a lesson. Development is still understood in terms of large projects at the cost of land, gene pool of bio-diversity and human beings. Proposed construction of a multipurpose project at Tipaimukh, which was granted notification in 2003, is also case in point. The entire lowland along the banks of three major river courses of Manipur—the Barak, the Irang and the Makru—which runs through the length of Tamenglong district, would be under perpetual threat of submergence (Churchill, 2006, 39). Following Table 11.5 shows the areas likely to be affected by the Tipaimukh Multipurpose Project.

There are no available data on land diversion in Manipur.[1] However, it is an observable fact that agricultural lands are largely converted into homesteads, private entrepreneurial sites, parking lots and so on. This phenomenon is not specific to the valley areas alone but also to the hill areas. Section 20 of the *Manipur Land*

Table 11.3 : Estimated Value of Average Yield/Loss per acre of "Phourel" Class of Land

Items	*Value*	*Remarks*
Average yield/acre	1200 kg i.e. 40 Sangpais of 30 kg each	Sangpai is the local term of measure of quantity
Value of yield/acre i.e. 40 Sangpais @ Rs. 90 per Sangpai of 30 kg	Rs. 3,600.00	
Cost of cultivation/per acre	Rs. 1,760.00	
Net value of yield/acre	**Rs. 3,600 (–) Rs.1,760.00 = Rs.1,840.0**	

Table 11.4 : Estimated Value of Average Yield/Loss per acre of "Taothabi" Class of Land

Items	*Value*	*Remarks*
Average yield/acre	1,000 kg i.e. 40 Sangpais of 25 kg each	Sangpai is the local term of measure of quantity
Value of yield/acre i.e. 40 Sangpais @ Rs. 90 per Sangpai of 30 kgs	Rs. 2,600.00	
Cost of cultivation/per acre	Rs. 925.00	
Net value of yield/acre	**Rs. 2,600 (–) Rs. 925 = Rs. 1,675.00**	

Source: Government of Manipur. 2006. *Report of the Committee of experts constituted by the Government of Manipur (vide Orders No. 25/15/99-power (HC) dated 22-12-1999 in pursuance of the Hon'ble Gauhati High Court's orders passed on 12-11-1999 (in R.R. No. 32 of 1994) to examine loss and damage caused by Loktak Hydro-Electric Project.* Imphal: Secretariat (Power Department), April 18: 7.

Table 11.5 : Areas likely to be affected by the Tipaimukh Multipurpose Project

Area of land likely to be affected (in hectares)	15,000.00
No. of villages likely to be affected	168
No. of villagers likely to be displaced	30,000.00
Area of natural habitat likely to be destroyed (in sq. km)	300
Length of NH 53 likely to be dislocated (in km)	60

Source: Compiled from, Laishram Churchill. 2006. Environment, development and social challenges: Scrutinising India's Look East Policy in Manipur. *Alternative Frames* I, III. April–June: 30–46.

Revenue and Land Reforms Act, 1960 with regard to diversion of land reads as follows:

(1) If any person holding land for any purpose wishes to divert such land or any part thereof to any other purpose except agriculture, he shall apply for permission to the competent authority which may, subject to the provisions of this section and to the rules made under this Act, refuse permission or grant it on such conditions as it may think fit.

(2) Permission to divert may be refused by the competent authority only on the ground that the diversion is likely to cause a public nuisance or that it is not in the interest of the general public or that the holder is unable or unwilling to comply with the conditions that may be imposed under Sub-section 3.

(3) Conditions may be imposed on diversion for the following objects and others, namely, in order to secure the public health, safety and convenience, and in the case of land which is to be used as building sites in order to secure, in addition, that the dimensions, arrangement and accessibility of the sites are adequate for the health and convenience of occupiers or are suitable to the locality.

(4) If any land has been diverted without permission by the holder or by any other person with or without the consent of the holder, the competent authority, on receiving information thereof, may impose on the person responsible for the diversion a penalty not exceeding rupees one hundred and may proceed in accordance with the provisions of sub-section (1) and if an application for permission to divert had been made.

(5) If any land has been diverted in contravention of an order passed or of a condition imposed under any of the foregoing sub-section, the competent authority may serve a notice on the person responsible for such contravention, directing him, within a reasonable period to be stated in the notice, to use the land for its original purpose or to observe the condition; and such notice may require such person to remove any structure, to fill up any excavation, or to take such other steps as may be required in order that the land may be used for its original purpose, or that the condition may be satisfied. The competent authority may also impose on such person a penalty not exceeding rupees one hundred for such contravention, and a further penalty not exceeding rupees four for each day during which such contravention continues.

The purpose of citing elaborately sub-sections of the appropriate Section is to emphasise that there are stringent laws applicable with the protection of the agricultural land. Original intent of the Section is to rationalise revenue creation on land. However, current demand on land due to raising population, urbanization, and so on make it pertinent to utilise these sections of the land Act to protect agricultural land from diverting into other purposes. Refusal for diversion of agricultural land could be affirmatively done using sub-section 2 of Section 20 on the ground of "public interest"; shortage of foodgrain is a public issue. Worrisome picture is the unavailability of records of land diversion due to lapses on the side of the law implementing agencies. At a deeper level, the abovecited cases must be seen at the backdrop of fluctuating area of rice and foodgrain under cultivation in Manipur.

Table 11.6 shows the area under cultivation of rice and foodgrain from 1990–91 to 2006–07. We witness a fluctuating trend in terms of areas under cultivation (both rice and foodgrain). On an average, over the select years, the average areas under cultivation for rice and foodgrain are about 160 acres and 165 acres, respectively. From year 1990–91 to 2002–03, there were negative growth rates (compound annual growth rates) of –0.23 per cent and 0.31 per cent for rice and foodgrain, respectively. However, from 2003–04 through 2006–07, we witness positive compound annual growth rates of about 1.97 per cent and 1.87 per cent for

Table 11.6 : Total Area under Rice and Foodgrain in Manipur

Years	*Area under rice*	*Total area under foodgrain*
1990-91	157.41	162.02
1991-92	160.30	164.29
1992-93	151.19	153.99
1993-94	161.87	164.59
1994-95	163.93	168.40
1995-96	151.19	153.74
1996-97	161.87	168.25
1997-98	157.90	161.47
1998-99	166.89	169.85
1999-00	157.05	161.39
2000-01	156.96	161.63
2001-02	162.57	167.63
2002-03	153.11	156.65
2003–04	157.83	160.20
2004–05	176.31	197.50
2005–06	166.23	169.10
2006–07	165.37	168.70

Source: Government of Manipur. Various issues. *Statistical Abstracts of Manipur*. Imphal: Directorate of Economics and Statistics.

rice and foodgrain, respectively. The improvements is largely on account of conversion of wetlands into agricultural lands by private players in three major districts such as Thoubal, Imphal West and Bishnupur. However, looked within a larger perspective, the scenario still reminds paradoxical given the fact that there were only ten public sector undertaking manufacturing units (all sick and defunct presently) and 113 Small Industries Development Organization (SIDCO) and non-SIDCO units in Manipur (see Table 11.7). Based on calculations from data given in Statistical Abstract of Manipur: 2004 and Economic Survey, Manipur: 2007–08, from the year 1997–98 through 2005–06, SIDCO and non-SIDCO units have negatively grown at a CAGR (–) 6.19 per cent and (–) 7.04 per cent, respectively.

Overall, there is a concern over the nature of utilization of land in India with regard to developmental projects including Special Economic Zones (SEZ). For example, in the year 2006, a 31 member Parliamentary Standing Committee was instituted under the Chairpersonship of Murli Manohar Joshi to review the Special Economic Zone Act, which was passed by the Parliament in 2005 and became a law in the year 2006. M.S. Swaminathan, National Commission of Farmers observed to the Committee that:

> Fertile lands must be preserved without fail and apart from the purposes of agriculture such lands should not be utilised for other purposes such as SEZ (industry). Such select programmes must be set up on non-agricultural infertile lands. Agriculture and industry should mutually benefit each other, not at one's expense (Web India, 2007).

The Parliamentary Standing Committee of Commerce called for sweeping changes in the SEZ policy to make it farmer friendly, including imposing a ban on further SEZs and review of tax sops provided under the SEZ Act. The Committee was of the view that SEZs should not come up at the cost of farmers and that the food security of the country should not get jeopardised at any cost. "There should preferably be a ban on the use of irrigated land, double-crop or multi-crop land for setting up SEZs. Only waste or barren lands should be used for setting up of SEZs. If the government is interested in ensuring that unrest among the farmers does not spread like wildfire, maintain food security of the country and sustainable development, then it should implement the recommendations of the Report". There is a consensus among all members on the Committee on the recommendations of the Report. Members of all political parties have been associated with the Report (Web India, 2007). By the year 2011, there is a growing debate on what constitutes the "public purpose" in terms of acquisition of land such as Nandigram in West Bengal.

Further, the Second Administrative Reforms Commission (ARC) headed by M. Veerappa Moily observes that the present approach of allowing use of prime agricultural land for establishing SEZs should be avoided. In this regard the ARC Chairperson M. Veerappa Moily said, "In establishing SEZs, use of prime agricultural land should be avoided. There is a need to amend the present approach to SEZs in this regard". The ARC report titled "Capacity Building for Conflict Resolution: Friction to Fusion", has suggested that the proportion of land permitted for use by the promoters of SEZs for non-processing activities should be kept to a minimum so that more land is put to productive use. Environmental regulations should be ensured, too (Thaindian, 2008).

Keeping these in mind, the Government of Manipur, too, must be guided by the logic of conservation and local needs while undertaking developmental works, not at the cost of agricultural lands, environmental destruction and human security. The trend of development undertaken so far in Manipur at the cost of agricultural land reinforces a classical example of Greek thinking and others, which embodies destruction is an inherent element of development. In its classical origin, and not only in ancient Greece, development was understood as a natural process in which phases of renewal, expansion, contraction and decomposition followed each other sequentially according to a perpetually recurrent cycle. In the modern world, a world in which it is artifice rather than nature that provides the analogue for the understanding of movement, development has increasingly come to refer to a discontinuous process in which destruction and renewal are simultaneous, as much as sequential. However, the essential unity of creation and destruction contained within the process of development has not changed; it still involves destruction (Cowen and Shenton, 2005, viii).

Need for Dispersal of Manufacturing Units

One way of overcoming increasing burden on land in the greater Imphal valley area, which is considered as the rice bowl of Manipur, is to establish manufacturing units in other areas taking into account availability of raw materials, logistics and so on. This can lead to rationalization of land utilization as well as generation of employment in the State. As such, dispersal of manufacturing units at district levels is not a new idea. The Government of Manipur in its policy announcement of 1990, decided to focus attention to the small scale and agro-based industries without discouraging the medium and large scale industries. It was expected to serve the objective of employment generation and dispersal of industries in rural and urban areas. The New Industrial Policy 1996 of the State has laid emphasis on creating a strong industrial base and employment opportunities in the State through provision of various growth inducing factors based on locally available resources such as raw materials and minerals. However, in this perspective, it is the State government that comes up with proposals and plans for setting up units at the local levels. Local governments are given mere administrative task.

Dispersal of manufacturing units should be located within the context of economic decentralization. This means that local governments should be allowed to come up feasibility studies as well as proposals to set up units. This can reinforce complementary and reciprocity between the "intention" of development on the side of the government and local or community needs. At the political level, a sense of ownership of resources and material benefits by the local community can harmonise conflict.

Some of the benefits that are associated with decentralization are discussed here. A benefit that has been stressed in decentralization literature is a presumed better match between bundle of goods and services provided by governments and the heterogeneous preferences of citizens. The better match of preferences and supplies is seen by some as having its roots in interjurisdictional mobility as in Charles Tiebout's model – A mobility permitted by decentralization (Tiebout, 1956, 416–24). By others, it is seen in some innate greater responsiveness of junior governments to the preference of people; by others still, it is seen in some greater motivation of local governments to seek to satisfy the preferences of their citizens. More recently, it has been seen as originating in the greater control that citizens at local levels can exert on their political leaders through the ballot box (Seabright, 1996, 61–89).

A second benefit of decentralization is an alleged greater propensity of government to innovate. To be more precise, the argument is that the risks associated with innovation are smaller for local governments; as a consequence, these governments will, other things being equal, have greater incentive to innovate. At least since Alexis de Tocqueville, local governments have been seen as training grounds for liberty and democracy. Tocqueville thought that local institutions are to liberty what primary schools are to science; they put it within the people's reach; they teach people to appreciate its peaceful enjoyment and accustom them to make use of it (Tocqueville, 1969, 63). John Stuart Mill who acknowledged an intellectual debt to Tocqueville,[2] especially on matters related to decentralization, stressed that participation in local affairs plays an important role in 'the public education of citizens.'[3] The argument is still used by institutions such as the World Bank as a way of encouraging the citizens of developing countries to participate in socio-politico and economic processes (Breton, 2000, 1–16).

Few important points that need to be kept in mind while understanding decentralization are given below. First, decentralization by itself is a source of interjurisdictional spillovers. Second, changes in the degree of decentralization, whether incremental or decremental, will generate what is, in effect, a particular sort of externality whenever constitutional powers[4] are complementary. Two powers are complementary whenever making use of one power calls for the utilization of the other. Spillovers and externalities can be internalized through intergovernmental coordination, an activity that is costly.[5] There are other costs of decentralization besides coordination cost. Among them, are the cost of interjurisdictional mobility and the cost of signalling one's preferences. But the cost of coordination are in all likelihood, the most important in constraining the extent of decentralization in governmental systems (Becker and Murphy, 1992, 1137–160). These being the issues, what remains are the question of finance and capital investment for setting up manufacturing units. One major handicap Manipur suffers is in this sphere. Since private investment is scarce in the State, the primemover has to be the Central Government.

Following the industrial policies highlighted above by the State government, manufacturing units were set up in different districts of Manipur. As mentioned above, industrial scenario presents a gloomy picture. There were only ten public sector undertakings manufacturing units (all sick and defunct presently). Moreover, based on calculations from data given in Statistical Abstract of Manipur: 2004 and Economic Survey, Manipur: 2007–08, from year 1997–98 through 2005–06, SIDCO and non-SIDCO units have negatively grown at a CAGR of (–) 6.19 per cent and (–) 7.04 per cent, respectively. It is beyond the scope of this chapter to analyse the reasons behind the failure of the manufacturing units, be it management or fiscal.

A total of 113 manufacturing units are found registered in Manipur during 2005–06 against 158 (132 SIDO and 26 non-SIDO) in 2004–05. Table 11.7 shows that among the districts Imphal East district has the maximum number of registered industrial units followed by Imphal West. The lowest was recorded in Chandel district. The district-wise SIDO and non-SIDO break-up of industrial units during 2005–06 is given below.

Table 11.7 : Growth of Registered Industrial Units and Employment in Manipur During 2005–06

District	*No. of units*			*No. of employment*		
	SIDO	*Non-SIDO*	*Total*	*SIDO*	*Non-SIDO*	*Total*
Senapati	6	3	9	24	6	30
Tamenglong	4	0	4	22	0	22
Churachandpur	8	1	9	29	39	68
Chandel	2	0	2	12	0	12
Ukhrul	3	0	3	12	0	12
Imphal West	24	0	24	124	0	124
Imphal East	29	5	34	236	31	267
Bishnupur	5	2	7	48	16	64
Thoubal	20	1	21	250	13	263
All Manipur	**101**	**12**	**113**	**757**	**105**	**862**

Source: Government of Manipur. 2008. *Economic Survey, Manipur 2007–08*. Imphal: Directorate of Economics & Statistics. 114.

Despite the introduction of the concept of District Industries Centre (DIC) as a developmental concept in pursuance of the Industrial Policy Resolutions of the Government of India adopted in 1977, no tangible improvement has occurred in Manipur. In fact, we find a regression in the total number of manufacturing units as compared to previous years as stated above.

Harnessing Opportunity: Case of Jiribam

While efforts should be made to set up larger number of manufacturing units in all districts of Manipur, immediate attention must be given to Jiribam. We remember Jiribam or the Jiri road only when the National Highway 39 is under siege or as the place where the last remaining members of Revolutionary Government of Manipur were arrested in 1971. Since time immemorial, Jiribam had been a place of strategic importance for Manipur. The kind of complex body politic prevailing in Manipur and neighbouring States reconfirms this historical fact and reminds us that the place cannot simply be neglected. Located at the border with Assam, it is the western gateway of Manipur adjoining Cachar District of Assam. It is approximately 80 km from Silchar, Assam. Moreover, available agro-climatic conditions and located at a buffer zone between two natural resources rich districts such as Tamenglong and Churachandpur make it conducive for undertaking horticulture and agro-related ventures therein. The demographic composition of the sub-division in terms of plurality is an added advantage for trade.

Historical Significance

Before the construction of National Highway 39 (Imphal-Dimapur) during the Second World War, the historic Tonjei Maril road, which passed through Jiribam from Imphal connected Manipur with the Western world. With the construction of the Old Cachar road (National Highway 53) by the British Government shortly after the Burmese War, it became the most important road before the British occupation of Manipur, leading from the Manipur territory (passing through Jiribam) to the British province of Cachar. The British maintained the road until 1865 after which the maintenance was done by the Manipuri kings.

Manipuris used this road for trade with the western world, pilgrimage to mainland India as well as a means to flee to Assam or Tripura during Burmese invasions. Jiribam's strategic and commercial importance can be garnered from the fact that earlier to British occupation of Manipur, all imports and exports of goods by Manipur took place through Jirighat.

However, with the kind of frontier politics shaped by the British in the form of construction of a new highway, for war convenience, the strategic relevance of Jiribam and Tonjei Maril was relegated to the background. After 1891, the cart road from Imphal to Dimapur gained more prominence with the extension of Assam-Bengal Railway till Dimapur. With this came a slow down in human interface between the two valleys (Imphal valley and Jiribam valley). Myths replaced reality and Jiri people were believed to be master magicians in popular Manipuri psyche. Nonetheless, Jirighat was preserved as a strategic location by the British and in the year 1909–10, Jiribam Police Station was opened on the Cachar border to prevent export of cattle and smuggling, and as check post to collect tax from traders and pilgrims.

During the second decade of the British rule, Manipur saw a quantum increase in its cross-border trade by the second decade of British rule (see Table 11.8).

The increase in import was well corresponded by the rise in export volume and as such, Manipur enjoyed positive trade balance

Table 11.8 : Import and Export of Goods through Jirighat and Mao Gate during the Second Phase of the British Rule in Manipur.

(*in Rupees*)

Year	*Import*			*Export*			*Balance of trade*
	Jirighat	*Mao Gate*	*Total*	*Jirighat*	*Mao Gate*	*Total*	
1901-02	121,608	68,988	190,596	121,985	120,822	242,807	52,211
1902-03	89,825	122,185	212,010	112,228	78,257	190,485	(-) 21,525
1903-04	100,271	246,064	346,335	25,730	136,817	162,547	(-) 183,788
1904-05	128,416	121,064	249,480	95,154	95,183	190,337	(-) 59,143
1905-06	93,998	116,029	210,027	164,422	138,637	303,059	93,032
1906-07	87,535	257,405	344,940	541,891	264,422	806,313	461,373

Source: Cited in Laishram Churchill. 2007. Manipur's Economy: Trajectory and transformation before and during the British period. *Alternative Perspectives* l. II, Issue IV. July–September: 13.

in most of the financial years. In terms of the volume of goods that passed through Jirighat and Mao Gate, we notice that there was reduction in import through Jirighat although some volume of exports occurred through this route. With the departure of the British, the significance of Jirighat was lost in antiquity except for minor contribution which is conditioned by happenings on the Imphal-Dimapur road.

Demographic Profile and Available Resources

Jiribam sub-division is spread over an area of 387 sq. km and has close to 70 small villages. As per the Census Report of 2001, Jiribam had a population of 37,792 (Urban and Rural). Males constitute 49 per cent of the total population and females account 51 per cent of the population. In Jiribam, 13 per cent of the population is less than six years of age. The average literacy rate is 73 per cent, which is higher than the national average literacy rate, which is 59.5 per cent. Out of it the male literacy rate is 80 per cent, and female literacy rate is 66 per cent. On the one hand, the sub-division is blessed with educated youths but unemployment which is a regular feature in the State remains a bane for the people of Jiribam.

Table 11.9 presents an indicative demographic profile of select wards in Jiribam for the year 2001. Majority of the population in the Jiribam valley are Vaishnavite Hindus comprising of Meetei and Bishnupriya Meetei. Hindu constitute more than 60 per cent of the total population. This is followed by Christian (18%), Muslim (12%) and Meitei Sanamahi (7%).

Jiribam is interlocked by hills and plains and is suited for agricultural, horticultural and forestry activities. The climate is warm and moist and Jiribam is rich in forest resources like timber, cane, tea, acrecanut, coconut, rubber, bamboos, brooms, etc. including a host of plants having medicinal values. Of the two tourist places identified in Imphal East, Jiribam is one, the other being Kaina. Thus, tourism also has a potential in this sub-division.

With the assignment of the administrative work of the sub-division, there was rapid immigration of the Government and semi-Government official in the town. With the development of transport and communication facilities in the region and their direct link with the town, Jiribam became a growth centre of its

Table 11.9 : Demographic Profile of Select Wards in Jiribam for the Year 2001

Ward no.	Hindu	Meitei Sanamahi	Muslim	Christian	Others	No. of households	Ward Population
1	2	3	4	5	6	7	8
1.	82	5	0	60	13	160	901
2.	122	17	1	37	1	178	917
3.	120	9	1	3	0	133	716
4.	91	8	4	4	0	107	474
5.	83	20	15	8	0	126	592
6.	69	3	52	10	0	134	737
7.	75	8	73	97	0	253	1,320
8.	124	14	0	24	0	162	846
9.	34	6	21	6	0	67	353
10.	78	7	1	0	0	86	401
Total	**878**	**97**	**168**	**249**	**14**	**1406**	**7257**
(%)	**62.45**	**6.90**	**11.95**	**17.71**	**1.00**	**–**	**–**

Source: Government of India. 2001. *Census of India*. New Delhi: Registrar General and Census Commissioner.

vast inter-State hinterland. With more than 725 of the working population engaged in the non-agricultural pursuits, Jiribam has dual characteristics; administrative and as trade centre.

Economy, Trade and Commerce

Industrially, Jiribam as a whole is a backward sub-division. There is not even a medium size industry in the whole of the sub-division. In 1985 Government of Manipur established an industrial complex at Kadamtala covering an area of 15 acres of land, which is supposed to boost the industrial development in the region.

Jiribam town has been known for its commercial activities since its inception. The Jiri Bazaar is well-known during the British period also. There are two bi-weekly market at Jiribam, one at Jiri Bazar and another at Gularthol. Inspite of its historical role as the centre of trade and commerce. Jiribam lacks basic facilities for commercial activities. Most of the shop buildings are kutcha and semi-pucca by nature. The markets are outgrown without plan and do not have basic amenities. A Market complex under the Ten per cent year marked fund for North East is nearing completion at the heart of the town.

According to the socio-economic survey conducted by Jiribam Municipality Council in 2006, there are about 609 shops and 775 vendors establishment in the town. The commodities dealt by these shops are grocery, hardware, stationeries, clothing, medicines, machinery spare parts, motor parts, electrical goods, construction materials, etc. These commodities are mainly brougnt from Silchar which is only 45 km from the town.

Reviving Industries in Jiribam

The failure of major industrial projects in Jiribam was on account of mismanagement and inefficiency on the part of the administrators. There cannot be any blame on non-availability of raw materials. The Manipur Government took up the construction of the tea factory at Jiribam Tea Estate with an annual production capacity of 300,000 kg of processed tea in 1996. Construction work on this project, with an estimated cost approximately Rs. 206 lakhs, started during the year 1996. The Manipur Plantation Crops Corporation took up the construction of tea factory at Jiribam based Manipur Tea Estate on a turnkey basis in three phases to produce around 300,000 kg of finished tea in the first phase, 600,000 kg in second phase and 1,000,000 kg of finished product per annum in the final phase when 425 hectares were fully brought under plantation. On completion of the construction the corporation incurred an expenditure of Rs. 178 lakhs. The factory also targeted to meet 26 per cent of the State's demand for tea in Manipur.

But soon after the commissioning of the factory, contrary to the targeted production and profit, the income generated by the factory could not meet the salaries of the employees and maintenance far exceeded the income of the tea estate. The annual deficit worked out to be about Rs. 50.72 lakhs. Since 2000-01 the Manipur Government declared that the estate had not been able to generate any income and government considered privatization of the estate (*The Sangai Express,* July 21, 2008). But till date the government has not taken any decision in this regard. The government has decided to revive the factory again and after reviving the same, whether it will be privatized or will be run by the government remains undecided as of now.

Investment Prospects in Jiribam

Manipur's industrial policy paper proposed eleven projects where there can be investment. Proposed projects include fruits and vegetables processing, ginger dehydration and oleoresin, spices processing plant, integrated mushroom processing plant, lime ginger plant, agri-export zone for passion fruit, Manipuri traditional liquor plant (distillery), integrated pineapple concentration plant, floriculture and custom farming (Government of Manipur, 2002). In this regard, Jiribam can take advantage in fruits and vegetables processing, ginger plant and, agro-export zone for passion fruit. Moreover, Jiribam can also enter into bamboo and allied industries. Table 11.10 shows the area under bamboo cultivation in Manipur.

Since, more than 65 per cent of bamboos are produced in Nungba, Tipaimukh, Jiribam and Tamenglong, from the logistic point of view, a bamboo and allied processing centre can be created in Jiribam. Traditionally, Barak River and Tuivah River are used as means for transporting bamboo, timber, ginger and so on up to upper Assam. The same can be encouraged and a processing centre can be set up at Jiribam. This can lead to commercial utilization of bamboo and bamboo shoots.

Table 11.10 : Area under Bamboo Plantation, Quantity and Annual Yield: 2007–08

Name of block	*Geographical area (sq. km)*	*Total bamboo area (sq. km)*	*Qty. of bamboo (in lakh MT)*	*Annual yield calculated on growing stick (in lakh MT)*
Thanlon	1238.4	387	10.14	1.69
Henglep	637.26	206.08	4.63	0.77
Nungba	1465.44	278.14	13.89	2.28
Tipaimukh	789.48	278.64	7.92	1.32
Jiribam	309.6	36.12	0.7	0.12
Tamenglong	1083.6	283.8	5.09	0.85
Total	**5523.78**	**1470.28**	**42.37**	**7.03**

Source: Government of Manipur. 2008. *Annual Administrative Report: 2006-07*. Imphal: Forest Department. 26.

Jiribam as a Full-fledged Revenue District

Most of the opportunities that lay in front of Jiribam can be realised only when the sub-division is converted into a full-fledged revenue district. A decision was taken in early 2008 by the Manipur Government to upgrade Jiribam as a full-fledged revenue district. This has been an inspiration for the locals. However, before the upgradation, the sub-division needs to have adequate infrastructure in place. The government is keen to upgrade Public Health Engineering Department sub-division, Jiribam, as a full division. In addition to various development projects being taken up in the sub-division, various other projects, including an Industrial Training Institute (Rs. 450 lakhs), a government housing complex, a city park, permanent helipad, and inter-State bus terminus are also to come up in Jiribam. The present government has also earmarked Rs. 1,000 lakhs for construction of Police Training Centre at Jiribam and Rs. 1,000 lakhs for construction of Rehabilitation Centre at Jiribam (*The Sangai Express,* July 21, 2008).

Jiribam's importance to the State will only increase in the future by virtue of its being the rail-head and an important trading point. Further significance will emerge once the Jiribam-Tupul and Tupul to Imphal rail link project, which is estimated to cost some Rs. 2,000 crore. The Jiribam-Tupul section is expected to be completed by the year 2012. Connectivity with Tipaimukh will be enhanced once Development of North Eastern Region project under Roads and Bridges Sector for Improvement of Jiri-Tipaimukh Road from 8 km to 48 km at an estimated cost of Rs. 18.56 crores is completed on time (*The Sangai Express,* July 21, 2008).

To facilitate convenient trading, a supermarket complex is being constructed at Jiri Bazar. The complex, work on which is being undertaken by the National Building Construction Company as implementing agency is nearly complete.

Present planned development works include; construction of a guest house at Jiribam proper, a bus terminus at Chandrapur, a railway point at Gularthol, the proposed Indian Reserve Battalion Headquarters at Yairolpokpi, and the proposed police training sub-centre. Upcoming projects include a 50-bedded hospital coming up at Ningsingkhun (Rs. 15.64 crores), sports complex at

Bidyanagar, and the ADC complex/mini secretariat now under construction at the Jiribam Headquarters.

Conclusion

There has to be reciprocity between "intention" of development and local needs. Much of the disillusionment with development policies in Manipur have been "development" getting misfired on account of development of parasitic sections of people within Manipur and lack of political will to sincerely implement any of the policies. Choosing an alternative paradigm of development becomes problematic as the State has not really tasted the fruit of success or evaluates the missing components as administrative lapses and politicization have been main source of discontent. Therefore, there is a need to give due cognizance to the centrality of meaningful utilization of land (agricultural). An alternative perspective on development in the State should foreground that fact that land is a primary asset for societies which conventionally thrive on agriculture. In this regard, we have analysed two relevant land policies which impinge upon utilization of land. Further, there is a need to make public total area of *Khas* land that have been converted into agricultural land or work towards conversion of more of similar land.

The anchoring point of policies on development in Manipur should be based on decentralization of development with sufficient attention to participation, specificity of culture(s), equity and durability. Implementation should also be through democratic means. In addition, development projects should not alter or displace the irreversible relationship between the cultural moorings of a specific society and their needs, and their dependence on natural resources. For these societies are capable of effecting substantial understanding and knowledge about resource management and draw "local" trajectories of development. With the making of development projects work at such a plank some of the immediate frameworks should be brought back as a major rationale of development discourse.

Corollary efforts must be undertaken for effective setting up of manufacturing units in districts of Manipur taking into cognizance availability of raw material, logistic viability and so on. Illustration on Jiribam is reference to indicate the opportunity it promises and as a means to divert misutilization of land as well as increasing pressure on land in the greater Imphal valley. The foregrounding of sustainable grassroot developmental economics is an urgency to stop and reduce pressure on arable land and fragmentation of the same. In the recent past the stubbornness on the part of the State to surpass these concerns has only resulted in stronger binaries. This binary is manifested in the form of sweeping neo-liberal economic pursuit, on the one hand, and people's resistance movements, on the other hand. Put simply, any serious look out for an alternative politics of an alternative economics should be acquiescent to issues at grassroot and, therefore, sufficiently democratise the perspective of economic development.

NOTES

1. *Manipur Land Revenue and Land Reforms Act 1960* states, "Diversion" (in this section) means using land assessed to one purpose for any other purpose, but using land for the purpose of agriculture where it is assessed with reference to any other purpose shall not be deemed to be diversion.
2. See John S. Mill, *Autobiography,* London: Penguin Books, 1989, p. 150, where the acknowledgement in respect to decentralization is explicit.
3. The complete sentence reads, "In an earlier part of this enquiry, I have dwelt in strong language – hardly any language is strong enough to express the strength of my conviction – on the importance of the portion of the operation of free (local) institutions, which may be called the public education of the citizens". From 'Considerations on Representative Government', *Mill on Liberty and Other Essays,* ed. John Gray, Oxford: Oxford University Press, 1991, p. 412.
4. "Constitutional powers" need not necessarily be explicitly entrenched in a written constitution. The term refers to all forms of authority that confer the right to design and implement policies in any particular domain.
5. That coordination can play that role, and that it is costly, was first modelled by Albert Breton and Anthony Scott (*The Economic Constitution of Federal States,* Toronto: University of Toronto Press, 1978).

CITED WORKS

Becker, S. Gary and Murphy, M. Kevin. 1992. The division of labour, coordination costs, and knowledge. *Quarterly Journal of Economics* 107. November: 1137–160.

Breton, Albert and Scott, Anthony. 1978. *The Economic Constitution of Federal States.* Toronto: University of Toronto Press.

Breton, Albert. 2000. Federalism and decentralization: Ownership rights and the superiority of federalism. *Publius* 30, 2. Spring: 1–16.

Churchill, Laishram. 2006. Environment, development and social challenges: Scrutinising India's Look East Policy in Manipur. *Alternative Frames* I, III. April–June: 30–46.

Churchill, Laishram. 2007. Manipur's economy: Trajectory and transformation before and during the British period. *Alternative Perspectives* l. II, Issue IV. July–September: 13.

Cowen, M.P and Shenton, R.W. 2005. *Doctrines of Development.* London and New York: Routledge.

Government of Manipur. 2002. *Investment Potential in Manipur.* North East Business Summit, Mumbai. Imphal: Department of Commerce and Industries.

Government of Manipur. 2008. *Manipur Gazette* 309. December 1: i–xxiv.

Institute for Human Development. 2006. *Manipur Development Report.* New Delhi: Planning Commission.

Kishan, Thingam. 2006. Economics of underdevelopment: Reading the Northeast. *Alternative Perspectives* II, I, October–December: 55—68.

Mill, John S. 1989. *Autobiography.* London: Penguin Books.

Mill, John S. 1991. Considerations on representative government. In *Mill on Liberty and Other Essays,* edited by John Gray. Oxford: Oxford University Press.

Sachdeva, Gulshan. 2000. *Economy of the North-East: Policy, Present Conditions and Future Possibilities.* New Delhi: Konark.

Seabright, Paul. 1996. Accountability and decentralization in Government: An incomplete contracts model. *European Economic Review* 40. January: 61–89.

Shukla, S.P. 1997, *Transforming the Northeast.* New Delhi: High Level Commission Report to the Prime Minister.

Singh, Ch. Priyoranjan. 2005. Manipur's economy: Historical roots and structural evolution. *Eastern Quarterly* 3, III. October–December: 149–60.

Singh, N. Manichandra. 2007. Foodgrain economy and food security in Manipur. *Alternative Perspectives* III, I. October–December: 4–29.

Thaindian. 2008. Avoid use of agricultural land for SEZs: Moily Panel. March 18. <http://www.thaindian.com/newsportal/business/avoid-use-of-agricultural-land-for-sezs-moily-panel_10028473. html>

Tiebout, Charles M. 1956. A pure theory of local expenditure. *Journal of Political Economy* 64. October: 416–24.

Tocqueville, Alexis de. 1969. *Democracy in America.* Trans. George Lawrence. New York: Doubleday Anchor.

Waiton Mamang Chingarel Loukol Kanba Lup. 2008. *Paojel.* August 10.

Web India. 2007. "Review SEZ policy to make it farmer friendly: Standing Committee". Friday, July 6. New Delhi. <http://news.webindia123.com>

12

Contesting Statist Version of Underdevelopment: Development and Conflict

Sanatomba Kangujam

Development discourse in Manipur more or less seems to follow the statist trajectory, which persistently tends to attribute the present state of underdevelopment to the existing conflict situation. Apparently perceived as a law and order problem, insurgency movements being launched by different shades of armed groups have been cited as the determining factor for the prevailing economic stagnation and underdevelopment in the State of Manipur and North East Region. Those at the helm of power have repeatedly stated in the mass media that development works in the State of Manipur are being derailed due to the rising spade of insurgent activities. A plethora of mainstream political leaders and intellectuals too always have held insurgency as the root cause of economic underdevelopment in the North East (Kumar, 2005, 129). Almost every case of economic underdevelopment—whether infrastructural backwardness, shortage of capital investment, stagnation in the tourism sector, lack of industrialization, trading bottlenecks or misappropriation of the plan money allocated by the Central Government—has been ascribed to insurgency.

The statist position holds 'law and order' problem solely responsible for the existing economic underdevelopment that Manipur is experiencing. It, however, becomes highly crucial to interrogate into the actual realities that form the basis of understanding of underdevelopment as predominantly caused by the prevailing conflict situation. Few questions are, therefore, being raised in order to unravel the truth concerning the insurgency and 'law and order' as main plank causing underdevelopment in Manipur. Does insurgency really hinder economic development or does it serve as a mere pretext for prolonging underdevelopment? Is development not possible in the presence of conflict? Would there be rapid economic development in Manipur had there been no insurgency? These are few questions that this essay attempts to answer in the subsequent pages for a clear understanding of (under) development debate in Manipur.

Ever since the end of the Second World War, countries across the world have witnessed different forms of conflict unprecedented in scale and numbers, though in most cases intra-State in nature. In a world predominantly characterised by scarcity of resources, unequal power relationship, incompatibility of interests, growing elite competition, absence of proper governance, preponderance of national powers and prevalence of exploitative social systems or repressive political regimes, one can only admit that conflict has been a norm rather than an exception.

However, one may wonder why development takes place in many parts of the world in spite of the existence of conflict situation. This can be partly explained by the fact that conflict is not an anathema to development or change, as it is generally perceived. The view that development has been stalled due to the existence of conflict (read insurgency in the case of Manipur) is grounded on the false premise that conflict and development are two antagonistic occurrences. Many people seem to overlook or inadvertently ignore the functional aspect of conflict in their obsession with the elusive notion of peace, which in reality is a mere utopia. Changes take place in society because of the conflict inherent in the social structure. Historical evolution of human society towards a higher socio-economic and political order manifests the role of conflict as catalyst for change.

Insurgency : An Instrument of (Under) Development?

A keen observation of insurgency movements in Manipur and their impacts on the overall development scenario in the State reveals an astounding picture that contradicts the claims made by the State. The frequent evocation of 'law and order' by State as a pre-condition for ensuring economic development is a mere strategy to absolve itself from the obligation of securing an all-round development to the people. The post-1949 political evolution and historical facts contradict the argument that insurgency is solely responsible for underdevelopment in Manipur. Ascribing the underdevelopment in Manipur and other States of North East Region to insurgency is tantamount to a diversionary tactics of overlooking the various factors responsible for (under) development. History stands as a living testimony on this count.

It can be argued that till mid-1970s, armed-insurgency was literally non-existent in Manipur despite the formation of Meitei State Committee (MSC) and the United National Liberation Front (UNLF) in the early Sixties as the activities of the former (MSC) were virtually nipped in the bud while the latter (UNLF) remained in a low profile directing its focus and activities mainly on building its organizational networks and social mobilization. After the aborted communist revolution of the Manipur Communist Party (MCP) led by Hijam Irabot from 1949-51, there existed in Manipur a relatively peaceful environment. Although, statehood movement could be witnessed during the said period, organized armed struggle was nowhere to be seen in the State. The period under consideration was quite conducive for any sort of development to take place. But what had taken place in Manipur in the period before 1975 did not demonstrate any substantive economic development. Leave aside any progress in terms of industrialization or any other sectoral achievement in Manipur; the Government of India (hereafter GoI) had failed to provide even the basic amenities such as electrification, basic health care system and water supply to the people of Manipur. Unfortunately, most part of interior of the hills and plain still remains deprived of basic facilities that constitute the defining criteria of the modern civilization.

Unlike Nagaland and Mizoram where guerilla armed movements became the order of the day, Manipur otherwise presented quite a different picture in the 1960s and the early 1970's where relatively peaceful environment prevailed. In spite of the relatively suitable environment for development initiative in the State, Manipur like most States in the North East Region was ignored by the Central Government for quite a long time.

The sum total of central funding, which Manipur received as a price of becoming a part of the Union up to the Fifth Five Year Plan did not reach Rs.300 crores margin (Datta, 1995, 299). Anyone can imagine as to how development could take place with such a meagre amount of central assistance. It was the time when Green Revolution had been taking place in Northern India with active and unstinted patronage from the Central Government. If development could be brought about in other parts of India, why could the same not happen in Manipur? Was it due to insurgency? It was not only in Manipur that the development failed to take place during these relative years of stability, the case of Assam also present a striking paradox of underdevelopment amidst the rich natural resources. The political situation in Assam until the late 1970s of the twentieth century was remarkably stable and provides suitable atmosphere for development to take place. In spite of such favourable conditions the per capita income of Assam *vis-à-vis* that of all India average had been not only declining but also widening. A look at Table 12.1 unveils the truth of the argument.

Table 12.1 : Per Capita Income of Assam and India at Constant (1980-81) Prices

(In Rupees)

Year	*Assam*	*India*	*Gap of Policies of Assam in Comparison with all India*
1950-51	1,173	1,127	(+) 46
1960-61	1,140	1,350	(–) 210
1970-71	1,221	1,520	(–) 299
1980-81	1,284	1,630	(–) 346
1990-91	1,544	2,222	(–) 678
1994-95	1,602	2,449	(–) 847

Source: Pukhon Girin, 2003. Ethicisation of Politics in North East India, New Delhi: South Asian Publishers: 29

This gap of per capita income is also visible between North Eastern States and some other developed States of the country. Imbalanced regional development of India's economy over the year is responsible for wide inter-State variations in the level of per capita income (Girin, 2003, 29). Although, Assam is the most resource rich in the North East, development failed to take root in the State as well. Besides, the political situation in Assam was relatively stable and calm prior to the launching of intense political movement against the 'foreigners' by All Assam Students Union and Axom Xahitya Xobha. The six years between 1979 and 1985 were the years of the 'Assam movement' – a campaign protesting what was alleged to be a *de facto* Indian Government policy of admitting and enfranchising 'foreigners' (Baruah, 2008, 115). The failures of the subsequent government including that of AGP to resolve the issue of immigrations created a fear psychosis among the Assamese population of losing their identity, land and economy to the foreign immigrants.

The origin of United Liberation Front of Assam (now Asom) and its intensive armed struggle for the 'sovereignty' of Asom is widely believed to be an offshoot of the anti-foreigners movement (Baruah, 2008, 115–43). Lack of development in Assam and Manipur during the period preceding the start of intensive armed propaganda by the insurgent outfits in both the States posit a critical question mark upon the fundamental premise of statist logic of underdevelopment as a result of insurgency problem in the State. The GoI owes an explanation to the people of Manipur regarding why development fails to take place during the period prior to the emergence of insurgency. Flaw in the premise becomes clearer if one studies the case of Assam having valuable natural resources such as tea, timber, natural gas, petroleum and fertile agricultural land. In spite of the presence of huge resource base any meaningful development rather than a few glittering centre with tall buildings and shopping centre in the city cannot be witnessed.

The correlation between underdevelopment and emergence of insurgency or law and order problem (as government claims it) is again not convincing if one looks at the number of factories that the States of Nagaland, Tripura, Meghalaya and Manipur have. It is a widely known fact that the State of Nagaland suffered the first spell of armed propaganda under the banner of Naga National Council, Tripura also witnessed the emergence of insurgent outfit in 1980's and unlike the three States that have been witnessing the issue of insurgency and its concomitant consequences, the State of Meghalaya have been experiencing relatively peaceful atmosphere. But according to the Annual Survey of Industries, 2004-05, Tripura has 275 factories, Nagaland has 113 factories, Meghalaya has 58 factories and Manipur has 55 factories (CSO, 2004–05. *Annual Survey of Industries, Factory Sector*).

The given data indicates the marked difference in terms of the number of factories between the two States of Tripura and Nagaland reeling under the spell of insurgency that far surpassed

Meghalaya and Manipur. There is no denying the fact that Meghalaya is one of the most developed States in the North East region due to plethora of factors. However, the case of Tripura and Nagaland is suffice to drive home the point that industrialization could take place to a certain extent despite the existence of phenomena of insurgency if there is stable government having systematic, well structured policy, a will to development on the part of ruling political class and relatively clean, efficient and transparent implementing agencies and administration; which are conspicuous by their absence in Manipur.

The process of industrialization in Manipur during those years of relatively stable social environment was virtually non-existent, it was only after the post-statehood period that a modest attempt to establish small and medium scale industries was embarked upon. Direct government participation in the process of industrialization in the State began with the incorporation of the Manipur Spinning Mills in 1974. It started its commercial production in 1980. The Manipur Small Industries Corporation was set up in 1969 for facilitating the growth of industries in the State and the corporation was finally upgraded to Manipur Industrial Development Corporation Limited (MANIDCO) in 1987. In order to facilitate the production and marketing of handloom and handicraft products in the State the Government of Manipur set up the Manipur Handloom and Handicrafts Development Corporation Limited in 1976 (Meetei, 2007:39–40). Besides the effort for industrialization in the State with commencement of Five Years Plan in India was very slow and meagre during the first-three Five Year Plans. The shares of the industrial sector in the total plan expenditure during these three plans were only to the tune of 0.66 per cent, 0.02 per cent and 1.49 per cent respectively (Meetei, 2007, 40–1). Moreover, total plan expenditures in the State during the First Fifth Five Years Plan were far too short for any kind of development activities to put them into proper trajectory.

Table 12.2 shows the total plan allocation during the First Fifth Five Years Plan in Manipur.

That the people of Manipur had been able to strike a rich bargain *vis-à-vis* the Central Government through the politics of insurgency was aptly demonstrated by the conferment of statehood to Manipur and subsequent fiscal treatment meted out to it.

Table 12.2 : Total Plan Expenditures in Manipur during the First Fifth Five Years Plan

Plan	*Total expenditure (Rs. Lakhs)*
First Plan (1951-56)	102.56
Second Plan (1956-61)	596.93
Third Plan (1961-66)	1281.28
Annual Plans (1966-69)	719.89
Fourth Plan (1969-74)	3100.00
Fifth Plan (1974-78)	6661.91

Source: Government of Manipur. Various issues. *Statistical Abstract of Manipur* Imphal: Directorate of Economics and Statistics.

Following the unceremonious merger or alleged annexation of Manipur to the Dominion of India in 1949, the status of a sovereign entity with two thousand years of historical existence was disgracefully relegated to a Part-C State and rein of Manipur administration was assigned to a Chief Commissioner for quite some time. Consequently, people launched a series of sustained democratic agitations demanding a responsible government and complete statehood for Manipur. The response of the Indian Government to the voice of Manipur people fell far short of the aspiration of the masses. In the midst of this political current, the irony of history once again got enacted when the injured pride of the Manipuri people was further made to experience another insult when the Indian Parliament passed the 23rd Amendment Act in 1963 for granting of statehood to Nagaland by amalgamating Naga Hills District and the Tuensang Frontier Tract, which earlier remained as Excluded and Partially Excluded Areas. The conferment of statehood to Nagaland was, no doubt, hastened by the Chinese aggression of 1962 which generated widespread security concerns in the Eastern front.

Nonetheless, the inauguration of Nagaland State was executed consciously as a political concession to Naga armed insurgency that threatened the internal security of the nascent India beyond expectation. It was primarily designed to marginalize the Naga National Council (NNC) from the masses into submission while simultaneously strengthening the integrationist elements as represented by the Naga moderates. It is worthnoting that the granting of statehood to Nagaland was a deviation from the principle of States reorganization on the basis of economic viability.

Of course, national security became more paramount than economic viability in those particular circumstances. But GoI failed to realise that it had committed a great political blunder in 1963 and for that it had to pay a heavy price in the years that followed. It led to proliferation of insurgency in the North East.

Right after the attainment of statehood by Nagaland, an insurgent group known as the United National Liberation Front (UNLF) emerged in 1964 with the objective to restore the lost sovereignty of Manipur. The formation of UNLF marked the culmination of people's desire for a higher political status. Meanwhile, the radical elements within the UNLF split away to form the Revolutionary Government of Manipur (RGM) to launch an armed campaign against the GoI and they went as far as East Pakistan (now Bangladesh) to get training and elicit foreign support and arms. It, however, proved abortive (Tarapot, 1993, 40–61). The rest is history, but the subversive activities of the nascent insurgent groups prompted the GoI to confer complete statehood to Manipur as a pre-emptive measure to prevent escalation of armed violence in Manipur. In fact, it is hard to imagine whether the Central Government would have granted statehood to Manipur in 1972 in the absence of insurgent activities in the 1960s.

From this perspective, insurgency serves as an instrument for ushering political and economic development in the State. It was only when the guns began to boom in Manipur in the mid-1970s that budgetary allocation for the State steadily increased. The huge increased in the Plan expenditures towards the State coincided with the steady rise in the activities of armed opposition groups or insurgent outfits in Manipur. The point of the argument can be substantiated from Table 12.3.

Table 12.3 : Plan Expenditure in Manipur from the Sixth Five-Year Plan onwards

Plan	*Total expenditure (Rs. Lakhs)*
Sixth Plan (1980-85)	24,312.32
Seventh Plan (1985-90)	51,732.77
Eighth Plan (1992-97)	122,450.97
Ninth Plan (1997-02)	184,865.10

Source: Government of Manipur. Various issues. *Statistical Abstract of Manipur*. Imphal: Directorate of Economic & Statistics.

Otherwise, it seems to be speculative that Manipur would not have been receiving a significant amount of central funding had there been no armed movements. Manipur badly needs substantial amount of central assistance for development to take place. But, New Delhi would never lend an ear to the democratic voice of the people unless compelled it to do under certain conditions. Central Government's insensitive attitude and non-responsiveness to democratic appeals leaves the people with no other options but to resort to the politics of insurgency. Nowadays, Manipur is receiving a good amount of financial assistance from the Centre as a price for waging armed movements. However, it remains to be clarified that pumping of crores of rupees itself is not development *per se*, but is certainly a means to attain it. If this is the case, there is no logic in claiming that conflict in Manipur, which takes the form of insurgency, is detrimental to development.

Anyone with a clear understanding of political economy of insurgency will certainly agree that the rise of insurgency has generated employment on a large scale. The last ten years or so have witnessed recruitment of a number of youths into police, army and paramilitary forces for counter insurgency operations. The only fear associated with this trend is that our society seems to be drifting towards a military economy. Insurgency, nevertheless, has proved to be an effective institutional factor for ensuring an equitable distribution of wealth in the society by effecting redistribution of the same. There was concentration of wealth only among the bureaucrats, white-collared professionals, businessmen, ministers and their henchmen in the earlier period. But of late, a new middle class is emerging as a social consequence of the ongoing insurgency movements and this is going to play a great role in shaping the future course of historical events.

Politics of Legitimization : A Case in Tourism Sector

Tourism is an important sector, where the notion of law and order figures prominently. It is needless to elaborate the potential of tourism in the State within the scope of this write-up as there is obviously no disagreement on this count. The crux of the issue, however, lies in the question pertaining to why this particular sector remains underdeveloped in spite of its vast potentials. The official explanation forwarded by the Government points to the fluidity of the law and order situation prevailing in Manipur. Outsiders are said to be constantly prevented from coming to Manipur by the apprehension of being kidnapped by the insurgents or by the fear of being caught up in the crossfire. Such a claim made by the State seems apparently true, but a deeper observation would reveal otherwise.

Foreigners have not ceased to visit Kashmir on account of the deepening crisis besetting the Northern State nor have any significant changes taken place in Mumbai tourism sector following the recent terrorist strikes.

Failure to introduce any significant development strategies in tourism sector is often sought to be legitimised on security ground. The Government cannot ensure security to foreigners and as such, it became imperative on the part of the Government to enact and enforce various Acts like the Protected Area Permit Act and the Restricted Area Permit Act, which discourage the entry of foreign tourists in the State. Here, one simply wonders how development in tourism could take place while legally preventing foreigners to enter Manipur.

One important reason, which is implicit in denying entry to outsiders, has been the policy of the Central Government to wrap up the armed conflict occurring here from the gaze of international community. The GoI is understandably trying its best to prevent any leakage of information relating to violation of Human Rights by the Indian Army and Paramilitary forces to the international media and Human Rights watchdogs. Otherwise, it would naturally come to the notice of the world that a hidden war is going on in Manipur and thereby cases relating to violation of human rights will be exposed to the world. In such a situation, the armed resistance groups will find it much easier to garner international support and launch aggressive propaganda against India, by taking advantage of the presence of foreigners in their midst. But, that will certainly cause embarrassment to the GoI, which as a matter of policy seeks to portray the existing armed conflict as mere internal law and order problem. In this context, one question worth asking is, why does not the GoI open up the region or the State to the international tourists and media and say that those people are terrorists who deserve to be treated as such? In that case, the GoI can even elicit international support to suppress the insurgent people of resurgent Manipur. But the GoI dare not do it. May be, because, the so called Militants/insurgents do have a legitimate cause.

The concerns that the GoI demonstrated for developing tourism in Manipur becomes quite obvious if one pays a visit to the famous 'Sendra', a tourist spot in the vicinity of Loktak Lake. The Indian Security Forces have been occupying the spot for quite a few years thereby inflicting serious blow to the development of tourism in Manipur. It not only incurred heavy loss of revenue for the State, but also deprived the people of their favourite pasttime. People feel psychologically seized at the occupation of an important tourist spot by the Security Forces and this is not unfounded. It is told that a few people including students who dared to venture out to visit 'Sendra' were ruthlessly turned away by those occupying the spot. One is compelled to ask why security post cannot be opened elsewhere other than the Sendra if such an arrangement is felt highly essential. But, the Government seems to do it consciously with a view to make the presence of coercive authority felt at the heart of the masses. If not, there is no plausible reason why an important tourist spot should be occupied forcibly. And ultimately, tourism sector remains politically victimised under the pretext of law and order problem.

Law and Order : Institutionalizing Class Domination

In the present juncture, insurgency has turned out to be a 'political dustbin' in as much as every ill of the society is generally attributed to it. Insurgents or those donning the mask of an insurgent or a revolutionary are always branded as extortionists. Any 'demand note' served on Government Departments, individuals or any institutions have to be entertained graciously. Failure to do it would certainly invite the wrath of those serving the demand note and this may range from firing of shots or lobbying of grenades at the residence of the concerned to kidnapping and abduction. This is a fact and nobody can deny it. But is the Government free from the same charge? The charge is that the Government, too, indulges in 'official extortion'. This may sound rather harsh for outsiders but for a native, this is an everyday experience. The present SPF Government of Manipur has become almost synonymous with a certain rate of 'Percentage Cut' for deducting a certain portion from the total amount of every scheme or work programme being implemented or executed (*The Sangai Express*, January 8, 2009).

Allocation of central funds hardly percolated down the poor masses. The Public Distribution System (PDS) in Manipur is a total failure not necessarily on account of interference from the insurgents, but rather due to institutionalised political corruption. Majority of the localities and villages in Manipur seldom get the facility of PDS. Few people in connivance with top bureaucrats and Ministers are robbing the masses through the back doors. It is also worthy of stating that a few steps towards industrialization were initiated in the past. In this regard, mention may be made of the Khandsari Sugar Factory, Loitang Khunou Spinning Mill and Hundung Cement Factory. All have failed miserably and the reason behind their failure was neither due to the existing law and order problem nor due to interference from insurgent outfits. It was purely a case of organizational mismanagement coupled with the lack of political will. The law and order problem has nothing to do with their failure.

A network of relationships of a few people including ministers, police officers, bureaucrats, contractors, suppliers and businessmen, engineers and doctors is already in operation. It is this class of people who are benefited most by the prevailing chaos and disorder. All the palatial buildings, luxurious vehicles, business houses, private hospitals and lands are owned by this class. Systematic exploitation of the society is sought to be fulfilled through high level co-ordination and application of State machineries thereby subjecting the whole society to their hegemony. The said class is in favour of the perpetuation of the present situation or existing conflict as they find it quite expedient to amass wealth and fortunes. It is primarily on this ground that they are conspicuously reluctant to portray the existing conflict as a political conflict involving two separate entities. Rather, they willingly followed the Central Government in terming the situation as a law and order problem. It is their strategy to misinform the Central Government of the ground realities so that they can reap the benefits of the armed movements by acting as broker.

The GoI responded to the situation in two ways. Firstly, it allocated huge amount of money to wage Counter Insurgency Operations (CIO) and also create more police and Paramilitary forces. Secondly, economic packages are granted to the State on a piecemeal scale to appease certain aggrieved quarters. In both the cases, it is the above-mentioned class who gained the most. The law and order problem, therefore, can be said as a mere creation or projection of this class for in its absence, this class can hardly prosper.

In their quest for class domination, the dominant elite groups of Manipur had successfully engineered into causing a series of ethnic violence in the last decade/century. The so-called ethnic conflict was nothing more than a middle-class phenomenon. The entire plot was hatched by the elites representing this exploitative class. Ethnic conflict served dual purposes for the dominant class. Firstly, the conflict and violence was a diversionary tactic invented by this class to divert the attention of the masses from their class exploitation, which was becoming obvious with the passing of each day. Ethnic strife was designed to camouflage class domination in the first place by mobilizing the common people on ethnic lines with a view to prevent eminent class war. Secondly, ethnic strife created a law and order problem. The containment of law and order problem can be seen as a covert operation of class suppression. On the pretext of maintaining law and order situation, the dominant class is psychologically as well as physically resorting to a sort of counter revolutionary measures to prevent possible eruption of class war in the foreseeable future. From this perspective, violation of human rights by the security forces can be viewed as a systematic application of State machineries for class subjugation and domination.

Towards Conflict Transformation

Conflict unlike dispute, is a deep-rooted problem involving interests which are not negotiable. The understanding of conflict slightly differs from one another depending on the approaches. There are at least three main approaches towards the understanding of conflict and its remedies.

Conflict Resolution approach holds that conflict arise over non-negotiable issues such as fundamental human needs, intolerable moral difference or high stakes distributional issues regarding essential resources like money, water or land. However, it argues that it is possible to transcend conflicts if parties can be helped to explore, analyze, question and reframe their position and interests

(Spangler, 2003). The general assumption underlying this approach is that conflict is bad hence the need to resolve the same. Conflict Resolution involves finding out a way that identifies and deals with the underlying sources of conflict through the intervention of skilled but powerless third parties to foster new thinking and new relationship. It means terminating conflict by methods that are analytical and goes to the root of the problem, as opposed to mere management or settlement, points to an outcome that, in the view of the parties involved, is a permanent solution to a problem (Burton, 1991, 82–3). Conflict Resolution is about how parties can move from zero-sum destructive patterns of conflict to positive-sum constructive outcome. It consists of a formula that appears acceptable to both the conflicting parties.

But, quite often than not, reasons galore as to why underlying causes of conflict may not be addressed. The causes of conflict are entrenched in the structure of the society. To achieve resolution of a conflict may require significant socio-economic or political restructuring of the whole system, which is a difficult thing to accomplish. Hence, conflict resolution may be a very distant dream. Nevertheless, it is necessary to do something to mitigate the conflict. It is here that Conflict Management approach appears. According to this approach, conflict cannot be resolved but can be controlled and regulated. It aims to manage the conflict situation in ways that make it more constructive and less destructive. Management is considered the most feasible where resolution seems out of sight. Sending peace-keeping force is an example.

There is still another school of thought that advocates the pursuit of conflict transformation as opposed to conflict resolution and conflict management. Conflict Transformation approach considers conflict as something rational, constructive and socially functional unlike conflict resolution approach which implies conflict as bad and, therefore, something needs to be done. Conflict Resolution holds a negative conception of conflict and fails to acknowledge its long-term character. On the other hand, Conflict Management wrongly assumes that people can be directed or controlled as if they were physical objects although it recognizes the long-term character of conflict.

The chief advocate of Conflict Transformation approach, John Paul Lederach, argues that conflict is a natural occurrence between humans who are involved in relationships (Spangler, 2003). Once, conflict occurs, it changes or transforms those events, people, relationship that created the initial conflict. This approach suggests that the destructive consequences of a conflict can be modified or transformed so that self-images, relationship, and social structure improves as a result of conflict instead of being harmed by it. Conflict Transformation is a process of engaging with and transforming the relationship, interests, discourse and if necessary, the very constitution of society that support the continuation of violent conflict. Conflict, in a constructive sense, therefore, can be seen as a vital agent or catalyst for change (Miall, 2004, 4). Of all the three approaches, Conflict Transformation Approach seems to be the most feasible and reliable way of engaging with a conflict situation such as the one prevailing in Manipur. And viewed from this approach, there appears to be hardly any contradiction or incompatibility between conflict and development. As we know, conflict by itself is neither constructive nor destructive. But what renders a conflict to be constructive or destructive depends on how we perceive or handle it.

Hugh Miall writes:

> Constructive conflict handling reinforces the society's confidence in its civic institutions, culture, and capacity to manage conflict peacefully. Further, it not only transforms relationships in conflict, it also strengthens society's system of governance and capacity for conflict handling and peaceful change (Miall, 2004, 11).

Nobody can deny that the situation in Manipur is deteriorating to a point at which people have begun to lose faith in everything. But as to why the situation has come to such an impasse is not far to seek. Concerned quarters have not so far applied or initiated any measures which aims at transforming the present conflict. It can be seen in the manner how the government is desperately trying to contain the situation. In the absence of a consistent policy to deal with the conflict, the GoI has excessively relied on military means and resorted to adoption of *ad hoc* policies based on political expediency that eventually resulted into further escalation of the conflict. Had the government properly responded to the situation taking full cognizance of the nature of the conflict, the situation would have been otherwise. One reason why the GoI resorts to militaristic approach rather than a political approach is the monopoly of the security establishments of India in the formulation of counter-insurgency policies. It may be pointed out that the top brass of the army, police and paramilitary forces are the ones that gain the most from the counter insurgency operations. Insurgency in the North East has become a gold mine in disguise. It is precisely on this account that they want to perpetuate the problem through excessive application of force without ever trying to resolve the crisis by identifying the core issue or the root cause of the problem. In the entire scheme of things, not a single thought is given on how to resolve or transform the conflict. The situation they had created is again made to serve as a convenient tool to cover up their governmental mismanagement. Perhaps, insurgency is being understood and propagated as a means to further the "reason of the State".

Conclusion

As argued above it is an utter oversimplification that conflict is the sole factor, which hampers development in any conceivable term. By interpreting the existing situation as a law and order problem, the dominant class is deliberately trying to justify lack of governance or misgovernment with the systematic application of this notion. The proliferation of armed groups provides a suitable ground to exploit the common people while shifting blame to the armed groups.

It will be wrong to make insurgency the sole scapegoat of the economic backwardness or underdevelopment the State has been subjected to. If it is in the opinion of the Government that economic development has been rendered difficult in the presence of conflict situation/law and order problem/insurgency movements, then is it not the responsibility of the Government to take up certain concrete measures to resolve the crisis?

Irrespective of how one interprets the situation as inter-State conflict or intra-State conflict, the truth, however, is that a conflict situation has already been there in Manipur for quite a long time. It does not matter whether the conflict is an internal matter of India or one involving two separate entities so long as it affects the lives of the people. The law and order problem is only one façade of the entire issue and a corollary of the conflict. This problem will always continue to linger until and unless the basic incompatibility associated with the conflict is resolved or transformed through sustained political dialogue and third party mediation. To facilitate such development, the GoI should at the first place admit without delay that the prevailing conflict is purely a political issue and should no more pretend to look the other way round. Deployment of army and enforcement of AFSPA 1958 are enough indicators to prove that the situation is no longer mere law and order problem.

Existing conflict situation should not be made a ground for prolonging underdevelopment in the State. Manipur, or for that matter, the North East is not the only place in the world where conflict prevails. There has been conflict in Northern Ireland, too, but development is taking place in that part of the world. Conflict and development, therefore, do not any longer constitute a binary opposition mainly in the context of conflict transformation process.

The GoI needs to acknowledge that there has been a conflict in Manipur and that it ought to be resolved or transformed at the earliest. If underdevelopment is besieging the State, it is not due to the prevailing conflict but the manner in which we handle it. It is high time to identify the core issue involved in the conflict and do something to end it. If we find it difficult to resolve the conflict instantaneously, steps should be initiated to transform the conflict in a way that shall prove beneficial to both the high contracting parties. Whatever, might be the claims and counter-claims advanced by the parties to the conflict, the basic principle underlying in both the claims always consists of development and welfare of the masses. As such, structural transformation of the conflict should be made in such a pattern as not to hinder but promote economic development. Informed engagement of the conflict in a constructive way is highly essential.

CITED WORKS

Baruah, Sanjib. 2008. *India Against Itself: Assam and the Politics of Nationality*. New Delhi: Oxford University Press.

Burton, John. 1991. Conflict resolution as a political system. In *The Psychodynamics of International Relationship: Volume II: Unofficial Diplomacy at Work*, edited by Vamik Volkan and others. Lexington, MA: Lexington Books.

Datta, P.S. (eds.). 1995. *North-East India and the Indian State: Paradoxes of a Periphery*. New Delhi: Vikas Publishing House.

Editorial of *The Sangai Express*, Imphal, January 8, 2009.

Girin, Phukon. 2003. *Ethicisation of Politics in North-East India*. New Delhi: South Asian Publishers.

Government of India. 2004–05. *Annual Survey of Industries, Factory Sector*. New Delhi: CSO.

Government of Manipur. (Various issues). *Statistical Abstract of Manipur*. Imphal: Directorate of Economic and Statistics.

Kumar, B.B. 2005. Perspective of security and development in the North Eastern Region. In *Perspective of Security and Development in the North East India*, edited by SK. Agnihotri and B. Datta Ray. New Delhi: Concept Publishing Company.

Meetei, Lourembam Sanatomba. 2007. Industrialization in Manipur: Retrospect and Prospects. *Alternative Perspectives* II, IV. July–September: 32–51.

Miall, Hugh. 2001. Conflict transformation: A multi-dimensional task. In *Berghof Handbook of Conflict Transformation*. Edited version by Berghof Research Centre for Constructive Conflict Management. <http://www.berghof-handbook.net>

Spangler, Brad. 2003. Settlement, resolution, management, and transformation: An explanation of terms. In *Beyond Intractability*, edited by Guy Burgess and Heidi Burgess. Boulder: Conflict Research Consortium, University of Colorado. <http://www.beyondintractability.org/essay/meaning-resolution/

Tarapot, Phanjoubam. 1993. *Insurgency Movement in North-Eastern India*. New Delhi: Vikas Publishing House.

13

Resistance and Development : Shaping of Counter-Discourse

Hidam Premananda

Political Constitution of Development Discourse

Discourse generally implies a series of mechanisms, a certain order of behaviours or mindsets that produce permissible modes of being and thinking, all of which orchestrated by the power relations involved and that disqualify and even give effect to make others impossible. Discourse includes language, but also what is represented through language. Following Arturo Escobar, it is a 'colonization of reality' that causes certain representations to become dominant, and indelibly shapes the ways in which reality is imagined and acted upon (Escobar, 1995, 5). For example, the Western discourse has constructed what is known as the 'Third World' through the practices of development. Discourse continues to be reproduced by its own course of circulation and distribution and thus development discourse can take on a life of its own. As common beliefs and mind-sets become established, and a consensus is reached on a particular issue, and becomes the dominant frame of mind which in the form of a model of thought gets reified as the absolute frame of reference. It becomes bounded by the prevailing theme, and new ideas or existing alternative ones are unable to alter the shape of the discourse. Protection of a particular development mentality is ensured through a series of mechanisms, knowledge and institutions, values and practices and in the course, new ideas become disconnected from imagination and are inhibited. In the same way, the term 'development' also becomes an invention with which the very existence of the notion of 'underdevelopment'of the non-west is, in fact, wagered, managed, and negotiated by arranging them around the politics of representation in the discourse of the west.

However, the effect of the discursive practice of development is as significant as its relation to idea of practice of resistance to it. Of course, the interplay of promotion and resistance is a character of every form of discourse and thus we need to see, in this sense, the ways in which development discourse becomes an interplay of both promotion and resistance. It means an attempt to understand development requires nuanced, historical, geographical account of the assumptions informing development thinking and practice, as well as an account of the specific paradigms and dimensions of history, culture, power and identity.

The effect of the discursive practices of development produces the grounds for contesting the categories which are constructed within the discourse itself. In other words, resistance to power and domination bears complicated relations between what is resisted and what is that which resists. In fact, the political meaning of resistance to development opens up new realities for scrutiny and negotiation. It also involves resurrection of histories of local struggles and subjugated knowledge. Attributions of grassroots development initiatives, community-bound definitions of tradition with an ability to combine cultural appropriateness and development goals are some of new zones which an understanding of development should take into account.

A critical account of the idea of development that is taking place in mundane affairs of our social life needs to see how particular development packages and devices are resisted and adapted in various ways, in global, national, regional and local contexts, varying with political economies, histories, and geographies. We need to see that development is engaged with various forms of different cultures of thought and practices. This kind of understanding highlights the insertion of development into the broader cultural, political and geographical grounding. In this account, the notion of development can be considered in a global field of multiple meanings and practices that inform the contested relations upon which development is built and policy prescriptions are devised. The general point is that an imagining of development may not be aware of the fact that it entails to the extent that the imagining of development presupposes the patterns of oppression. It suggests that resistance is contextually bound to the social and political structures that are being resisted.

Thus, development discourse and resistance to it is concerned with power, and is intensely material. It is to see that development is a politically constituted discourse. This view leads to examining the ways in which resistance occur—resistance which is capable of recreating cultural identities, and that which relies on its intent in making visible a source of power previously hidden. To put it in David Couzens Hoy's words, "the resistance of completely powerless 'Other' is perhaps paradoxically the most powerful form that resistance can take" (Hoy, 2005, 16). We need to interrogate into the terms on which the efforts to bring development into the social realities are constructed. The terms are multiple and produced in communities of intent and meanings, institution and language. This will enable us to outline the political nature of development for the latter opens to a field of contestations of meanings as well as meanings of contestations.

One of the ways to see the nature of displacement and reconfiguration of the notion of development is to get into the specificity of that which constitutes development as a way of political life of those for whom are devised huge resources of policies and interventions. The notion that development is a fact of life and a true 'descriptor of reality' should not be uncritically embraced. Development does not have to be considered to exist 'out there', solid and material. It inscribes in the social reality, and cannot be utilised to give to accept an effect of harmlessness. The seemingly uncritical tendency of a dominant development mentality is in fact a desire to define, categorize and bring order to a heterogeneous and constantly multiplying field of meanings (Crush, 1995, 2).

Again, the qualifiers of the term 'development' have multiplied rendering nature of the term problematic. Development is a language that is used to define the meanings it has produced. It is constitutive of the social reality within which experiences of difference, dissent and aspiration come to play as a force to become what can be considered broadly as the reality of politics. Therefore, unproblematic nature of development needs to be destabilised for it is development that paradoxically regulates both the grounds to protect and also to modify the social order. The discourse of development, the form in which it makes its arguments and establishes its authority, the manner in which it constructs the world, is profoundly problematic: it has made possible a cultural politics of domination as well as resistance. Development makes visible the 'silent violence' embodied in the understanding of project of domination and the 'unplaced voices' about material conditions, history, culture and identity embodied in the resistance to domination. Development discourse including both its functionaries of power and ruptures of their working needs to be seen not as a reflection of social reality, but as constitutive of it; it is one among many other discourses through which social reality inevitably comes into being political.

Resistance and Representation

Resistance to development is not be construed as anti-development. It is rather the opening up of new spaces of authority, sites of experience and ways of 'defamiliarization' of the established categories and authority. It is through resistance that the notion of development is brought to the critique of the knowledge and in..tutions that protect the silent violence. Resistance produces heterogeneous language of acting and understanding the configuration of domination and subjection. It confirms or modifies interpretation of the world of those who are subjected to an unrecognized, unclaimed zone of existence. It reclaims a subversive means of transforming and reconfiguring the complexity of their being 'non-placedness' into the capacity to speak in a language that seeks to destabilize the very complexity of relations involving knowledge and institutions. This act of relocating the position within the very discourse of development is what is involved in the idea of transmission: something about knowledge, capacity, energy which is on the one side, in the collective sensibility that must be transferred onto the 'Other', into the dominant authority and its definition. The presupposition is that the process of transmission is not only what resistance does but also effecting crossing of the borders as a means of questioning the grounds for domination.

There are a few things to say about representation. It plays significant role in shaping of the politics of resistance.

Representation involves an unpacking of relations most profoundly built with inequalities, domination and subjugation. It is due to the critical aspect of the relation between the two that is important to consider here a little more. This aspect is what we may see as the role of the presence of resistance whenever, there is a form of dominant categories that tend to define others as representable only through its perspectives. For example, the notion of orientalism is a case in point. Orientalism, as Edward Said understood, is the systematic 'body of theory and practice' that constructs or represents the Orient (Said, 1995, 6; see also Said, 1993, xxiii; and Said, 1985, 248).

'Theory' means the Western imperial episteme—the West's intellectual and cultural production, including research, writing, ideas, arguments, images; and by 'practice' he denotes the accompanying socio-cultural institutions and structures—the colonial administration, universities, museums, media, etc. (Said, 1995, 3, 5 and 332). Westerners tend to be produced as characteristic of 'rational, peaceful, liberal, logical' without natural suspicion and easterners or the orient as 'irrational, degenerate, primitive, mystical, suspicious, sexually depraved' and so on. What is important is that these representations are not neutral. In this sense, 'Orientalism' is the enormously systematic discipline by which European culture manages and produces the Orient politically, sociologically, militarily, ideologically, scientifically, and imaginatively. Partly in response to this tendency, Bhabha suggests an extended understanding of how representations are produced in ambivalence in his study of post-colonial discourse of identity. In fact, Bhabha makes 'hybridity' the keystone of his subsequent elaborations. Hybridity describes the way in which colonial and imperial discourse is inherently unstable, 'split' in its 'enunciation', so that 'in the very practice of domination the language of the master becomes hybrid' (Bhabha, 1994, 33). Bhabha illustrates this instability through an analysis of the 'colonial stereotype', which he considers an instance of the deployment of imperial authority. He shows how these stereotypes—the 'noble savage', the 'wily oriental' are meant to be accepted as 'fixed' and 'natural'; yet they are endlessly and anxiously repeated and reconfirmed by the colonizer.

Often these stereotypes are also contradictory. For example, the colonial subject is 'savage (cannibal) and yet the most obedient and dignified of servants; he is mystical, primitive, and simple-minded and yet the most worldly and accomplished liar' (Bhabha, 1994, 82). This means that representation is both incitement and interdiction, relational and negotiated. It also implies that discursive practices always enable a form of subversion, founded on the undecidability that turns the discursive conditions of dominance into the grounds of intervention. Subversive intervention demonstrates that representation is cultural and that is why it is political. It involves estranging, contaminating or repersuading the dominant discourse, by imposing suppressed knowledge as unanticipated alterations with the overall effect of denying or subverting dominant authority. It should be noted that it is this emergence of the unavoidable collusion and complicity between the dominant and emergent practices that gives to see that representation is always a negotiation.

The core political issue in the resistance to development in the final analysis is about setting a critique of representation and the manner in which the representations are actually encountered. The implication is that development thinking and practice constitute a complexity in that is built an essential denial of the tendency of its being solely owned by a particular authority. Resistance as a form of critique and way of encountering representation reflects multiplicity of source of power, hidden and manifest, and a relation between powerful and powerless, and enables the retrieval and recognition of difference in the social realities that appropriate development in different fashions. The object of looking into the representative character of the discourse of development is to deny binary categorization such as in this context, coloniser-colonised, global-local, modern and traditional, expert and ordinary, etc. Rather it is to see that politics of resistance destabilizes the practice of development by invoking multiple sites of shaping differences and aspirations, thereby ensuring a counter discourse of development. It is on this account of the transformative character of resistance that it becomes the object of negotiation through representation. For example, markers such as 'local' and 'traditional', in this context, are sought to negotiate with dominant understandings of these terms by intervening into the vary practice of production of knowledge, values and institution, that is to say of the counter-formations.

Development and Local Dissent

The power of development discourse and its material effects on the lives of people is subject to development policies. Mainstream development thinking is mainly founded on the notion that the logic of development as problem-solving is universal. Policymakers design programmes that are culturally appropriate. They provide unique skills necessary for collecting primary data necessary for planning and formulating policy; and they project and assess cultural and social effects of intervention. They correct interventions that are underway. They conduct evaluations that contain valid indicators of programme results and also reconsider that which will be economically unfeasible and face community opposition.

The question is how to contend the dominant discourse produced under specific political and structural conditions. The answer lies in the opening up of discursive spaces for the local to imagine and struggle for what may be considered as alternatives, or even making of an aspired world of existence. This aspiration that focuses on both the hegemonic and counter-hegemonic discourses demonstrates the dialectic nature of knowledge production which in fact is what is happening in various parts of the world. Active rebellion and attempts at secession mainly in the form of armed resistance by many groups for example, resistance of the Sudan People's Liberation Army to the government in Khartoum in Sudan, the Zapatista rebellion in Mexico's Chiapas State, and the Karen hill people's struggle against the brutal military regime in Myanmar are all cases in point.

Politics of resistance, as discussed above, confirms the ways in which the authority of dominant ideology is being challenged and brought to a field of contestation. An approach to the study of politics of knowledge production as the foreground of bringing the local dissent to the globalised meaning of development will lead to a more comprehensive and nuanced understanding of development as both discursive and counter discursive. Bringing local dissent to the centre of engagement is perhaps one way to see how development is largely a cultural politics of emergence and submergence, of displacement and replacement, ideology and counter ideology. The dissents which are reflected in various articulations provide a series of other possibilities, such as tensions between change and the preservation of cultural integrity; resistance to development and the selective adoption of innovations in order to maintain a degree of cultural and ecological balance; between shared cultural practices and significant heterogeneity; between local boundaries and the increasing need for regional and national alliances; and between traditional craft and its impact on cultural reproduction.

Local dissents rise as both social and political movements, press for a combination of cultural autonomy and democracy, and the construction of material and institutional structure to improve local living conditions. This does not mean to simply say that development should be bottom up or rather be culture specific. It means in larger contexts of political economy, history and power, these are all contributions to the shaping of the politics of resistance as the enunciation of the mode of development discourses.

For example, the currents of social movement that is associated with the construction of Mapithel dam of Thoubal multipurpose project in Manipur is a case in point where the whole movement against the rationale behind the project is being put into question. The project that commenced in 1980 with the approval of the Planning Commission is now challenged on the ground that it did not have proper consultation with the villagers who are severely affected by it. The question of food 'sovereignty' and security, pollution, livelihood and degradation of agricultural activities due to shortage of water have been gradually put to the front. This resistance to the very authority of the experts of the government does not mean to reflect that the villagers and the 'other' experts of the movement are more capable of imagining an alternative policy. Instead it brings forth an idea that the politics of resistance produce new sources of knowledge that in turn shape an entirely new field of meanings of what actually development should be in the eyes of those who have experienced the hardships of such projects. Another way to put this understanding is perhaps a reformulation of relation that is established between those who define development and those for whom development is defined. This field of relation is altered when there is resistance and as a result the discourse of the notion of authority is open to a possibility of problematization, thereby interrogating the notion of development.

Conclusion

The accounts of resistance to development that is presented in the essay need not be synthesized with anthropological critique of development and political programmes of critique to neoliberal ideas of the present world economy. However, the idea of giving some light on the critical role of resistance in the development practices and thinking raises a few intriguing questions that are being addressed by way of conclusion here. What does it make sense of resisting a particular mode of development? What would make development a political practice?

A brief answer to the first question is that the main threat is felt differently now that the proscribing power of the authority of the government is challenged in many ways and unravelling of its being contested by the language of popular struggle has marked a serious rupture within the establishment of development thinking. The struggles around the issues of food, corruption, land, despite their invisible and unarticulated, may be considered to remain within the framework of the resistance to development thinking. At best these struggles challenged development politics in their rhetoric and in the deployment of the institutional mechanisms of redressal but never went beyond the confines of the idea of people's interest. The politically inscribed power of the powerful class and their continuing stranglehold could never be challenged within the sanitized institutional mechanism of redressal but without an articulation of a form of popular movement. That is where the value of resistance both at the level of ideas and practices.

The second question is little more significant than the first for it is within the discourse of development that the very shaping of the politics of resistance is taking place. It can be answered in this manner. Development policy is conventionally concerned with the mainly governmental institutions and arrangements for promoting welfare through the amelioration of individual and collective needs as demanded by the imperatives of 'security'. Development is closely tied to the production certain types of knowledge about security and welfare. The very alliance of security and knowledge of welfare is so characteristic of various developmental policies undertaken by the government. Security's astonishing production of knowledge which gives it license to render all aspects of life transparent has been closely brought to an arrangement of a network of relations between development and surveillance. The government provides welfare with an institutional and governmental interest through the endorsement of a particular model of thought, values and knowledge. This makes it possible for the kind of development to be in the manner it should be and only in the way it is. While on the other, there are common senses, series of a type of knowledge which are brought to a close link to the idea of welfare. The government achieves its identity, in part, through intervening in problems of a group or individuals or a locality, or the larger society. This intervention is most fully portrayed in its accounts of development policies articulated in a number of ways. It has a direct relation to efforts to improve the quality of life through development programmes like building schools and hospitals, airports, dams, hydro electricity projects, digging wells for clean water, providing funds for people to start small businesses, population control etc. There are interventions to create jobs, strengthen local democratic political institutions, and address competition over natural resources. These ideas of welfare however are not innocent. One should not be taken in too much by the seemingly innocent models of development endorsed by the government. Hegemonic projects of the government are ambiguously built on specific relations between welfare and security, and in the ways in which the State is sought to relate to the civil population.

A remarkable point in this regard suggests that the State is related to the civil population in a way in which 'illegality' marks a representation of the relation in a society where there are popular struggles. Or to be precise, there are development programmes to address issues of crime, terrorism, and violence. These programmes seek to claim that anti-government activities can take root and grow in fragile conditions where 'hopelessness' and 'lawlessness' prevail. Those who challenge to certain development policies of the government are profiled as anti-national, insurgents and are thus organized and managed within the logic of the police. Hence, controlling of these forces while at the same time strengthening the stand to promote the particular government projects to which they resist. It makes development all the more political in this sense.

However, resistance, as stated above, transforms the nature of the ideological expressions of dominant developmental model by putting its authority into the grounds for intervention. It exposes the relation between development policies and the policies of marginalizing the unplaced voices further to the point of extinction. We can also see the ways in which the politics of resistance is being shaped in the tools or activities and the fury unleashed against a despotic authority whom they enjoy hanging or burning in effigy, in protest and marches in order to avoid avowing openly and honestly that ideas behind the act of resistance is culpable or unworthy of notice. Resistance as a form of critique contributes to an understanding of how to make crucial transformation by referring it to the terms of debate of development discourses. It is important to bring to the centre an understanding of the politics of resistance in order to see that development can be a negotiated discourse, to see that development is not the product of grand narratives but of diverse struggles that questions the patterns of domination and repression.

CITED WORKS

Bhabha, H.K. 1994. *The Location of Culture*. New York: Routledge.

Crush, J. 1995. *Power of Development*. New York: Routledge.

Escobar, Arturo. 1995. *Encountering Development: The Making and Unmaking of the Third World*. Princeton, New Jersey: Princeton University Press.

Escobar, Arturo. 1997. Anthropology and Development. *International Social Science Journal*, 49, 4.

Hoy, David Couzens. 2005. *Critical Resistance: From Post-structuralism to post-critique*. London: The MIT Press.

Said, Edward. 1993. *Culture and Imperialism*. New York: Vintage.

Said, Edward. 1995. *Orientalism*. London: Penguin.

Index